Tom Weir M███ ███ ████ ███ █████ █ ████ █ Scotsman. Born
in Glasgow, he w█ ████ ████ █████ ███ of working class
outdoorsmen, his ea███ y████ w███ ███████ █oring the Scottish
Highlands on days off from his job as a grocer's boy. Always intent
on making his way as an explorer and climber, writer and photographer, his progress was interrupted by service with the Royal
Artillery in World War Two although his first book, Highland
Days, was written while still in uniform.

Tom's dec █ation took him from impoverished Glasgow to the ends
of the ea█ █. He climbed and explored in arctic East Greenland,
northern █orway, the High Atlas of Morocco, and Kurdistan. In
1950 he w █ a member of the first post-war Himalayan Expedition
(*The Ultim █e Mountains*) and, in 1952, one of the first mountaineers
to explore █e hitherto closed ranges of Nepal (*East of Katmandu*).

For over f █ty years his feature 'My Month' appeared in the Scots
Magazine reflecting his fascination with Scotland, its remote
corners, p █ple and wildlife. Between 1976 and 1987 he hosted the
popular t evision programme *Weir's Way*. He won the Scottish
Television █ersonality of the Year Award in 1978 and, in 2000, the
inaugural █ohn Muir Lifetime Achievement Award.

In the co█ █se of a long lifetime Tom Weir wrote many books and
articles o █ the subjects and places which were close to his heart:
Camps an █ Climbs in Arctic Norway, *The Scottish Lochs*, and a fine
autobiog█ phy, *Weir's World*.

Hamish █ █wn (1934–) is a mountaineer, lecturer and photographer █ █o has written or edited many books. He was the first
person to █alk all the Munros in a single trip, the story of which,
Hamish's Mountain Walk, has inspired generations of walkers and
climbers.

One of Hamish Brown's teenage inspirations was Tom Weir's *Highland Days* and, later, he was lucky to know and sometimes work
with Tom and has travelled to many of the places Tom describes.
Hamish was delighted to put together this selection of Tom's work.

Other books by Hamish Brown
published by Sandstone Press

Hamish's Mountain Walk
Hamish's Groats End Walk
Climbing the Corbetts
The Oldest Post Office in the World

TOM WEIR

An anthology

Edited by

Hamish Brown

SANDSTONEPRESS
HIGHLAND | SCOTLAND

First published in Great Britain in 2013 by

...eproduced,
stored, or transmitted in any form without the express
written permission of the publisher.

The publisher acknowledges subsidy from
Creative Scotland towards publication of this volume.

ISBN: 978-1-908737-28-1
ISBNe: 978-1-908737-29-8

Cover design and photographic layout by Gravemaker + Scott, Edinburgh.

Typeset in Linotype Palatino by Iolaire Typesetting, Newtonmore.
Printed and bound by Ozgraf, Poland.

For Rhona

CONTENTS

6   From Norway to Corsica

7   A Variety of Interests

8   Tom's People

9   Always the Naturalist

LIST OF ILLUSTRATIONS

Section One

1. Tom Weir, aged three, in Springburn Park, Glasgow
2. Tom on Doune Hill in the Luss Hills looking down to Loch Lomond
3. Tom, with Harold Raeburn's ice axe, when president of the SMC, 1984–86
4. Inspecting the tool chest made by A. E. Robertson (first Munroist) when AER was fifteen years old
5. Two worthy hill gangrels: Tom Weir and Syd Scroggie (the latter lost his sight and a leg in the last days of World War Two)
6. Tom's sister Molly and wife Rhona at a standing stone on the Island of Jura
7. The world that lured four Scots lads, all self-supporting, on the first post war Himalayan expedition
8. Porters in the Rishi Gorge, described in Tom's book, *The Ultimate Mountains*
9. Men and women porters on a Himalayan glacier as described in *East of Katmandu*
10. The coastal area described during Sir John Hunt's 1960 expedition to Greenland
11. Rhona at a camp in the Jotenheim, Norway
12. On a ridge in the Toubkal massif of Morocco's Atlas Mountains
13. Ringing gannets on the Bass Rock

Section Two

INTRODUCTION

This is a selection from the many books and some unpublished material written in the course of a long and active life (1914 – 2006). It is not a biography; Tom's own *Weir's World, An Autobiography of Sorts*, written in his eighties, is his personal story, the telling of which is a tour de force: very readable, often exciting, sometimes moving and of growing historical interest. Much of what he wrote is about what he did, what he saw, what he thought: head, hands and heart writing.

Tom's autobiography does not follow a strict chronological order and this selection does similarly, taking some of the dominant themes he followed, sometimes briefly, sometimes with a lifelong dedication. He wrote with considerable passion, an earnestness which perhaps hides the vivacious, often amusing side of his persona. He 'made good' by unstinting hard graft and bore the disciplines of his way of life with good grace.

When people turned on their TVs to watch *Weir's Way* they invariably smiled in anticipation. Tom was enthusiasm personified on TV. The stocky figure with trademark woollies and toorie top was a friend to thousands. The erudition was there of course. Few had travelled more or had studied more about Scotland, its history, its people, its wildlife.

What many won't realise is how much research went into his work. He was not only immersed in the geography of Scotland but in its history. "He kens aboot awthing" was a viewer's comment I once passed on. But the fluency of his TV work and the factual detail in articles came from the hard graft of researching. All writers are readers. He absorbed Scotland whole – and gave it back in words and on the TV screen in a unique way that endeared him to everyone.

I encountered his perfectionist demands during the making of one of his Weir's Way series. I had just completed the one-off walk over all the Munros and he wanted to cover this in one of his programmes. We drove up to the Loch Sloy dam and, dressed as I was for the walk, pitched the tent and scattered the correct gear as if relaxing at the end of day, mug of tea in hand. Tom then trundled down to me with a "Hello, Hamish" to which I had to look up and reply "Oh, hello Tom". There were ten takes of that scene before he was satisfied.

Among the questions asked about Tom are those wanting to know how he started out as a writer so I'll use this introduction to recount something of his early life with its inexplicable initial inspiration and steely ongoing determination. The spark came early and the flame never dimmed. At a lecture question time when he was in his eighties someone began, "Now you're retired . . ." only to have Tom snap, "I'm not retired!"

Tom was born in Springburn in 1914 and never knew his father who had been killed in Mesopotamia (as had the father of W H Murray). He was brought up by his Gran while his mother worked painting wagons in the railway yards earning just enough to support Tom, his sister Molly and brother Willie. His mother had a love of hills and early Campsie days would spur on his first dreams of the outdoors while Glasgow itself had plenty of green places and rivers where children roamed and learned in a way regrettably missing today. Interestingly, Tom won through his early hill explorations without any mishap yet, as a boy, broke his collarbone when hit by a motor bike and was seriously concussed when falling down the close stairs.

He drank deep of the books of Shipton, Tilman and Longstaff, devoured volume after volume of Seton Gordon, took every chance to head for the hills by bus and bike and thumb, exploring further and further afield, meeting other inspiring stravaigers like Ritchie Wallace and Matt Forrester and befriending people who lived in the remoter Highlands. This passion for the hills by hard or easy routes turned Tom into a lifelong gangrel, exploring Scotland as few others had done, in a way unknown today, and setting his characteristics, moulded by people and places encountered. That so many men, older and more experienced, accepted, befriended and led Tom in his adventures, points to a strong outgoing character already there. Tom just didn't dream; he put legs to his dreams.

Tom left school at fourteen and had ten years of unhappy security in a Co-op grocery, necessary until his older brother qualified as an engineer and could support the family. Determined that he would become a writer he learned to type by taking lessons from sister Molly (at 2/6d a session – she was an equally 'with it' Weir) and buying the correspondence course booklets of the self-improving Pelmanism scheme. He also attended some nightclasses on writing skills. He persevered. "I could have papered a house with rejection slips" he once said (At the same stage I had a shoebox below my desk inscribed with a double misquote: "All that glitters is not sold") but how greater the satisfaction when work begins to be accepted. He would see a million and a half words appear in the Scots Magazine in the 48 years he wrote "My Month" (1956 – 2004).

Molly Weir's 'Shoes Were For Sundays' gives a vivid picture of their early life and is worth reading. Theirs must have been a lively home with three youngsters bursting out of their chrysalises to spread wings for such disparate flights.

Tom was struggling to survive once he left his grocery 'job for life', finding time to write, and explore, while earning something at whatever he could. If you are writing you are not away doing the things you want to write about, if you are away you are not hammering at the typewriter. Oddly, it was the war that gave him time to write what would become his first book, typing it after being demobbed in 1946. With his background as a gunnery surveyor he soon found work with the Ordnance Survey which happily had him roaming the hills of home again.

As a youngster keen on the hills I read Tom's first book *Highland Days* not long after it came out following World War Two – and have read it on many occasions since. Like Borthwick's classic *Always a Little Further* it painted a picture of a world utterly remote and different to today's: traditional and settled in character, kindlier in social manners, a world uncrowded and, for visitors like Tom, as unexplored as the Arctic or Himalaya. The book is a gem. For years, every time we met, I would urge Tom to try and have it reprinted (it eventually was in 1984). When I said it was the best thing he'd ever written he grinned back, "So you're saying everything I've written since then is rubbish?"

Tom always called himself a photojournalist rather than a writer and studied hard to make himself one of the best. The commissioning editor of Scotland's Magazine when discussing an eleven part series by Tom, under the name Ward Clarke wrote, "We know that we will get a good sound job from you – that it will be true to the facts, informative, readable and all we wish our material to be" – a good summation of Weir's writing. But I always recall many gems of description brightening climbing or wildlife features: "... clinging to avoid becoming part of the wind ... thick lips of snow cornice ... the wind was a scream ... blackcock with Glengarry bonnet tails ... divers, low as battleships in the water ... guillemots, like rows of bottles in a press."

He progressed from using a cheap boyhood camera to become a busy professional, illustrating all his own features and books, with his own darkroom and writing sanctum from which all distractions were barred. Rhona became headmistress of their local primary school and the pair took classes on memorable hill outings.

Tom and Rhona settled in Gartochan after marriage in 1959, a hamlet with its own wee hill, the Dumpling (Duncryne 463 ft/142 m), and, at the mouth of the River Endrick, flowing into Loch Lomond, an area of outstanding bird interest and recently bought by the RSPB.

Tom was a bonny fighter when he saw thoughtless or perverse commercial wrong being done to the environment. Hydro schemes and forestry could – and should – benefit local people and look attractive but when tax benefiting blocks of trees were planted in the Flow Country of Caithness or a hideous track scarred a view or a dam was proposed across the Nevis Gorge, he would fight hard to prevent such unimaginative desecrations. I recall Tom's scorn when a power line from Skye was built and was taken through to Kinloch Hourn by the only glen in the west free of man's handiwork, a fact which should have been its safeguard but to the planners was the reason for going that way.

Reading dozens of obituaries after Tom's death I was struck by the variation of perception and conception and, too often, simple errors of fact. What I've written I've tried to verify from prime sources and personal knowledge. Myths start so easily, Tom's wife Rhona gave me an example.

She and Tom visited Foula in 1959 on their honeymoon, an eight hour uncomfortable boat journey (Tom was not a good sailor) then, when she returned recently – by air – the welcoming folk recalled the first visit and where they had pitched their tent and how Tom had presented Rhona with a bunch of red roses when landing. "As if Tom would."

Recently I met a strange myth. During the war Tom reputedly wrote a book about climbing in the Alps (which he'd never visited) as an aid to escaping POWs, and sent to them in Red Cross parcels. Comments, such as 'from the Dufferspitz the view to the NE reaches as far as Looniberg 80 kilometres away', could be read 'backwards' to gain useful geographic information for escapers. All very hush hush; not even the family knew.

Tom had started off in the Cowlairs Co-op as a message boy and then working in the shop. More than a decade on he left to work in Willy Paton's grocery where the incident with the scales occurred (see Nine Years to Happiness) and he walked out. He went to work on an Arran farm, struggling to write and explore in the limited time available. Then came the war.

The war, as mentioned, gave more opportunity to write: hours were often regular and pay certain (his discovered love of opera dates from this time) and danger and boredom were relieved by looking back to the good days in the past.

'Sitting writing this in a guard-tent in the blazing heat of a Belgian July I find it hard to believe that my memories are thirteen years old. "Is it thirteen years," I ask myself," since I fearfully traced out of Abraham's British Mountain Climbs dotted lines up the face of Buachaille Etive Mor, and produced diagrams of likely routes I could climb solo."

Tom was no saint. He could be 'thrawn' and argumentative, determined to do what he wanted, when he wanted. He liked his day's routine unchanging. He had strong views because he'd read and thought his way to them. But what strong characters are not prickly at times? His really close friends of many decades were all robust characters who could give and take. Sadly, he outlived most of them, his declining powers a frustrating burden. Duncryne was hardly the same when its climb was a struggle with two sticks but "better than the alternative". Tom was also very much part of a couple to those who knew them and Tom without his wife Rhona unthinkable. She was his great support and aid throughout 47 years of marriage – and in her nineties she is still attending meets of the Ladies Scottish Climbing Club. She used to joke that Tom was the only married bachelor she knew.

Tom and many of his friends were members of the Scottish Mountaineering Club and, in his early days, often wrote for its Journal (listed in the bibliography) and two articles are included: p98 and p129. One of the pictures shows Tom as club President (1984 – 86) with one of the club's treasures, the ice axe of Harold Raeburn. Traditionally the club president leads a walk on the day following the dinner and I recall Tom, then president, refusing the excuse of a ferociously wet day, leading a group of us from Strathyre up and over the shoulder of Beinn an t-Sidhein to Glen Buckie and back round by Balquhidder – and setting a cracking pace.

My first encounter with Tom would lead to several projects where he involved the Braehead School children. This was a junior secondary school in the mining coast of Fife where a team of inspirational teachers were giving new heart to a depressed area, my part being to take them into the wilds, to explore their world, to climb their dreams.

Descending to Loch Monar in the Sixties we came on a "bouncy wee man" (one lad's description) whom I recognised as Tom Weir from the Scots Magazine and *Highland Days*. He later confessed to being astonished at the encounter with such lads in such a remote spot. Typically, he at once pointed out a kestrel *keeking* up on a crag and much bird talk followed. If the kids thought him "great", he was impressed by their knowledge and enthusiasm. "I was seeing myself again as a laddie when all things were possible."

When Braehead had closed and my *Hamish's Mountain Walk* was published I asked Tom about the idea of trying to make a go of writing, as he had done. His reply was, "Don't" – so I did, passing his test of my commitment perhaps, where becoming a casualty in the reality of such a life was all too likely. Tom, in the best notion of the term, was a self-made man, working unendurable hours for very little return in a chancy and very limited field. If he hadn't the monthly assurance of the Scots Magazine – and a working wife – he might not have survived.

Writers in this field do not become rich! Strangely, not so long ago a youngster asked me the same question, and received the same reply. Tom endured, Tom stayed the course and, with the inspired engaging him on TV, became one of the best known and loved figures in the outdoor world.

Tom was one of the first members of the Scottish Wildlife Trust and of the John Muir Trust, the latter presenting him with a Lifetime Achievement Award in 2000; in 2001 the

Outdoor Writers Guild gave him their Annual Golden Eagle Award. He was Vice-President of the Scottish Rights of Way Society. In 1976 he received an MBE and in 1978 won the Scottish Television Personality of the Year Award.

Tom kept a low political profile (though admired by and giving advice to many, including Tam Dalyell and John Smith) but was all for taking Scotland back to her own destiny with independence. In an interview in the Scots Independent (2005) he was asked, "Do you believe in God?" He is sure of his answer: "No, Everyone has one life. That's all it is. No spirit looks after you beyond death. I was lucky not to have been killed in the war. I was lucky not to have been killed on Ben A'an. I don't believe the world will be in existence in another 100 years. Man is outliving himself." Perhaps you need to be a pessimist to be an optimist, to whom everything is a surprise, a marvel, and life taken with a big heart, like Tom.

This is a collection for dipping into and I hope will encourage readers to seek out copies of his books still in print or those less easy to find. Details are in the bibliography. The only liberty I have taken with the text is to have abbreviated at times, space being at a premium. Any comments of mine in the text are in square brackets and introductory or other notes are in italics. Tom's spellings have largely been followed as long as the meaning or name is clear.

Tom's later work as a photographer and on TV is well remembered so pictures have been chosen to show the younger photographer, his friends, and the wide range of topics he covered, both at home and abroad, a representative selection from a vast archive and of increasing social and historical interest.

My thanks to those who encouraged along the way: to Rhona first of all; to Robin Campbell and other Scottish Mountaineering Club members who brought some order into Tom's archive material; to the St Andrews Sustainability Institute for a grant to help with part of the research; to the

Trustees of the National Library of Scotland and the staff of the Library where it is now housed (Acc. 13059), for their patience and helpfulness over many months, to Sheila Gallimore and David Ritchie for the typing, scanning, etc, of an unruly text; and to Robert Davidson of Sandstone Press who bullied the complex work along.

Hamish Brown
Burntisland 2013

I

LIFE TO WARTIME YEARS

During the war years Tom tried his hand at writing fiction which, as with most early essays in fiction, leaned heavily on a limited personal experience. The two pieces following give vivid pictures of life in Springburn in pre-war days. 'Nine Years to Happiness' is scarcely fiction at all, he is Allan, the frustrated shop assistant and Jock is the very recognisable Matt Forrester, mentor and friend.

Tom wrote very little about the war so I include three very varied pieces which, in different ways, will be familiar to anyone who served in the ranks. Typically Tom gave his home address as Glen Brittle House, Isle of Skye, when much of the Highlands was a restricted area. 'Across Sutherland Hills' was one of his explorations when on leave.

That, and 'An Epic' are from Highland Days, *his first book which was written during the war, as was W H Murray's* Mountaineering in Scotland, *though the latter was written in the worse boredom of a POW camp.*

NINE YEARS TO HAPPINESS

Monday morning. Beyond the sugarloaf brilliance of the housing scheme and its forest of red roofs towered the craggy ridge of the hills. A thin spiral of silver veined it. Snow. The hooter of the engineering works sounded. With a start he bounded into a run. He had five minutes to get to the shop.

All the assistants were at their counters when he got in. Quickly he pulled on his coat stiff with white starch and seizing a broom, began sweeping the back shop. The gag was sometimes successful but not this morning. He knew it when the boss came into the back shop.

"I was wondering where you were hiding," he said. "Did you think I didn't see you?" Allan pulled out a box, swept under it but didn't look up. "Well I'm waiting for an answer. Another thing; that's already been swept."

"I'm sorry, I thought it hadn't." He made to go out to the front shop.

"Come here Smith, I'm speaking to you!" His rubbery lips had a smirk of self-satisfaction and the sight of his double chin quivering as he spoke roused a wave of hatred in Allan. His name was Wheeler. He was a tall man going bald at the front and developing a paunch. No one ever succeeded in liking him.

"I don't like telling you off Smith, but we can't let you get away with it all the time. This is the fourth time in less than a week. What's up? Do you go to bed too late?" It was no use explaining. "I'll try to keep better time," Allan muttered. "Well try then. This is a good job and you don't want to lose it."

"Give McKend a hand with these orders." With his

3

thumbnail he scratched a grove in the barrel shape of butter newly out of its cask and popped the wrinkled accumulation between his thick lips. He went to the cash desk where five girls were adding up figures and checking their cash. The assistants talked in low voices for Wheeler maintained that you couldn't both work and talk.

With jobs so scarce he knew how to make them toe the line. Beside he had a reputation for managing successfully on a smaller staff than any of his predecessors. That was why the firm had given him their biggest shop.

At the age of sixteen Allan should have been sacked and replaced by a non-insured youngster of fourteen. As a message boy he had hated Wheeler. He knew too, how the counter hands hated the job. He could sense only too well the servility the customers expected and got from the grocers.

Then came the offer. There was a superannuation scheme. A guaranteed job. People always need groceries. (Look at the number of unemployed engineers.) What will you do if you don't take it? The deciding factor was his mother. She was a widow. Other places he had tried for a job had ignored him, so he became a grocer's assistant.

It wasn't too bad at first. There was a lot to learn; prices, where the various things were kept, what all the drawers held, how to weigh goods accurately, how to fold paper bags so there was no possibility of the contents escaping, how to keep tobacco moist with the help of a cut up potato, how to 'gas' eggs, and then there was window dressing and the arranging of show cases inside the shop.

"Intelligent anticipation saves time," was another of Wheeler's sayings. That meant that shelves never had to go empty and cause a hold up at the counter while a new case was being opened in the back shop. It was a crime in his eyes to run out of goods. Allan was responsible for tea. No matter how busy he was these tea shelves with all the different blends had to be fully represented. He made it known how many men he had sacked for this neglect.

A favourite trick of his too was to withdraw from a cus-
tomer under some pretext, packages of some expensive stuff
like coffee or tongue, which had just ben weighed. It would be
reweighed in the back shop and woe betide the unfortunate
assistant if it was even a fraction overweight.

At home, he never mentioned the shop unless asked. "Your
mind is always on these hills. If you'd take more interest in
your work instead of reading about hills and going away
every week-end climbing hills you'd get on better. Coming
in here with a bag of wet stinking clothes every Sunday. And
you can't get up for your work on Monday."

His was a grand respectable job his mother thought. If only
if he'd take after his younger brother Willie a bit more. He
was an apprentice engineer and wrapt up in his job to the
exclusion of all else.

It was true though that Allan had a passion for the country.
After the shop shut on s Saturday night he would catch the
last bus out and from the terminus walk across the hills to
pitch his tent in darkness by some little hill stream. To wake
up in the morning to hear the gurgle of the burns and to look
out to the green curving hills was the most joyful thing he
knew. From the day he stood on Earl's Seat and looked over
Loch Lomond to the mighty summits stretching from west
to east in a ragged blue line, he had been an addict. He read
everything the public library had on the Scottish Highlands.

About this time he met Jack Brown, an enthusiast like himself. He was a butcher with the same sort of hours and ideals.
They met on the train and spent the weekend together. Brown
was an ornithologist and an advanced thinker. He fancied the
simple life. To be a wage slave was all wrong. "If you don't
like the job you are doing change it." Since he enjoyed the
butchery trade it was easy enough advice for him to follow.

They had some great times together: they crossed the
Cairngorms, climbed the Cuillin of Skye, wandered across
Sutherland, explored the wilderness of Wester Ross, visited
Harris of the big hills, and each of these journeys was done

in their annual ten days holiday. He taught Allan to identify birds and in a thousand ways added to his education.

But at twenty three Allan was still a grocer. He was in charge of the provision counter by then and if anything, hated the job more than ever. Now that his brother was a tradesman, his mother was reasonably well off, so in short, he was free from responsibilities.

And how little things affect our destinies.

The shop was pretty busy and Allan was at his counter answering various calls for bacon, boiled ham or black puddings. Now it happened that the schoolchildren were fond of foregathering in Allan's corner. The bacon cutting machine fascinated them and the man behind it was always friendly. Wheeler frowned on Allan's popularity. On this day a youngster was holding down the other side of the scale on which Allan was trying to weigh something. He made a playful lunge to slap the hand of the offending youngster, slipped on the greasy floor and with a thud and a crash of breaking glass, scales and Allan hit the floor. There was commotion in the shop.

Wheeler took command, order was restored, and when the shop had cleared, Allan was ordered into the back shop. He owed an apology and intended delivering it. The broken scale was prominently exhibited, and when Allan came in, Wheeler pointed to it. "I thought you would do something like this," he began. "Do you know how much this cost?"

"It was an accident sir," said Allan diffidently enough, "and I'm sorry," "Not much use in being sorry is there, after doing your best to smash something." His voice was at its nastiest.

"I slipped on something and fell. That was all. It was just bad luck bringing the scale down as well."

"I saw what happened. You were capering as usual with these damned youngsters. I'll need to report this to the general manager. There are a few things I have to tell him about you while I am at it."

"Well, if the general manager is dealing with it, that will be all." Allan moved to go.

6

"I give the orders here. I've a few things to say to you. Your mother came to me and asked me to do my best for you when you were a message boy. I kept you on. I've closed my eyes to a lot of things, coming in late in the mornings, going away sharp at night, slip-shod work. And what thanks do I get?"

"You don't want thanks for condemning me to a life of this, do you? Let me tell you that it was the worst thing that ever happened to me, getting kept on at this job. Now you are trying to make out that it was only your generosity that has kept me working here. You are incapable of generosity and if my mother did speak to you, then it must have accorded with your wishes to keep me on. You are not the man to sacrifice anything. But you haven't spoiled my life yet though you've tried by fault-finding and watching my every action. Well, I'm finished here. And the sooner you let me leave the better!" Allan's face was white when he left Wheeler. The following morning he sent in his resignation.

There were four days left till Saturday. Four days, and Allan worked as he had never worked before. He wanted to show them what a good man they were losing. He was in on time and out after time.

Saturday night came. He turned down his hams and bacons on to their marble slabs for the last time, draped cloths over everything, and went into the back shop. Wheeler stopped him going out the back door. "It isn't too late to change your mind," he said. "Stay on with us. You belong here." He held out his hand. Allan shook his head. "Goodbye Mr Wheeler," he said.

Brown did not applaud his action. He looked grave when Allan told him he had packed in. "It's all very well to talk, "he said, after a bit, "but now you are out of a job and jobs are scarce. I hope I didn't influence you."

"I expect you did," said Allan gaily. "I spoke to my mother about it. She was against it but told me I knew what I was doing."

That weekend wasn't so enjoyable as usual. For the first

time the full seriousness of his step really came home to him. Twenty three years of age and he was trying to change his job. Brown has made it all sound so easy. Now he hadn't a job.

Monday he scanned the adverts and saw no jobs to his liking, Tuesday, he signed on at the Labour Exchange, Wednesday he wrote after various outdoor jobs he saw in a county magazine, Thursday he signed the Exchange, Friday he went away by himself for a long weekend. By Monday he proved that a life of leisure is not a life of pleasure.

The following weekend he got a lift north in a milk wagon. Rain was sweeping in grey veils across the sodden hills. After a few miles he decided to brew a can of tea under cover of a friendly barn, and with that object asked the farmer if he could have some boiling water. "Come inside," said the farmer. They were a friendly couple and soon he was sitting at the table telling them his story.

"You are better out of it," said the farmer. "What would you like to do if you could?"

"I don't know, but I fancy the simple life, at any rate an outdoor job where I could see the seasons and the country and get away from the artificiality of the town. I don't want to work under eyes all the time."

"What about farming? Did you ever think of it?"

"You need to learn an awful lot."

"A willing man can always learn and I'd rather have a willing learner than an unwilling expert."

"Yes, maybe *you* would."

"I'm offering you a job. I'll pay you the standard agricultural rate and there is a bedroom in the house here, I need a man to help me. I've just broken up some new ground. The two of us can manage it. Can you start now?"

"What's doing?"

"We'll riddle some spuds, and when the rain clears uncover a wee stack I'm selling."

So Allan started on his new life. The farmer found him a keen man and quick to pick up the art of harrowing, ploughing, cultivating, rolling and sowing. He was happy, and of a weekend the barn is a great place of outdoor men, hikers and climbers. But as well as giving advice on where to climb or hike, he'll tell you the secret of successful living. "Be happy at your work and if you don't like it, move heaven and earth to change it."

Typescript in the National Library of Scotland collections

Tom was an extremely active youth. He joined the local boxing club in the hope of increasing his height – and for their excursions to Campsies and Ben Lomond. He joined the Boys brigade while underage in order to play the drums, an enthusiasm that only waned when the more serious business of learning to write began.

TOUGH JOINT

'Wanted. Hot band for Saturday night dancing. Four or five members, terms moderate.'

A reply to this advert in a Glasgow newspaper secured us the job, and on a dirty Saturday night, five men with an assortment of cases might have been seen scouring one of Glasgow's less choice districts for the hall. We were late, fearfully late.

"Here's the bon," was the prelude to finding the place and with sinking hearts we were hurried through a pend and up a wooden stair by five or six toughs who had been sent to look for us.

"Come on, boys. Hoff past eight. Whit kep' ye?" greeted us in angry tones. The toughness of the crowd made our already quavering hearts quail and the women looked as unpleasant as the hard-bitten, hands-in-pockets, dandified toughs, resplendent in flashy mufflers. Resentful faces scowled at us as we crossed the dingy dance floor to gain the platform. We were an hour late and expected a razor attack at any moment for daring to keep them waiting.

Never did the band get going more quickly and we soon had the crowd swinging into a foxtrot. This was better we thought. The dancers seemed to like it, and with some feeling of confidence we waited for the MC to announce the next dance.

He did, shouting from the middle of the floor but we could not make sense of it. Expectantly the crowd awaited the band starting up, the women nipping their fags and lodging them behind their ears as their partners claimed them. Frantically our leader signalled the MC. "What was that you announced?" he asked. The MC bawled something unintelligible. "Say it slowly please," the leader said, his face more ruddy than usual with the stares of the mob. "La Fanatique," the MC retorted peevishly, "Ur ye coren beef?" "OK," said the leader, then turning to us, "Have any of you boys ever heard of it?" No one had. "Right then. 'Dark Town Strutters' at this tempo." He beat out a tempo about Palais Glide speed.

Before the first dozen bars were over we knew we had blundered. Scowling faces passed the platform. Suddenly a raucous female voice rang out, "Aw quicken up the bon there!" The pace quickened and we scrapped through. But that was only the beginning. For the first time we learned to play 'modern select' as it is called. Many of these dances are exclusive to the joints and owe their origin to ingenious, if misguided, MCs. Windsor tango, Happy landing foxtrot, sequence rumba, and a host of un-nameables were asked for and somehow we managed to dish them up. But the crowd did not like us.

The band platform however was a popular place, for behind my drums was the favourite spot for consuming bottles of beer. I had visions of being made a target for an empty.

It was during the last dance a scuffle broke out near the door and in a moment it was an all-in affair, the women standing on chairs for a better view.

As is the custom during a disturbance, we kept playing, but everyone abandoned the dance floor for the better fun of

10

the fight. Like a rugby scrimmage the struggling mass gradually moved doorwards and down the stair. Raised voices and
oaths and the clatter of bottles showed the fighting was still
fierce. The hall was deserted so we packed up.

An ominous stillness marked our departure. The MC met
us in the lobby and paid us our wages. He was in no way
perturbed and seemed to regard the whole affair as normal.
"It was only a 'barney' and it clears the hall."

Typescript in the National Library of Scotland Collections

AN EPIC

It was fourteen years ago on a Loch Lomond bus that I first
met Richie. I was sixteen at the time and my ambition was to
be an explorer. I had read everything about the Arctic and
the Antarctic that I could lay my hands on and here, for the
first time, was a kindred spirit. I can see him now as I write,
a quiet, rather grim looking man with yellow hair going a
bit thin on top. His quietness was noticeable, for the busload
were singing their heads off after a successful Easter weekend.

He leaned across and asked me if I had been climbing, for
although dressed as a schoolboy complete with a cap – in order
to get half fare on the bus – I was carrying an army pack. I
confessed my enthusiasm as is the way of youth, and he took
me seriously. Indeed, he confessed to similar ambitions.

I did not expect to see him again, but by a coincidence met
him later at Rowardennan one moonlight Saturday night as
I searched the foreshore for a camping place. We shared the
tent and got on famously. Richie seemed to know every part
of the Scottish Highlands. He had been a cyclist and had just
taken to walking and climbing.

He was unemployed and spent most of his time outdoors,
going back to Glasgow from Tuesday to Thursday to sign
his name at the Labour Exchange. Politics entered my life at

11

this time too, for Richie was embittered against a government that had no work to offer, and rather than walk the streets he walked the hills. He was a plumber and in his kit he carried a few tools of his trade, so that he could pick up an odd penny by wee jobs such as repairing milk cans and so on.

He was a little chap, not more than five feet six in height, but very strong. [*Tom was five feet one.*] Weightlifting and wrestling were his hobbies, and I remember that weekend there was a health-and-strength club camping in the bay. We were sitting on the foreshore when a big chap, stripped to the waist and of magnificent physique, offered to 'pull' any one of the party. No one spoke and after a short silence Richie said he might have a try. It was a David-and-Goliath sort of tournament, but I have a vivid recollection of the big chap's shoulders being forced down on the gravel so mercilessly that blood streamed down his back. Later, when weightlifting with boulders, Richie capped all their efforts by doing a 'bent press' with an enormous stone!

That, then, was the man. As well as revolutionary ideas on politics, he had revolutionary ideas on walking. He wanted to do it the hard way, the explorer's way, across Scotland by the mountain tops, self-supporting in food and sheltering where one could. This was what I wanted, and Richie had an idea for a tour, provided I could get my holiday when he was allowed off by the Labour Exchange.

It was all worked out, and late one night a man and a boy might have been seen boarding the Oban train. Probably the watcher would even have permitted himself a laugh, for the boy, small for his age, was carrying a Bergen rucksack of huge bulk that reached far below the proper place in the small of his back. To counteract its weight he had to bend nearly double, the motion being as near turtle-like as makes no difference.

Taynuilt was our destination and in the grey of the morning we fortified ourselves with a meal. When I say 'fortified' I mean 'fortified' – at least as far as Richie was concerned. He prided himself on being a good trencherman. He was more than that. In amazement I watched as our store of food dwin-

12

dled as Richie "packed it away", to use his own expression. Our food was supposed to last a week, but I knew there and then that it would not.

Ben Cruachan, whose tops we were supposed to promenade over to Ben Starav, was in cloud. Also its slopes looked fearfully long and steep for our heavy bags, so we decided that, since there was nothing to be gained by going up into the mist, we would go up the seldom visited west side of Loch Etive. There as a track marked on the map, but the toil of that rucksack made each step a separate effort of will.

I can remember little of that walk except a pair of dogs that Richie antagonised by swinging a stick at them and hissing like a cat. He antagonised all dogs in fact, so that I was in terror each time we came to a house. What I can remember is that evening at the head of Loch Etive. All the toil was worthwhile just to be ringed around by the great hills, rocky and green, and seamed with innumerable cataracts that filled the air with sound. How delightful to be free of the sack and to be at last 'exploring'!

Morning saw us take to the hills in rain by a wild pass, the Lairig Eilde, which at length led into Glen Coe. An impression of cloudy gloom and fierce, toppling crags remains distinct from the glen as I know it today. Under a rock we ate the last of our food and were joined by a tramp.

Richie was not flattered at being asked if I was his son, and answered rather sharply to the contrary. Prematurely thin on top myself at thirty I can understand how he felt at twenty-eight to be mistaken for the father of such a precocious youngster. I had many inward chuckles later as the same mistake was made time after time by people whom we met.

Richie's interest in the tramp was more than passing, for he had a hankering to try the life himself, and he questioned the tattered-looking fellow on the technique of the craft. It was a mean sort of existence, of begging and labouring, and of model lodging-houses in big towns when winter came. The tramp's last words were, "Keep off the game, it's only for

13

down-and-outs like me." As he shambled down that bleak moor in his rags, purposeless and alone in an inhospitable world, I found my first romantic picture shattered.

It was afternoon as we climbed up a heathery hillside, the north-enclosing face of the glen. We were on route for Loch Leven. What went wrong I don't know – our map was a motoring one, three miles to the inch, so I suspect that had something to do with it – but for hours we crossed an expanse of heather and bog, 'God- forsaken and man-forsworn'. At length a long slash of water gleamed. We thought it was Loch Leven but tasted its water to make sure. It was fresh and sweet, therefore not Loch Leven water. We scanned the map and decided it was the Blackwater.

On its shores I was seized with a trembling of the lower limbs. I did not say anything but my weakness was apparent to Richie, for I was lagging behind. I had 'the knock' he informed me, a complaint common among hard-pushing cyclists. Food was the only cure but we had none, so he bravely shouldered my pack in addition to his own, and we pushed on. Later that night we camped at the foot of a huge, thundering waterfall, the biggest I had ever seen, and in my imagination now as big as Niagara. We came far that day.

But Kinlochleven was not far off, and after a breakfastless start, we got there around midday. Richie bought the groceries while I went to a house for water. 'Is it tinkers?' she asked as she handed me the brimming can. We got the stove going behind an outhouse and, regardless of the curious townsfolk, had a meal that is an event in my memory.

A convenient bus took us to Fort William and that night saw us in the half-way hut on BenNevis. It was a beautiful evening and the silver lochs to the west and the massive peaks of the Mamores to the south enraptured us. All the charm that the Scottish hills have for me is conveyed in that fragment of memory. It is too indefinite to explain, but I can see a collection of giant hills and lochs probably more akin to the mountains of the moon than to reality.

Right through the night people kept coming into the hut on their way to the top for the sunrise. It was cold up there wrapped in a solitary blanket and we were glad to get moving ourselves. Mist had crept down to us and up into a thickening gloom we climbed. Somehow I hoisted that pack to the top. Below us were the dripping wet crags of the wildest place I had ever seen.

Our plan was to traverse the mountain into the upper part of the glen, so we were not at all careful where we went down. Anyway we got entangled on the crags. I suspect that we descended quite a bit of the north-east buttress for I have a fearful recollection of crying for help as I sought for handholds, while the weight of the bag nearly dragged me to perdition. The crags seemed to drop away sheer below us, yet we kept on going. Fate looked after us more kindly than we deserved, for we got down.

Richie was elated. 'We'll climb Aonach Beag,' he cried. We left the bags and we seemed to float up it, so easy did it feel after our bag-hoisting efforts. There was nothing to see except for dirt scarred snow-beds, hard as ice, in the hollows. Actually, I think it was Aonach Mor we climbed, but whatever it was we enjoyed it. How we bounded down that peak, whooping with delight at our achievements and the release from the bondage of the packs! There was something unutterably satisfying about these great green slopes seamed with wild mountain torrents and scattered with boulders.

We were soaked through, not relishing the prospect of camping, when a miracle in the shape of a little tin bothy at the junction of two rivers gave us the shelter we needed. It was cold on the concrete floor but we did not complain. The purring of the stove was cheery and we felt the warm glow of comradeship.

The rain still fell as we pushed towards Loch Treig in the morning. There was no track, the floor of the glen was sodden and the river in wild spate. At last with the rain running out of us we came to a lonely house, unfortunately on the wrong side of the river. We had an urge to get in to a barn or shed, and maybe we could get a few eggs.

We surveyed the stepping-stones submerged by a swirling brown flood. I shall never forget that crossing. As a foot was submerged to reach a stone, the force of the river would sweep it aside, and the movement of the water tended to confuse the senses. Luckily they were flat stones, but in mid-stream I felt as isolated as a man all alone in a coble in mid-Atlantic. I could see myself bobbing up and down in that brown rush to be flung in cataract into Loch Treig. But I got across safely.

The people in the house were friendly and gave us eggs and flour. We could use their barn if we wished, but they recommended going on to Loch Ossian where a house had been put at the disposal of walkers and climbers. This was news to us so we pushed on. I will draw a veil over the short cut we tried to take to reach the house. Short cuts can never pay on Rannoch . . .

The door was locked but we entered by a window. We felt we were expected. On a table stood a jar of almonds and raisins and there was an enormous store if firewood. Soon all our clothes were on the pulleys and a great fire was roaring up the chimney. Over it we made pancakes with our eggs and flour and Richie initiated me into the mysteries of French toast. That was a happy night. We sat in our birthday suits while our clothes steamed merrily above us. An abundance of blankets saw us warmly through the night. I learned afterwards that the building was called a Youth Hostel. This was my first experience of something that was to popularize the whole outdoor movement. [*Loch Ossian is still an SYHA hostel*]

We had decided to go down to Rannoch and climb some peaks from there. At Corrour, next morning, a convenient train was standing in the tiny station, so we piled into it as we had no time to buy tickets. The first stop was Crianlarich so our plans were spoiled. We walked along the railway line to near Tyndrum, and, as the weather was wet and cloudy, parked ourselves in a railway bothy, the key of which had been handily placed under a stone.

Richie was in a quarrelsome mood that night and told me off severely for 'filthy habits' when I licked a blob of condensed milk off the edge of the tin after pouring some out. I explained that I had picked up the habit from him but he did not take it kindly.

The atmosphere was rather tense when we went to bed but Richie's temper was to find an outlet in the morning. We were awakened by a loud thundering at the door with an angry command to know, "Who the hell is in there?" Our fire had been seen. "Don't answer," said Richie. He pulled on his trousers.

"Open up at once or I'll have the police on you," the voice shouted. "You have no business here at all."

Richie flung open the door, chin thrust out in a look of angry determination that would have daunted the boldest. "Who do you think you are talking to?" His voice was quiet.

The man continued to shout. "Listen," said Richie. "Get the police. Get who you like but don't stand there shouting at me. I'll not have it. Get out!" He took a step towards the man. The man fled.

"Now for a quick getaway," said Richie. We made off up the slope of Ben Lui, traversed its misty top and dropped into Glen Falloch. Richie's bad temper had gone, so I was grateful to that railwayman.

I was rather puzzled though when Richie suggested sheltering from a few drops of rain that were falling. We slipped unseen into an outhouse. "Eggs," explained the lad briefly. Now, I have said nothing of Richie's activities as an egg collector for he had practised it long before I met him. It was his boast that he had taken eggs in every county in Scotland and I believed him. He got out his tea-can and disappeared into a shed from whence came the sound of hens. It was unfortunate that the farmer met him coming out . . .

Next day saw us back home. My mother was quite shocked by my appearance. She declared I was like a greyhound, skin and bone. Certainly an examination in the mirror showed a pinched appearance and an emaciated look about the face.

But I enjoyed that trip, and even now as I write after all these years, I still catch something of the high adventure of exploring. The Highlands were my Himalayas, and no intrepid spirit wandering new valleys in Kashmir or the Karakorum has reached a higher plane of exultation in the joy of the quest. The hardship served only to make it seem all the more worthwhile.

I have a lot to thank Richie for. He went to work in England shortly afterwards and our hill-partnership was severed. He was a good companion and a character. I have tried to draw him as he was, with his weakness for argument and eggs, his huge appetite, and his generosity in carrying my rucksack when I was ill. Richie was an unconventional type of man, but no one delighted more in the wild beauty of the Highland hills, and his spirit of adventure was forever an inspiration to me.

Years later, heading for the Fannichs, I was cycling through Strathconon. It was early May and snow showers and a vicious east wind made a winter's day of it. My bike was loaded with food and camping equipment. Whisking down a hill with my load wobbling I saw a bald head bent over the handlebars, and a pair of bare knees moving up and down. He looked up as I approached and I jammed on my brakes. It was Richie – a delightful surprise. We shook hands heartily and exchanged ideas.

He was unemployed again, and had been out of Glasgow since Friday afternoon. This was Sunday. He had left Glasgow at four o'clock in the afternoon, slept in Crianlarich, pushed through Glen Coe and up the Great Glen, through Glen Sheil and by Loch Duich to Strome Ferry on Saturday, and now he was en route for Fort William to spend the night there so as to be in Glasgow on Monday.

I gasped. A motorist would consider this a good tour and Richie was doing it by pushbike. He looked at my ancient bike with horror and wondered how I managed to push such a load on it. I reminded him of my early training in pack carrying at his hands. The snowswept hills seemed very bleak after Richie passed.

HIGHLAND DAYS

In World War Two Tom was stationed on the south coast of England, a surveyor in the Royal Artillery preparing batteries for repulsing the likely German invasion, a not too onerous time. With that danger receeding, he crossed the Channel to Belgium and also served in Italy. With his five foot one height he once joked to another wee companion, "Just look at the bullets we'll miss." (Small he may have been but he had the stride of long practice and immense fitness) He still had a couple of close escapes. 'I was in a cinema in Germany and there was an explosion and the whole screen blew right out covering everyone with the debris. We fought our way out again. There was the time too when I was in a top bunk and another chap was on the lower. We were bombed and the bomb went straight through the bunks between us.'

INSPECTION

There was a flap on. The annual inspection of the C.C.R.A. was due. C.C.R.A. stands for Corps Commander Royal Artillery and the Battery Commander would rather face an angry German than submit the battery to his eagle gaze.

Since the 'warning order', bullshit had been our order of the day – or weeks. Cinders fresh and black lay on the paths between newly trimmed grass verges; fire points shone in pristine red paint; the brass on the stirrup pumps was polished to perfection; swill tubs were sparkling their whitewash to dazzle the eye; the cookhouse smelt of new paint and the gleaming stove reflected its cream and white; battery offices were scrubbed and the tables neat with empty trays and clean squares of pink blotting paper.

But this was only a dress rehearsal for the real show. Our rifle drill, march past, fit of equipment and state of blanco and battle dress was to be tested.

At last it was all over. Battle dresses had been changed, drill smartened up, charge sheets made out and C.B. awarded, and all we were waiting for was the big day – the easiest one of the lot for us for our Lieut. Col. is windy and we know the C.C.R.A. will be easier to please than him.

Reveille was at five a.m. on that fateful morning. Nothing gets a soldier down more than constant inspections. Tempers were frayed and arguments numerous before each bed was the replica of the Regimental Kit Layout, barrack room floors scrubbed and stoves blackened and walls washed.

Dinner was at eleven thirty so that we could be on parade at one o'clock to be ready for the big cheese himself at three o'clock. We 'right dressed', 'opened and closed order march', 'sloped and unsloped arms', 'stood at ease, easy and attention' until we were all blue with cold and furious with the irk of it all. "Fifteen minutes to go," I breathed to myself at last. At that moment a dispatch rider roared in, saluted, and presented a note. Our O.C. was a long faced man with an expressionless countenance. He stood regarding us all for a moment, then he slung down the note and kicked it to the wind. "It's all off, He's coming tomorrow," he bawled. "Parade dismiss . . . And go out and get drunk." For the first time since the bullshit began no one abused him. He felt the same as we did . . .

Typescript in the National Library of Scotland Collections

ZERO HOUR

It was 3 a.m. All night guns had rumbled and crashed in a fierce barrage. Very lights and rockets lit long coloured tails in the sky over the battle area. Round a tea bucket dim figures of men were having a last drink. Zero hour in another hour. The gun sheets were off, and the huge super-heavy equipment, muzzles at a sinister angle, looked gigantic in the semi-darkness.

In the command post – a dugout fourteen feet wide and eight feet long with just enough room for your head – there was activity. Gone are the days when you faced the enemy and sighted your guns on him. Artillery problems are mathematical problems now. Only the observation officer and his staff see the shells fall as a rule. Gun programmes would be handed to each sergeant in charge of a gun and an immense amount of work go in to their compilation. Switch from zero line, gun timings, rates of fire, fuse lengths, etc. must all be accurate if the gun is going to carry out its battle task. The latest weather report had come in and right now the command post staff were crouched over a couple of tables working out by lamplight the range correction and deflection necessary to counteract the effects of variations in the temperature, barometric pressure, speed and direction of the wind etc. No easy job in bad light at 3 a.m.

Tea over, a subdued excitement was in the air. No one was allowed to talk except in a whisper. It is a tense job waiting for a big something about to happen. The last check up in the command post was completed. Numbers one were handed their gun programme. All that had been done, the surveying in of the gun positions, laying out of lines of fire, calculations to get the gun on its target, would now be put to the test. Wireless sets were netted and somewhere in sight of the enemy was the Battery Commander waiting to observe the effects of the fire and send down corrections if necessary. His observation post had been dug in the night. A trying task. Only those who have dug a hole in the dark in hard ground within sound of the enemy know the difficulty and discomfort of the job.

"Take posts." There was no sound except the faint click of the winch as a monster shell was hoisted into position. "Halfway." Not the usual urgent shout. The shell was ready for its final ramming. "Home." A heaving of arms on the long rammer. With a faint ring its driving band bit into the

21

rifling of the barrel. The huge breech mechanism closed on the charge. For the gunners it was the culmination of hard training and intense work.

"Three 0 seconds to go!" No need for the G.P.O. to subdue his voice now. "Ten seconds to go." "Five ... Four ... Three ... Two ... One ... FIRE!" In the orange tongue of flame the detachments were squirming silhouettes in fantastic shape as their bodies took the recoil of the gun.

The earth shook with the terrible blasting roar of the explosion. In the command post a smother of chalk and earth covered everything. Flying dust rising in a cloud obscured the gun.

"Load!" And so it went on for an hour, an inferno of noise, dirt and the smell of cordite.

That was just the beginning. At 0930 hours the real programme started. The artillery were massed in order of size. 25 pounders – the Germans' poison because of their deadly accuracy and rapid fire power – were for'ard. Behind them came heavier stuff of widening barrels and longer muzzles until you came to the super-heavies at the back. The guns were ready.

A rocket was the time signal, flickering and sailing white through the air. The guns thundered and belched fire and smoke. A salvo of such a number of guns must be heard to be believed. Imagine the loudest peal of thunder you have ever heard being echoed back by rocky mountains and prolong that ear-splitting crackle for hours on end and you will have a faint idea of what modern artillery can do. Nothing in the whole of the last war compares to a 1945 concentration.

From the O.P. a moving sea of earth tossing madly in the shrill whine of a shell storm was the result. Then came the first canisters of smoke falling like a rain of meteors trailing gigantic tails. In billowy masses the smoke built up. Then came aircraft. The pe-ow of their bombs was lost but into the foam of smoke they went like gannets diving into a pearly sea.

22

The O.P. was hazed over in a gauze of mist. Under its cover the infantry were advancing, ghostly figures spiky with the edges of war. Their Zero Hour is now.

Typescript in National Library of Scotland Collections

Tom notes, 'This is an account of an actual barrage' but 'avoiding names or places which could be of slightest use to the enemy.'

II

THE HIMALAYA

Douglas Scott had served in the army in India during World War Two and before returning to the UK made a trek into the Garwhal. He couldn't wait to return and soon found fellow enthusiasts. The Scottish Himalayan Expedition of 1950 to India was the first expedition to take up where Shipton and Tilman had left off before the war and was followed up in 1952 with an expedition to Nepal. The first party was Tom Weir, Douglas Scott, Bill Murray and Tom Mackinnon, the second included George Roger as Murray had become involved with the notable exploration of routes to Everest with Shipton, Hillary and others in 1951/52 – which led to Everest being climbed in 1953.

Tom MacKinnon was a member of the successful 1955 Kanchenjunga expedition. With hindsight the momentum from such small post-war beginnings is remarkable. We are lucky that Tom recorded that unimaginably different world in The Ultimate Mountains *and* East of Katmandu. *Just how different is pictured in this first extract describing the challenge of even reaching Katmandu. Tom, Douglas and Bill all resigned from good jobs to mount this first expedition, not something done casually when in their mid-thirties in the grim post-war years of high unemployment. Sponsorship was unknown then but a Weir/Scott feature in the National Geographic magazine funded their second Himalayan expedition. The description following brings home just how things have changed.*

FIRST REACH KATMANDU

September; stifling heat and humid air, and we wilt in the Bombay Customs House, feeling that if hell has an earthly likeness it must be the interior of this dismal place of corridors, iron grilles and inmates who sit at wooden tables trying to sort out a man-made inferno of regulations; papers that rustle in front of worries faces – Anglo-Indians mostly, who talk with Welsh-like accents, and who certainly do not intend to meet us half-way. They want us to pay duty on 1200 pounds of food and equipment. We are a Himalayan Expedition (such is our grand title) and for the hundredth time, it seems, we give our reasons why we will not part with the fabulous sum of rupees demanded. All they seem to understand at present is that we are Scots, and so they are determined to attempt the impossible by trying to take the breeks off a Highlandman. For the umpteenth time we explain that we are the Scottish Nepal Expedition, that we are going to Katmandu to explore the region west of Everest, that our 1200 pounds of boxes contain merely tents, old climbing clothes, primus stoves and iron rations. Every item is listed, and since we have been granted duty free entry into India, and anyhow are merely passing through India to get to Nepal, please can we get on, get out, and leave them to pester someone else?

There are four of us concerned. George Roger, who has never been to the Himalaya before, is a gentlemanly type from Gourock on the Clyde, and we watch with interest to see how long his reserves of good nature and politeness will take to break down under the strain of Indian inefficiency and unwillingness to make a positive decision on anything. Douglas Scot and Tom MacKinnon are old companions of

27

the 1950 Scottish Himalayan Expedition, men of patience and determination, who know when to stop smiling and get down to business; as for me, impetuous by nature and quick to anger, my impulse is to wrest our goods from the Indian Customs by any means.

Our expedition is a democratic one, with no appointed leader. Jobs get done by someone undertaking them rather by anyone formulating a plan or laying down an order. In fact there is something quite miraculous about being here at all. In June we had done nothing except mark time for getting a political pass into Nepal to explore – applying not very hopefully when Nepal first threw open her doors on 500 miles of unexplored mountains hitherto closed to generations of mountaineers.

Our luck was that W. H. Murray, who had been with us in Garwhal in 1950, had been chosen to reconnoitre the south face of Everest with Eric Shipton, and thus was one of the first mountaineers to see a terrain shrouded in mystery until his visit. The party came home with a tale of a fantastic land; of spectacular gorges in whose depths travel was even more difficult than over the snowy passes to Tibet; of Sherpa villages perched in incredible places below the highest peaks in the world; of a mountain with the name of Amadablam supported on razor-sharp ridges and easily the most formidable peak ever photographed.

Their fascinating job had been to puzzle out the topography of the Everest massif and find a route to the summit if possible. The splendid ultimate result of this reconnaissance is known to the world, [*Everest climbed in 1953*] but how many people remember the magnificent exploration achieved by this party which comprised of Shipton, Ward, Murray, Bourdillon, Riddiford and Hillary?

What attracted us most was the description of a great gorge they had seen, a sheer-walled canyon called Rolwaling, into whose depths they had peered for 7000 feet, down an ice crest above a basin not unlike the Nanda Devi basin, in the centre

28

of which was a peak of pale granite and ice which they named the Menlungtse Peak. The gorge at their feet was called Rolwaling after the furrow made by the plough, and it was on the glaciers of this region that they found the prints of the Abominable Snowman.

That was in 1951. The plans we made for 1952 were to explore this gorge, and try to climb some of the magnificent peaks that Shipton and Murray had described so well.

In the Himalaya, of course, everything hinges on getting a political permit, a more difficult thing to achieve than the summit of many a peak, as we know from our previous experience in 1950 we had to set sail without it, and miraculously tracked it to earth once in India.

Waiting for the Nepal pass was interesting for me, because I had three strings to my bow. First was the Himalaya, but if no permit came through by June I had the option of a place on a sledging expedition to Spitzbergen, then in May, while still waiting for the permit, I was invited to go on the British North Greenland Expedition to Queen Louise Land. Advanced stages of dithering were suddenly ended by the arrival of the permit. We were on – to Nepal – and there was not a moment to lose, because our application to explore was granted with effect from August to January, which left us only two months to prepare.

Hectic months – getting tents – buying food – arranging import and export licences – pulling strings to get the berths to Bombay – working out a plan of campaign – then on the day of sailing for India to be told that there was political upheaval in the country and that all travel to Nepal was temporarily restricted. Can you imagine us returning home? Certainly not. We sailed, and put all unpleasant thoughts out of our heads for the duration of that delightful voyage over 500 miles of tranquil ocean.

Now in the Bombay Customs house it seems we are hammering our heads, not against a brick wall, but against something more rubbery, composed of ignorance and stupidity against which one only rebounds, and not even the United Kingdom Commissioner can batter through. But he brings us good news. We are being allowed to proceed to Katmandu; and to speed us on our way H.M. Government are prepared to act as guarantors that duty will be paid on our food and equipment if this is found to be necessary.

This should be sufficient for any Customs House. But instead of accepting it they now lay down a contrary policy, involving the relisting of all our stores under two headings, consumable and non-consumable, so at the end of another day we are no further forward, despite the fact that they know and we know that New Delhi has granted us duty-free entry of all our goods.

We have nearly reached the fighting stage by now, and violence is almost done when next day they demand yet another set of lists, with prices of every item this time. Even the peaceful George recognises the last straw when he sees it, and when we go in a body to see the chief of the Customs House he wilts visibly at the sight of our outraged faces. He listens respectfully, and we expostulate with as much arm-waving as hillmen deprived of backsheesh, and to out astonishment he does not put up a defence. "Enough," he says. "Tomorrow you can go." And we do, pausing only a moment as we board the Frontier Mail – not to offer up a prayer for our deliverance but to wish the Bombay Customs House a soldier's farewell – and settle down for a tranquil night, or as tranquil as one can reasonably expect on a hot and heaving Indian train.

We awoke on the plains, in the gold of a September dawn, and from the railway carriage window looked on swirling rivers in brown monsoon flood, gay with lines of snow-white egrets. India is in fact a land of birds, so numerous that they are a physical part of the landscape, in their grace, flashing colour and infinite variety, from grass-green bee-eaters and slim wren warblers to long-winged marsh harriers and hovering vultures. The pleasure of being an ornithologist is that no country is ever empty for you, and to Douglas Scott and myself it was like coming amongst old friends to see little cormorants sunning themselves on high banks, wings outstretched like their larger brethren on the Clyde. Near and far we could see patient paddy birds, sombre coloured like stones until they slowly opened white wings and became graceful birds like miniature herons. In the air were glossy king crows and ragged kites flying high above the bustle of busy minahs, the latter like so many busy starlings. Kingfishers, pied or vividly blue and orange, dashed on whirring wings over the water. Blue jays, shrikes and bee-eaters occupied the telegraph lines for mile after mile.

The vastness of India! So much of it flat, green, empty of human life. Monotonous mile after mile until suddenly a weird rock escarpment breaks the unending landscape. Now and then there are lonely figures of herdsmen with cattle or goats or water buffaloes, or ploughmen plodding behind their labouring oxen on the sun-scorched plain. Humid air and wilting heat – hothouse greenness, so different from the dry dusty desert of May in the pre-monsoon period of our first Himalayan expedition, when the land was on fire and crying for water and we sat around a block of ice with the screens of the carriage drawn, as we do around our own firesides on a winter evening at home. How in such a climate can people live in shanty-town villages of tin huts like air-raid shelters, devoid of protection from the ferocious Indian sun?

It is always a surprise to run into a railway station in this sort of country. Here, in contrast to the sleeping country, is hell let lose in babbling humanity – the cries of vendors, the whines of beggars, the slamming of carriage doors and the shouts of coolies competing for trade. When we reached Lucknow on the following day there were even acrobats and performing monkeys to divert the traveller and part him from his rupees.

We were on our last lap now to the Nepal border, speeding through an absorbing country of river, lake and flood water – a region where every tree had its growth of weaver birds'

31

nests, and tall stacks of sugar cane grew thickly – rice and banana country, with fields of tall Indian corn so good to eat when roasted.

The long independence of Nepal was favoured by the notoriously unhealthy country that stretches north of the Indian railhead at Raxaul. What we saw when we got there was a dismal place of flooded rice fields and palms, dotted with sugar factory chimneys, occupying a plain only 350 feet above sea level, and with dismay we learned that we would have to spend the night in this hot and smelly place. There was no train to the Nepalese town of Amlekganj until the following morning.

The only highlight of Raxaul was a cold bath that washed away the sweat of two and a half days in the train. But we shall not readily forget the one night we spent in the Nepalese Rest House adjacent to the station. Poor George Roger was not only bitten it seemed by every known variety of insect but when we went for a walk he was attacked by a monstrosity of a duck-goose that hissed at him, snapping with outstretched neck at his khaki-clad legs.

He had further grounds for invective when we went for a meal at the station restaurant, which was dark except for an oil lamp on our table that attracted winged shapes from all points of the compass. George was tackling a curry of unappetising appearance, and as he lifted a portion of meat on his fork a large armour-plated insect like a buzz bomb exploded on his plate, wings flailing and drumming. Douglas's statement that it was 'only a dung beetle' was scarcely mollifying, and George was in the act of saying so when a long green animal like a flying banana ricochetted off the table lamp to cannon from his neck on to the plate. For the first time in our lives we saw him really ruffled as he sprang to his feet and grabbed his hat.

Outside we were confronted by an amazing sight. On the velvet blackness of the night darting lines of red were criss-crossing like some incredible firework display, or an infantry attack with tracer bullets. Not for a few moments did we realise we were looking at fireflies tracing their movements within a few feet of our faces, We thought we were accustomed to the insect noises of the Indian night, but the chorus of cicadas and bullfrogs at Raxaul was the loudest and most ceaseless vibration of clamouring sound we had ever heard – an evil sound in the hot sticky air of that place. Above we could hear the sound of a drum beating, and faintly in our ears – almost in echo of the whining of a mosquito – was the shrill voice of a woman singing a wavering song charged with emotion and sex. There was no doubt that we were in the East.

We retired to bed, but not to sleep, for the mosquitoes droned in our ears in weird harmony with that shrill song, and we had no nets to ward them off. We simply had to lie and be bitten. An incident occurred that may have been real or imagined, for I had been reading a story by Jim Corbett [*author of the classic* Man Eaters of Kumaon] about cobras and what I thought was real may have been the result of a dream. But I awoke in panic in pitch darkness with something slippery slapping my face, something that felt reptilian. My hand went to my face and at the same moment there flashed through my brain the thought 'a hooded cobra!' I tried to keep still to let it slide away, then gave the alarm. Everyone was awake instantly. A light was flashed and I told my tale, but there was nothing to be seen. "That is all I needed," said Tom MacKinnon. "I've had enough of this. I'm going to sit outside on a chair rather than lie and be bitten in this hell-hole."

Next day we moved into Nepal, climbing gradually through rice fields into the Terai on a narrow-gauge railway. Times have changed since this was all unhealthy swamp and jungle. Reclamation has turned much of it into prosperous farmland and it is now renowned as the granary of Nepal. The rice harvesters were busy on their flooded fields, and on the pasture were herds of goats, pigs and water buffaloes. Houses of red clay with thatched roofs made neat little settlements.

Soon we were enclosed by jungle – the sal jungle which is

said to be the haunt of elephants, tigers, panther, leopards, black bears, wolves, jackals, wild buffalo, hog deer and four-horned antelope. The Indian rhino is supposed to exist here too and it is to be hoped it is true, for with the passing of the Rana regime it seems unlikely that this teeming region will ever be hunted again on elephant back as of old with hundreds of these beasts closing into a ring to trap everything contained in it. For six months of the year this is the most unhealthy jungle in India or Nepal, and the Tharus tribes which live within the forest would be extinct were it not that they are partially immune to a deadly brand of malaria known as *awal*.

Quite suddenly we were finished with railways. We were at Amlekganj, and the train exploded people, all hell-bent on getting on to three ancient busses standing outside the platform. It was a battle of umbrellas, for the rain was teeming down, and the unfortunate ticket collector stood more than a little chance of having his eye poked out.

We chartered our own bus, a decrepit vehicle with tyres innocent of tread and windows patched with wood and paper. But though it rattled and vibrated alarmingly it went with a will into the lash of the rain and swirling clouds, climbing ever upwards, until suddenly we were in a ravine with chir pines askew on ragged crests above us – truly in the Himalaya at last. Grey langur monkeys with black faces crossed the road in front of us. Waterfalls poured from the hills and mud avalanches obliterated the road in places. Workmen were still busy clearing the latest of these where a vast slope of red clay sheered down to the river, and we had to wait while they cut an opening for our vehicle.

The roadway comes to an end at Bhimpedi, where a busy little town is compressed against the main wall of the Siwalik, the first of two mountain ridges barring access to the Vale of Nepal and the fabled city of Katmandu. The ridge rose above us as an uncompromising green slope cleft by gullies, up which we could see a wavering path dotted with the bent backs of coolies.

Theoretically we should have been able to get coolies to carry for us over to Katmandu, but not that night except at their price.

The old truth that every man is a capitalist was promptly demonstrated when the few nondescript characters available knew that we wanted to get moving immediately, and in ten minutes doubled their charges on their scarcity value. We were indignant and were telling them in no uncertain terms what we thought of them when we were rescued by a distinguished-looking native bearer in the employ of the British Embassy at Katmandu who urged us to leave the luggage to him. He would superintend its delivery to Katmandu.

How the devil looks after his own! Such a piece of luck was not to be scorned, and although we were departing from the good rule in India of never separating from your kit, we accepted his offer gratefully, relieved to be done with the trains and busses and the gabble of wrangling tongues. To face a green slope and get some exercise, even if it was only putting one foot in front of the other, was the perfect antidote to the trial of patience which is the first test of the Himalayan traveller.

We were surprised to find ourselves climbing in the gathering darkness with speed and enjoyment, for first days in the mountains are usually a penance. In a steep village where drums were beating and men were singing we were directed to the Rest House, sited like a deserted mansion in splendid isolation. Someone from out of the dark took it upon himself to find the caretaker, and within half an hour we were inside, listening to the death cackle of a fowl which appeared on our plates in a remarkably short time.

What a contrast to Raxaul! Life there had been a sweat bath. Here at over 600 feet we were pleasantly cool – so cool that in lieu of bedding, which had not yet caught up with us, we had to don socks and pullovers to get warmth enough to sleep, and we did not need any lulling, for it had been a tiring and anxious day.

The air felt fresh as spring in the morning. Birds were singing and slow moving coils of mist drifted over jungle walls patterned with incredible rice terraces, built like staircases into the mountains. Far beyond the valley up which we had zig-zagged by bus lay the Indian Plains – as pale as lavender seas stretching away to infinity.

It was a strenuous Himalayan march that lay ahead, twelve miles of ups and downs on a path whose borders were worn smooth by countless bare feet – an Asiatic highway packed with scuffling goats and slow moving buffaloes, strings of coolies bent under heavy packs, parties of Gurkha soldiers going and coming on leave, wealthy people reclining on litters or sitting perched in the huge baskets which are the taxis of this part of the world, powered by hill men and women who certainly earn their living the hard way. We had stepped into the seventeenth century, but for the giant funicular of an electric ropeway which spans the valleys, shuttling from hill top to hill top swinging baskets bearing trade goods from India, and (we hoped) some of our luggage.

There were cunningly sited tea houses on the top of steeper rises, designed to tempt the traveller to stop and buy a brass tumblerful of hot sticky-sweet tea at city prices of two annas a cup, and we only wished we could talk a common language to the round smiling Nepali faces eager to be friendly. It was a stiff pull up to the ragged edge of the final pass, and it was with excitement that we climbed to its jungly crest to look across the vale of Katmandu not to mountains but to towering banks of cumulus, a tremendous cloudscape that even as we looked flamed with sunset, filling the sky with incredible pillars of fire. On the plain below, tiny, remote, in the vastness of encircling ridges, lay Katmandu. We stood spellbound, looking down on the twinkling lights of this last great city of Asia, as the turmoil of clouds deepened the encroaching darkness, swallowing up one by one the mysterious waves of ridges and valleys.

Below our feet was Asoka's Staircase, spiralling down a fierce jungle wall loud with the dusk cries of Himalayan

36

barbets. (Asoka was the Emperor who in 261 A.D. proclaimed Buddhism to be the state religion of India, and established monasteries and temples throughout the land, himself becoming a monk) We plunged downward on this 2,500 foot staircase, pausing not a moment either for breath or to pick off the leeches that attached themselves wherever they could, for it was a race with darkness and we did not know where we would sleep that night.

But we reckoned without the kindness of the British Embassy. Colonel Proud, the Second Secretary, had been notified of our coming, and had his men out patrolling to waylay us and bring us to his house. We were seized, whisked into a motor car and, rather dazed by it all, found ourselves with drinks in our hands, a hot bath waiting for us, and the best dinner we had faced for years . . .

Motor cars are an anachronism in this atmosphere of the Middle Ages, especially as each one has to be carried bodily over the Chandrigiri Pass and set down in this flat land of the vale, but a jeep road from India to Katmandu has just been completed, and this will speed up the westernisation of this city once so remote.

What did the Tibetans think of it, we wondered, as we watched a caravan drive their sheep into the Durbar square – men in pigtails, skin-clad, cloth-booted, sturdy, slant-eyed, broad-faced, in contrast to the smaller and more neatly dressed Nepalis who went about the city centre. For the Tibetans this would be journey's end – from the Tibetan plateau across a hundred miles of Himalayan mountains to this most fantastic corner of Katmandu, where on four sides there are the finest creations of a thousand years of oriental art, in pagodas, temples of richly carved wood, red-orange bricks, beaten brass roofs, slender pillars, steps bearing quaintly carved animals, a weird figure of the evil-looking god Kali . . . What a contrast to the Gurkha city of hospitals, prisons, modern palaces, and crude statues designed in the nineteenth and twentieth centuries!

37

It was a pleasing surprise to learn that our six Sherpas had arrived from Darjeeling – the first Sherpas we had ever seen. Not so small in stature as I had imagined, they advanced in a smiling body, and from their midst stepped Nyma, apparently the sirdar ... Had we only known it, the real sirdar was Dawa Tenzing, Tibetan in appearance, with a long drooping moustache and shiny blue-black hair wound horizontally round his brow. Normally he wore it as a pigtail, and this horizontal winding was merely a concession to the sophistication of Katmandu. A red tartan shirt, R.A.F. blue trousers and smart brown shoes gave him a rakish appearance. Dawa, we were to discover was the prince of our Sherpas, and was later to distinguish himself not only on the ascent of Everest, when he went to the South Col, and later as sirdar to Hillary's 1954 expedition in the Makalu region, but also as headman to the successful Kanchenjunga team. [*of which Tom Mackinnon was a member*]

Mingma, Ela Tenzing, Ang Dawa and Kamin were the others. Ang Dawa was a good looking youngster who we at once nicknamed the Boy Scout (good at making omelettes). Ela and Mingma were first-class men, reliable types who could climb and carry.

A pleasant piece of news was that they had brought four Sherpas from Solu Khumbu who would act as porters for us. These were excellent young men, with one exception called Huma, a woman of uncertain age. How old she was we had no idea, but she was incredibly ugly and much attached to the tallest of the porters, whom I nicknamed Kharab Joe because he wore a long-suffering, browned-off look. Before the end of the expedition he was known to all Sherpas and sahibs alike as Joe, and a fine character he proved to be.

Coincident with the arrival of the Sherpas came news from the Embassy that the bearer entrusted with our precious baggage had seen it safely on its way, and that some of it should be at the terminus of the electric ropeway, while some of it was in his personal charge in Katmandu. This was great news, and with the Sherpas' help we rounded it up, doing some sleuth work among a mountain of gear at the foot of the Chandrigiri Pass. Only the kerosene had come to grief, though someone had ransacked a case and stolen Scott's best jacket.

Now we had something positive to do, sorting out loads and getting everything in order for the march, and after a good day we were invited to a cocktail party at the British Embassy at which the highest in the land were to be present, including B.P.Koirala, one of the two brothers who had led the revolution. Slim and distinguished looking, young in appearance for his thirty years, he wore a khaki frock-coat buttoned up to his neck and his legs were encased in tight pyjamas.

Most of the others wore finely woven jackets and waist coats of semi-European cut over their fine silk shirts and pyjamas: pillbox hats were worn even inside the house. Most of the officials we had already met were present. Some seemed very nervous and neither ate nor drank, others talked incessantly in peculiar broken English and the word 'democracy' popped like a champagne cork out of every corner. A big surprise to us was a lecture on Imagination in Literature, given by Dr Philips who had been flown especially to Katmandu. Kubla Khan was the subject of his talk and he described how the poem came to be written under the influence of an opium dream. It was a good talk but it left us wondering how much of it got across to the Nepalese, for their command of English is not good.

Of outstanding interest to all our party was a meeting with Peter Aufschnaiter, the famous German climber who had been with Heinrich Harrer in Tibet after their epic escape from the internment camp at Dera Dun. They had been interned on their way back from a climbing expedition to Nanga Parbat, and about the middle of the war they escaped and made their way through Kumaon and Garwhal to Tibet, enduring incredible hardships and bluffing their way through the most difficult country in the world to Lhasa. (The story graphically told in Harrer's book *Seven Years in Tibet*)

As well as becoming civil engineer on water schemes and general improvement plans for Lhasa, Aufschnaiter was made official cartographer to the Tibetan Government and allowed to go into regions never before visited by a white man. He usually travelled alone, with yaks to carry his baggage. He told us that he felt completely happy in that country which he regards as the most fascinating in the world. His eyes lit up and his rather solemn face became animated when he spoke of views he had seen over hundreds of mile of shining ice mountains, mostly unknown and unexplored. He had no wish to go back to Europe. His yearning was for Tibet and he would never have left it if the encroaching Chinese had not forced him to cross the Himalaya into Nepal to seek sanctuary.

We had become quite resigned to awaiting the end of the festivities, since we could get no change out of any of the coolie contractors, when one of those unexpected things typical of the East happened, and we suddenly found ourselves with a crowd of ragged Tamil coolies to choose from, a small host having invaded our lawn. Yes, they were prepared to start right away, provided our loads met with their approval, so we let them loose among our gear, and after a deal of wrangling each man chose his load. We had the riff-raff of the bazaar without a doubt, but we were in no position to pick and choose, and our departure was timed for the morning. So we settled down cheerfully to our last night with Colonel Proud and the kindly staff of the British Embassy, who had done so much to smooth our path through Katmandu.

EAST OF KATMANDU

THE TESI LAPCHA

Himalayan expeditions depend heavily on local porters and both Scottish expeditions were much impressed by the character and skills of the Dhotial, Malari, Bhotia, Rolwaling and Sherpa men – and women – who carried heavy loads over challenging routes to make their wanderings possible. There's a lovely incident when the porters were drumming and Tom asked for a shot and then astonished them with his expertise. In this extract the party is crossing from the Rolwaling to the Solu Khumbu by the 6000 metres Tesi Lapcha.

Like all hill people the Rolwaling men and women use headbands for supporting the weight of their loads. This is the ideal way of carrying a burden on dangerously steep slopes. A special rope with a broad band for the head is adjusted round the baggage at the point of balance. If danger threatens a Sherpa need only throw back his head to get rid of the load. Also, the neck is tougher than the shoulders and can sustain a load for a longer time.

On the debit side they cannot swing their heads or get more than a very restricted view.

This traverse led to a very formidable rock buttress up which we could hardly believe the route went. It was a place for a rope, we thought, but they waved it aside. The women climbed in their bare feet, probably to save the yakskin soles of their boots on the sharp rock, but whatever the reason it was soon obvious that they were very much at home on the crags, even with sixty-pound loads. But we died a thousand deaths watching them, imagining all to vividly what would happen if one peeled off – the body hurtling downward to be smashed on the debris of the glacier below. It was astonishing to see how the women used their feet, spreading their prehensile toes and gripping with them as if they were fingers. Every upward movement was studied and carefully

41

controlled. There was no panic as they mounted for 200 feet what would be classed in Britain and the Alps as a difficult rock climb. The crux was a corner where the rock bulged, then rose vertically from a sketchy foothold. In this recess Nyma stationed himself and guided each Sherpa round by means of a stick pressed against the rock in lieu of foothold. Each man curled his toe around the stick, bent his neck to his chest to prevent the load slipping, and swung round the difficult bulge. There were no scared faces, but for the first and only time Kharab Joe's girlfriend Huma was without a smile. Most of them seemed to think the climb was a great lark.

Above this the angle eased to another rake zig-zagging to a niche between precipices – not a place for sleepwalking. It was four o'clock and we had apparently arrived at a camping place, for there were caves and hollows to shelter some of our team. Water was reasonably close at hand and we were fairly safe from stonefall – though the coolies threw themselves to the ground when one did take place. The stones shone like diamonds when they pinged through the air for a couple of thousand feet to whistle into the depths of the couloir we had recently abandoned for the rock wall.

Our height now we judged to be about 18,000 feet, [5486m] and the situation was impressive. Immediately behind us to the north, was a rock face cradling a narrow glacier hanging like a frozen waterfall. On the south side, across the rubble we had marched on all day, were the rock needles we had likened to the Cuillin of Skye. Now they were seen to be formidable mountains in their own right, yet they were mere outliers of the ice ranges behind them. South-west of us, blocking the whole valley, was the Kanchenjunga-like mass that blocked our path and forced us to make this detour. Ideally we should have contoured up the icefall under this face if we were to make the most direct approach to the Tesi Lapcha, but how impracticable this route was we now fully appreciated, for the cataract of ice was riven and contorted between narrow dangerous walls.

The Rolwaling folk had no eyes for any of this. They were hard at work removing stones and digging out holes to make caves or sleeping quarters for the night. We gave the women our bungalow tent and were glad to turn in to our own without undue lingering, for a wind had risen, forcing us into our sleeping bags to get warm – the first time on the trip that we had foregone supper rather than stay out in the cold.

To our amazement, when we went out to see how the Sherpas were faring we found a number of them lying out under the sky with no more cover than their homespuns. They were asleep and when we asked them in the morning if they had been cold they shook their heads and said they had been warm. They must undoubtedly be amongst the toughest people in the world. That night was the most comfortable I have ever spent in a high camp, proof that acclimatisation was coming at last.

To awake in this eyrie and look out on a cloudless sky was to get what we had prayed for in the crossing. All going well we should be on the other side of the pass by nightfall. Everyone was in high spirits except two firewood carriers whose luggage had now been used up. By agreement they were now due to return, but they wanted to stay and were downcast when we refused their request. By half-past eight we had said goodbye to them and begun the climb to an arch of granite curving against the blue sky a long way above us. There were traces of yak dung on these slabs, and we learned with amazement that despite avalanche danger and stonefall yaks are sometimes brought up the couloir and manhauled up the admittedly easy slabs of rock and scree we were now climbing. No one can say that the Sherpas are not enterprising. From the summit of this rock crest we looked down into a great glacier basin draining a spectacular array of snow peaks, and not for a moment or two did we realise that this glacier was in fact the upper part of the huge rubble-covered ice-field we had been following for the best part of two days. We had bypassed its seracs and crevasses by climbing over

43

this rock wall. And we would have to descend to it again, where it was now a shining highway curving into an infinity of unknown mountains.

Across the glacier we could see the pass over the main range – a narrow saddle between two sharp ice peaks, a cleft defended on one side by a thick wedge of green ice that topped a line of cliffs like icing on a cake, and on the other by an icefall. This was the Tesi Lapcha. It was even more of a mountaineering route than we had supposed. We descended into the wide glacier basin in a traverse of a mile of boulders and slabs. Dropping a thousand feet to find ourselves surrounded by glistening peaks. We crossed the glacier, sinking deeply into the surface snow, and climbed up towards the pass.

Dawa Tenzing was excited for he had been at this very place with Shipton and Hillary in 1951 and 1952, and he pointed out to us where their party of three sahibs and four Sherpas had turned up this glacier where it swung northeast, to have a look at what lay around the corner. In passing they had climbed the sharp ice peak forming the south flank of the Tesi Lapcha, an example of the skirmishing type of mountaineering in which Shipton excels, demonstrating his boundless energy and instinctive topographical sense of going to the right place. What a wealth of knowledge of this hitherto unknown region of Nepal he had brought back from two expeditions! And what a brilliant piece of work was his party's reconnaissance of the Everest route which paved the way for the Swiss and for the final climb!

Some of the Sherpas without sun glasses were suffering from the glare here, and it was interesting to see their natural way of overcoming it. They merely took strands of their long hair and pulled it over their eyes, and very effective blinkers this improvisation seemed to make. While they took a meal of tsampa we examined the icefall up which we would have to climb. We were in luck. The surface that could so easily have been clear ice, involving us in hard step-cutting, was covered in a layer of firm snow giving good foothold. By keeping well to the left side of the pass we would clear all obstacles. After an initial steepness the hill rose steeply to a shoulder. This was a slope that Hillary had found difficult with clear ice, so we congratulated ourselves on our good fortune.

The heavily laden Rolwaling folk found this lift very hard, for with sixty- and seventy-pound loads they were grossly overburdened for climbing at this unaccustomed altitude. But they went up with a will and made height steadily towards the gap between the mountains. On our north side a great sheet of reddish granite shot to a pinnacle. Flanking us on the other side was Shipton's peak, a soaring snow-point trailing a plume of spindrift which stung our faces as we got into its backlash; this made the going harder, for we sank into drifts caused by it. Sinking deeply and heads down to the wind the women came battling on.

It was an inspiring moment to step over the windy col [the *Tesi Lapcha*, 6096m] and look on a horizon of new mountains standing above cloud seas and steaming vapours that simmered like porridge in a pot. This was Solu Khumbu, the fabled home of the Sherpas, a world of ice, sheer walls and spires, where it seemed only a race of great mountaineers could live, for the visual impact was one of relentless savagery. It was too cold to linger. The slope below bent away icily, swept clear and polished by the wind, making it slippery going for the Sherpas with only yakskin soles to their boots. Some of them joined hands for greater stability. Others with axes started to cut steps, the women being particularly nervous and grateful for assistance. Soon the slope became an ice cliff with gaping folds like a concertina, but there was a cunning corridor down, with a rocky couloir hard against its edge. Descent of this difficult portion was no more than a steep and slippery scramble, well clear of the natural line of avalanches from above. Once down the little rock pitches of this place we were on a gentle incline, then another icefall bent away steeply. Local knowledge was invaluable here, for

45

Dawa Tenzing knew exactly the outlet to choose from this high basin, and soon we were plunging down broken rocks and scree, crossing ice patches and descending snow slopes to another hanging corrie. Temper-breaking work began here, for the whole lower part of the corrie was treacherously loose, piled high with rubble as far as we could see. Keeping as far as possible to a rock shoulder, we kept traversing to the right, to hit a moraine like an embankment which was firmer under foot. It took us down to about 16,000 feet, [4877m] to a tangle of rock-strewn hillocks which we could not avoid, where we were forced up and down over their steep sides – back-breaking work at the end of such a hard day's carrying. It seemed an eternal wilderness of stones but at last we came to a cairn, then to a path leading to grass, and the first welcome slope we could descend comfortably to a glen with a stream and thankfully select a camp site.

The place was good enough to be a mirage – a hollow with caves and dwarf juniper to provide heat and shelter for our whole band. One by one they struggled in, tired, but not too tired to give us a salaam when we shouted "Shabash!" for a truly great day's work. They had been carrying for ten hours, and as we issued them with baksheesh in the form of tea, sugar, soup and pemmican we told them they could take a long lie in the morning and get their strength back after such a fine lift.

We were in grand spirits. The Tesi Lapcha had been a highlight of the expedition, a superbly interesting pass, and now we were in the Solu Khumbu country with Everest just around the corner. There was gaiety and laughter round the little fires twinkling in the dark, and we could hear the slap of chapati-making and the busy clatter of cooking. Above us the moon was a pale sickle glistening on a ribbon of snow 5,000 feet sheer above, and we felt with the coolies in their song that life was good.

EAST OF KATMANDU

UJA TIRCHE

Uja Tirche, 6,200 m, facing the Lampak peaks above the Girthi Ganga gave the most successful climb of the 1950 Garwhal expedition.

Then we saw Uja Tirche.

It rose above the boil of monsoon clouds, a narrow summit rising thousands of feet above the Girthi in rock bands and ice bulges. Even as we looked the clouds shifted, disclosing twin sickles of ice fringing the cliffs, sweeping down to rock splinters, pinnacles which we knew must be of great size to show from here.

What excited us was the possibility of climbing this peak. It looked difficult, promised mountaineering of the highest order, and the height of 20,350 feet [6,200 m] made it a worthy peak. We camped that afternoon on the stones of its glacier, marvelling at our situation close to a great waterfall in the midst of a horseshoe of unclimbed mountains, the same mountains we had seen from Dunagiri.

The Malari men had done well. We were all friends now, even the headman's sullen look had given way to positive enjoyment. Goats unloaded and saddle-bags neatly piled, they lit a fire for us before departing, assuring us that they would return in three weeks' time for the traverse of the Girthi.

We lost no time in sorting out three days' food supply for an attack on Uja Tirche. We had enough food for three weeks' climbing, and ten unclimbed Himalayan giants were ringed around us. We were fit and the weather at last seemed to be on the up.

Morning saw us climbing upwards with six of the coolies. It was a delightful approach, first by a traverse over flower-covered meadows, then by a steep grass slope to a snowy corrie. The coolies were making heavy weather of it however.

47

I took my own line on the left flank of the corrie, sliding on abominable scree to reach a little peak on the spur of Uja Tirche. Behind the camp we had left, clouds were piling up, breaking open now and then to reveal 7,000-foot ice walls, fragments of summit ridge, and sharp pointed tops suspended in space.

Suddenly I was on the ridge looking into the other world of Tibet. It was indeed another world, a world roofed by the clearest sky I have ever seen, a sky of pale brittle blue. And rolling away to infinity, range after range of autumn-coloured hills, vegetationless snow-covered hills, curiously reminiscent of Scotland, particularly the view south from Cairn Toul in late March when spring has stripped all but the last snowfields from the hillsides. This was the desert of Tibet, a contrast indeed to the snow peaks and green-clad Himalaya on our side of the watershed.

The disintegrating nature of the ridge had troubled me as I traversed across. If the pinnacles of Uja Tirche – now in cloud – were a continuation of this ridge as I suspected, then we could look out for sparks, for I had never climbed on rock that needed more delicate handling. Herds of bharral, the wild mountain sheep, stood on the snow gully connecting my ridge with the right arm of the corrie. Gratefully I joined the ridge.

I sat up here to await the others. Scott appeared with bad news. The coolies were going badly. One was sick, and all of them were feeling the altitude. The rattle of scree sounded above us and Tom McKinnon appeared out of the clouds. He had been up amongst the pinnacles and described them as the craziest things imaginable, but he had cairned a route until stopped by a great Sphinx head, fully two hundred feet high and obviously difficult.

Even as we talked, Bill Murray and two of the coolies appeared. Heroically the coolies returned for the abandoned loads while we built tent platforms from the stones. Our height would be about 17,000 feet [5,300m] and we felt more energetic than in previous high camps. The reward for being up here came at sunset when the enveloping clouds wreathed upwards and peak after peak stood clear, pink-shafted above cloud-filled valleys where night had already fallen.

Breakfast in a high camp is not a jolly affair. Getting out of a sleeping bag is not as bad as the business which precedes it, forcing biscuits and lukewarm tea down one's throat, the latter from a flask filled the night before. Boots and other preparations seem a confounded nuisance at such times, and it is a brave man who will say anything controversial. At 5.30 a.m. with this behind us we set off on two ropes for the pinnacles, Tom McKinnon and myself on one, Bill Murray and Douglas Scott on the other.

The pinnacles were indeed a weird sight, towering out of the clouds, tottering spires, Old Man of Hoy shapes, Storr Rock forms, and the Sphinx head which marked the end of McKinnon's valuable recce.

McKinnon lost no time in descending to its west face, where he had detected two wide cracks rising one above the other, the top one banked with snow, but offering the possibility of ascent if frozen enough to permit cutting of hand- and foot-hold.

It was a good choice of route. The first crack went easily, and there was a hitch for the rope to safeguard the leader on the upper section. I joined him, and we forced the final part of the climb by a combination of step-cutting on the hard-frozen snow-ice, and using hand-holds on the edge of the rock wall. We beckoned on the others and looked round the corner.

The way ahead looked feasible, but involved us in much up-and-down work on rotten rock, till at last we were at the bottle-green ice of the couloir, virtually part of a hanging glacier which we knew marked the beginning of the ice ridge. We retraced our steps to a steep rock chimney, climbed it, and marked the spot with a cairn, climbed over some easy rocks and found ourselves on the ice ridge.

With glee we noted that the snow was hard, suitable for crampons, so we laced the ten-point spikes on our boots and started up the arête. The spikes gripped beautifully, saving us the job of step-cutting, and we made height quickly. The altitude would be about 18,000 feet [5486m] and thick mist enshrouded us.

The arête was an exciting place, with the west cornice overhanging space and the east eave falling away steeply to – we knew – crags and hanging glacier. The need to take a breath at each step indicated that the ridge was steepening, and a rift in the mist confirmed this. We were below a point where the narrow sickle of the arête swept upward to join with the vertical handle of the second sickle. There was no direct ascent. We must traverse across the ice wall to join another arête on the right, which made a wedge with the other part of the ridge. It was corniced on the far side and the angle looked high, but it did not look impossible.

McKinnon led across. At such times it is reassuring to have a good anchorage on the mountain, such as a well-driven ice axe with a turn of rope around it. In this case, a few inches of axe-head had to suffice. It looked insufficient, with a drop below of thousands of feet. But if it could be climbed I felt sure McKinnon would do it, and if it could not, then I had enough faith in him as a mountaineer to know he would return.

Cutting hand- and foot-holds he moved across the wall, stopping half-way across to ask me if I was happy. He told me he was fairly enjoying himself. Forty feet outward and he swung himself out of sight over the cornice on the far side. Far minutes passed and I heard his cheery cry, "Come on".

The traverse was not easy, extremely awkward in its last move over the bulge of the projecting cornice. Round the corner I found Tom poised on an excessively steep slope with the same kind of belay as I had had myself, a few inches of axe-head in the ice. Some sharp step-cutting and we were on the easier crest of the ridge, but we could see ahead of us a replica of the thing we had climbed, but with a larger section of ice wall to cross.

We did not feel dismayed, neither could I say enthusiastic.

50

Our main feeling was one of astonishment, that we had been able to rise to such a standard of difficulty at this altitude, and hardly notice it during the excitement of climbing. The time factor was our chief worry. We had been going seven hours and the summit was by no means within grasp yet.

The second ice wall went as the first, but this time we climbed it united as a party of four, to gain the advantage of additional anchorage. Above that the arête seemed to go on and on, till suddenly a thin snow blade loomed ahead, the summit.

It was snowing as we crowded on to its narrow top, to look down ice walls disappearing into gloom. In such a situation one does not feel a conqueror, quite the reverse. The climb had taken eight and a half hours, and, apart from being too cold to linger, we were going to need all our time for the descent. Five minutes up there and we were off.

It was a treacherous descent. The thin snow surface had deteriorated, causing the crampons to gather a slippery sole which slid on the underlying ice. We took them off and used a different technique. McKinnon was a sheet anchor, and he stood firm while Murray led downward to be followed by Scott and myself. Then we dug in till joined by McKinnon. In this way the party were always anchored, and a slip, whether from above or below, could always be checked.

The first ice wall went well, though a certain amount of rope engineering was called into play to safeguard the last man. It was a different story with the second step. The dangers of this traverse were all too apparent, not least being the lack of safe anchorage to protect the leader and save the others from being pulled off on the event of a slip. We cast around for an alternative, deciding to follow the slope downwards to where it became a rock buttress. Solid footing on the rocks to give safety to the party was what we wanted. We got it after a few hundred feet of excessively steep descent. Two hundred feet of ice wall separated us from the ridge.

We took turns at cutting a passage, McKinnon first, then

51

Murray, then Scott and myself, then Murray again. It was an uneasy crossing, the ice watery and unreliable, difficult by its splintery nature to shape into steps with the ice axe. McKinnon tried crampons on it and was shot down forty feet to be stopped by the rope when a step broke under his stamp. Our safety-first tactics had not been in vain.

But around us a minor miracle was taking place. The mists which had enveloped us all day were dropping to the valleys, making us forget the shivering cold. In waves of movement peaks were breaking through, Kamet signposting the Badrinath range in a great wedge of silhouette, immense against fire-tinted clouds. Even as we looked, the warmth was withdrawn from the sky and the cloud sea paled to a shadow. The immensity of depth, of incredible space, is something I am never likely to forget, a feeling of being not on earth, but on another planet.

Meantime, at the end of two hundred feet of climbing rope, Murray was fighting his last battle with the gap. It was a fine piece of mountaineering. Picking steadily, cutting hand-holds and foot-holds, he had worked harder than any of us on this traverse, and a triumphant shout told us he was across. Fastening rope slings to the stretched rope we crossed in his steps. The method was unorthodox, but the only one practicable with all our available rope out. We gained the ridge in moonlight, thanking the Providence that looks after drunken men and mountaineers.

Mentally we had prepared ourselves for a night out, thinking we should need to squat down on the first suitable place. Thanks to the moon we revised our ideas. Further, our safety was greater since a frost crust was rapidly binding the arête, giving certain foothold. It was a wonderful moment when we stepped off the ice on to the rocks of the pinnacles traverse.

Here McKinnon came into his own. Quickly he found our cairn marking the first chimney – now glazed with ice and calling for care – and we were soon on the route of the morning. It seemed fearfully hard work, sliding on stones, climbing and contouring among these queer moonlit shapes, with the worry of the Sphinx at the back of our minds. This descent went surprisingly well, McKinnon coming down last man, safeguarding us all from above and descending himself unaided. A few complications traversing right and left, and we passed the last pinnacle nine hours after leaving the summit. We reached the tent eighteen hours after leaving it.

Curiously, no-one was hungry, despite having eaten almost nothing on the mountain. Dutifully the coolies had kept a fire going and they were soon out of the tent bringing the kettle to the boil for tea and soup. That was Uja Tirche. Looking back on it, I remember no other mountaineering day to equal it for suspense and sustained interest. Even the camp was a delightful place, perched on the Tibet border and commanding the sunrise and sunset, when at dawn the desert of Tibet was flooded in seas of warm colour, or in the evening when Tirsuli and the ring of peaks above the Uja Tirche glacier were suffused in Alpen-glow.

THE ULTIMATE MOUNTAINS

ENDINGS

All good things come to an end and, having spent months circling among some of the greatest mountains on earth, the second group came back to their starting point.

That day we covered ground that had formerly taken two marches, and we camped at our old camp on the Sangasoti Danda. What a view had been hidden from us in the monsoon! Now we looked on the whole frontier ridge of Nepal from Annapurna past Manaslu and Gosainthan to Gauri Sankar. We seemed to feel the pulse of the earth that night, as darkness deepened and a rich wave of fire lit the crest of the Himalaya, to be dowsed by the rim of the earth. The light of the sky ebbed visibly, in sharp pulsations, violet light deepening to envelop the pale peaks and bring a sparkle to the first stars.

There was a curious ceremony round the camp fire that night. Poor Ang Dawa had been unwell for several days, and although Tom had been doctoring him steadily, the medicine was having no effect. This good-looking youngster was not merely sick but quite ill, and daily we watched him grow weaker. Despite long prayers at every chorten we passed, and the tying of little prayer flags on every suitable pole, his supplications to Buddha were having no effect. We saw him go through many peculiar rites, from prostrations before small shrines to the offering of rice and grain. Tonight Ang Dawa stood with a bowl of rice in hand praying earnestly, touching his forehead with handfuls of the rice and scattering it at his side. Beside him stood Dawa Tenzing with a little tray on which had been set up candles and some little figures like plasticine puppets, cunningly manufactured from stiff tsampa dough. Without saying a word he held the tray out for my inspection. The tray was arranged as a little stage, with the figure of a lama beside two chortens and an unlit candle. Between another two chortens and facing the lamas were the figures of a man and a woman. The Sherpas around the camp fire looked towards Ang Dawa, their lips moving in prayer like his. In the flickering firelight it was a strangely impressive scene, becoming invested with a touch of magic when rice was scattered on the flames and a burning brand was taken from the fire by a wild looking Sherpa called Ang Phutar. With it he lit the candle on the tray. The sick man continued to pray while Dawa Tenzing walked slowly round the fire, the candle on his tray illuminating the strange little stage. Then he changed direction towards Namche Bazaar, and at that same moment Ang Phutar with his burning brand seemed to go into a frenzy, slashing at the heels of Dawa and yelling fiendishly at the top of his voice. The devil tormenting the sick man was being driven back to Namche. After this there was a long series of prayers, sung rather than spoken, the chorus being punctuated with handclaps and staccato passages marking changes of tempo. There must be a traditional pattern in all this, learned from an early age, for every man knew his part. Unfortunately it did not cure Ang Dawa.

. . . .

How we remembered the first bathe of the expedition, when we had banished the feeling of torrid heat, by floating blissfully in a pool of the deep river, as it flowed in a series of waterfalls through green ricefields. The river had practically disappeared and the fresh green of the rice had gone. The fields had been harvested and were now a neutral grey. But the calling of a sandpiper, and a sight of this little bird of the Scottish glens, sent our spirits up. Our Sherpas were feeling the heat in this lower country, and Dawa raced round like a whippet, seeking out a chang-house in every little village we passed through. He was taking his responsibilities as sirdar very well and kept us informed. If he said he was breaking for half an hour, then half an hour it was. There was a happy spirit about our party that made the daily marches a joy. Unfortunately, this was the last camp of the march, for on the other side of the ridge we expected to catch a lorry next day. As though in honour of it Mingma put on his last great feed for us – a roast chicken done to perfection. And I finished it off by making a last giant dumpling.

At eleven o'clock next day we were picked up by a lorry, and for some of the Sherpas who had never seen a motor vehicle, let alone been on one, the most exciting part of the journey was still to come. It must have been an extraordinary experience for them as we scraped the walls of houses and crushed through narrow lanes never meant for motor vehicles, with chickens and pigs flying for their lives. But they were enjoying it, and the eyes of those who had never seen a town before were big with wonder as we whisked through the streets of Katmandu by roundabouts, statues and electric cables, to swing into the Embassy grounds and pull up before its magnificent pillared front.

What a welcome the ambassador and his wife and staff gave us! We had expected to camp or go to the Government Rest House, instead we were plied with mugs of foaming beer and each given a suite of luxurious rooms. It all seemed too good to be true, especially when a bag of mail was put into our hands and we relaxed in armchairs to read. It is good to be denied the comforts of civilisation if only to savour them again after abstinence, and how Mr and Mrs Summerhayes spoiled us with huge meals, wines, and morning tea in bed!

. . . .

Yet at what speed do events move. A way of life that has lasted hundreds of years has changed dramatically in less than a decade. How could Dr Longstaff have forecast, for example, that his chapter on Nepal in *This My Voyage* would be out of date by the time it appeared in print? Take the sentence: 'Mysterious Pokhara, tropical, low-lying by a lake and closely backed by the immense peaks of Annapurna, is still beyond our ken.' Annapurna was climbed in 1950, the year the book came out, and in 1953 an air service was established at Pokra, where two medical missionaries are now at work. The veil of mystery is not being merely withdrawn but rent apart.

Hillary's expedition in 1954 climbed twenty-three peaks in the course of a single season, mapping and exploring the region east of Everest, while national expeditions in other parts of the range were attacking the great peaks of Manaslu and Dhaulagiri. Cho Oyu (26,750 feet) was climbed. Gauri Sankar was attempted, and as I write the Nepal face of Kanchenjunga has just been climbed – the greatest piece of mountaineering in this century – Tom McKinnon having played no inconsiderable part in its conquest. A sign that we ourselves were not a moment too soon in entering Nepal was the arrival of seven bulldozers across the Chandrigiri

Pass, the first vehicles ever to arrive in Katmandu under their own power.

The pleasant time at the Embassy passed all too swiftly, listening to symphonies and fragments from operas played on long-playing records, and being royally entertained ...

The path to the Chandrigiri Pass was as busy as Sauchiehall Street, with Indian sappers and coolies toiling to prepare a way of descent for the bulldozers, which were now over the col and facing the worst part of the route. Landslides had now taken place at one or two points, and we had to keep a sharp lookout for falling stones, which buzzed through the air and bounded through the trees.

It was a relief to get clear of all of this and climb along a ridge to camp in a small clearing, looking over a gossamer cloud sea whose tide was gradually filling the Vale of Katmandu and chilling the air around us with damp. The view we had hoped for was reserved for the next night, when we least expected it. Three thousand feet below us was the road-head where we would catch a lorry to take us to the railway, but there was a little peak that looked as if it might give some sort of view, and we climbed to it. Instead of a little view, a vast panorama was spread before us – ridge upon ridge mounting in grey blue to become the crest of the Himalaya. Laid out before us was the route of our journey, signposted by Gauri Sankar and the square-cut flank of Rolwaling beneath which had been our base camp. We filled our eyes with it, imprinting it on our memories, conscious that tomorrow it would be only a memory, but one to treasure to the end of our days.

EAST OF KATMANDU

III

HIGHLANDS AND ISLANDS

His wartime journey through Sutherland's hills, following, would still be an impressive venture and is worth following on the map: Landranger 9 and 10. It gives the lie to the notion that past weather was always so much better than today's. He might not be so happy with the new bulldozed tracks everywhere he tramped but, on the whole, the people of such remote regions have benefited from developments.

ACROSS SUTHERLAND HILLS

"The third of June and look at it."

Rain battered the train windows, washing them as though by water thrown in bucketfuls. There was nothing to see: all the clouds in the world seemed to be massed on the Cairngorms. And this was my embarkation leave and I was bound for the wilds of Sutherland with food for a week in my rucksack and no tent. I had fooled myself into thinking that in June a sleeping-bag, stove, and food was all that was necessary.

What of my fine plans if the weather were like this for a week or more? I had worked out a route across Scotland's most northern mountainland and it was beginning to look as if it would be a rout and not a route. This northland does not offer tourist accommodation, in fact it shuns it, and such inns as were once convenient to climbers have been closed for many years. It is an old Highland story – like the Clearances – and is almost as effective in keeping the land for the few.

At Carr Bridge my sorry ruminations were disturbed as a new traveller got in. Even for wartime his dress was bizarre – from his wrinkled red tartan tie to his much patched rubber boots. Within two minutes he told me that he was going to try to get his wife out of Inverness Infirmary where she had been for five weeks. He had the soft speech of the west and I was not surprised to hear that he came from North Uist.

"The Lord will help me this day for He knows that I am on His side." He looked at me intently and added with some heat: "Yes, I know the Book from Genesis to Jeremiah and the Lord is revealing it to me more and more every time I read."

I had nothing to say.

61

"Yes, I know the Bible better than all your scholars, lawyers, and doctors. God is in me here." He pointed to his heart. "I don't want learning." Up went his hand in a dramatic gesture. "May the Lord give me understanding, understanding and the knowledge to do right."

He pointed at me. "Where is your learning today? See what it has brought you. It is the devil's work and Armageddon is at hand. I know it. The Lord has revealed it to me." The accusation in his eye and certainty in his manner were rather startling. Then in a quieter voice he told his history.

"Nine and a half years in the army. I was eleven and a half stones in those days and as strong as a bull. Yes, and the finest sportsman in the army, not in the regiment, but in the whole army. Every prize I took. Yes, and even yet I'll outfight, outrun, outswim, or outdrink any man of my age."

He struck an attitude with his fists clenched in the manner of a boxer and gave us a pantomime of all the jaws he had broken; of how when all his money had been spent on drink he had walked in the dead of winter all the way from London to Inverness.

"I can make a pair of trousers and vest as good as any tailor. But not the jacket. I was never taught the jacket. I'm knacky with my hands, knacky. Yes, I can do any job at all, any mortal job, working a croft, carpentering or building."

His financial position quite distressed me. Twenty seven and sixpence [*less than £1.50*] was the total income of the two of them, his wife and himself. There was no bus from the cottage and he had to walk seven miles each way, even in the snow, to draw his pension and carry his groceries home on his back. He had an idea of getting some timber and building a cottage near Inverness. "I will look for a place when I am in Inverness for I have the timber for the asking." He had no doubts about his ability, a frail old man, lost without his wife but full of zeal as to the future, Armageddon or no Armageddon.

When Lairg was reached I was told that there was no mail-car to Durness for another six hours. Luckily they have a café in Lairg so I spent the time drinking tea. By 2 p.m. the sun was shining and the mists of morning were floating as beautiful cumuli, dappling the blue hills with racing shadows. Lairg, by its verdant green and fine woods at the edge of Loch Shin, came as a surprise, for on the map it looks a bleak place on the edge of a peaty nothing. Impatiently I waited for the mail-car, full of the expectation that this strange land of Sutherland arouses. At last the mails were loaded, passengers aboard (a full complement of two, including myself) and we rattled away towards one of my lifelong ambitions.

All this land was new to me and my heart rejoiced to recognize Beinn Klibreck and see Ben Loyal leap from the moor in rocky spires. The vastness of these moors made a profound impression: warm-coloured by the sun and threaded by blue streams and dotted by little gems of lochs. But all too vividly I could picture them, sullen and waterlogged, beaten by wind and rain.

Altnaharra, a long climb up to a high point on the road, and I recognized Loch Coulside. Ahead was a tiny house marked on the map Inchkinloch. This I had chosen as my jumping-off spot. I paid my dues and slung on my heavy sack. My way lay over the shoulder of Ben Loyal, by what I had anticipated would be bad bogland, to a little loch set in the heart of the mountains. This loch had a peculiar hold on my imagination – for no reason at all except its setting. I made my way towards it invigorated by the joy of being at last in this great country.

What an evening that was! An evening of blue-washed hills and bluer lochs, lochs the colour of blue dye that had seeped into the very burns. For contrast there was the near mass of Klibreck, a great sweep of russet patched with shadow. Shadows in Sutherland, this bare land, assume the significance of physical features, like the vasty sky that domes this edge of Scotland where it fringes the northern seas.

My prediction as to the wetness of the ground proved accurate, for above Loch Coulside by the saturated ground that held Loch Haluim, I found a morass that was barely passable.

63

But for compensation there was the beauty of waving bog-cotton and the peak of Loyal, an upstanding rock pinnacle towards which a birch gully twisted. My watch said 7 p.m., so parking my bag, I followed up that gully by birch greens to rock. The sun had been behind clouds but broke through as I popped my head over the top.

Below me was the Kyle of Tongue, yellow sands and green woods floodlit against the vivid sea. Beyond Loch Eriboll, reaching back in waves of increasing bulk inland, were shaggy rollers of mountains, blue-black against the sun, Ben Hope, my legendary peak, was opposite, supported on three rocky pillars clung with birches. Above a little loch at my feet was a sensational crag, rising to another of Loyal's peaks. All that was missing was Orkney.

Happy now, I got back to my bag and pushed on by another loch and a burn that cascaded amongst birches and willows. Then my loch, Loch an Dithreibh [Dherue], hove in sight, straight below me and fringed by an oasis of green amongst golden whins. Perched on the shore was a house.

How I wish Matt had been with me! Often he told me that in his POW camp he had pictured the little loch with its birches and sandy shore by Cul Beag where we had caught the fish. Here was his dream come true: a sandy shore, steep crags hung with birches, and high hills for company.

Over Ben Hope the sun was setting in streamers of gold that filtered the purple of its shadowed face. The loch, still as a mirror, held all the yellows and reds of the sunset sky. Around me, snipe were at their nesting note, a sign that I always associate with great days on the hills, sandpipers were calling and flitting over the water, and a twite was singing its linnet-like little song as I turned into my bag at midnight. The song of a willow-warbler, repeated time after time and note for note, was my coming to consciousness. It was 10 a.m. before I got up for I needed the sleep. Breakfast and a sandwich and I was off for Ben Hope. Rain was sweeping the hills but the air was mild and blinks of sun gave encouragement.

64

I traversed the peak from the south, and all the time I felt I was racing the bad weather, for thunder was sounding in the west, and creeping inward were huge black clouds below which the peaks of the Ben Hee group were wan. I won the race by about a minute, just in time to get shelter. Over the Kyle it was sunny and the moorlands glittered. The tide was out and long sands reached out to sea.

It is a fascinating place to be, this high peak above the north tip of Scotland. Loch Hope, black as ink, was three thousand feet below me, and over a peaty tongue of land was Loch Eriboll. Fionn Bheinn [Fionaven] and its rain blurred neighbours looked tremendous, rising in rock to shapely peaks linked by inviting ridges. My only company was a ring ouzel that sang its staccato phrases to cheer me.

Down over rock debris and other signs of glaciation I came to the floor of the upper corrie, a place of little lochans and strewn boulders. The bad weather cleared away and I sat warm in the sun watching a greenshank and some sandpipers at the water's edge. I thought of climbing Ben Loyal for the sunset and waiting for the sunrise but on the way down it started to thunder and before long a downpour had blotted out everything.

I mentioned a house earlier; this was uninhabited but securely locked up. In view of my bedraggled condition and need for shelter I decided it was justifiable to enter., This was accomplished, after searching for a key under all the local boulders and in the niche above the door, by forcing myself through a tiny window high up, whose latch yielded to the deft twist of a pocket knife. Inside were a couple of couches, a bed, table and chairs. Obviously the place was in use, probably during the lambing season and sheep gathering. A good fire going and a meal on the hob made it seem a cosy spot indeed. By candlelight I read, with the flickering fire for company, F.B.Young's epic poem, 'The Island'. I would not have changed my digs for the most palatial hotel in Britain.

The sound of rain thrown on the window by wind awoke

me in the morning. By the time I had eaten a leisurely breakfast, juggling with dried eggs and the synthetic stuff a war
forces on a camper, the sun was beginning to break through.
A traverse of Ben Loyal was indicated and the obstacle of the
burn being negotiated by a tightrope act on twin strands of
loose wire, the hill was all mine.

I went in and out amongst boulders torn from the steep
crags above and supporting, somehow, a forest of silver birch
and mountain ash. It was more like an April morning the way
the sun played hide-and-seek with the clouds. From the loch
came the weird sound of loons, blackthroated divers.

I now skirted north-east, heading for the most seaward
peak of Sgorr Chaonasaid, so as to traverse the mountain from
north to south. Looking back, I could see Sgorr a' Chleirich, a
tooth of grey rock as sensational as the third pinnacle of Sgurr
nan Gillean. The steep slope I was climbing was a colourful
garden of globe-flowers, tormentil, violets, buttercups and
daisies, broad-leafed willow-herb, bluebells, spotted orchis
and even wood sanicle. Tree pipits were singing from the scattered birches and even at 1,500 feet I saw robins and thrushes.
From under my feet a woodcock rose, quite possibly nesting
up here.

I had hoped for a rock-climb on my peak but the intense
vegetation extended to the rocks. Every known lichen must
have hung on the crags. It was evident that I was on bare
rock covered by a skin of moss, for large areas of foot-hold
kept slipping away. But this dangerous traverse was made
worthwhile by the glory of cushion pinks and starry saxifrage
that made a rock garden of the mossy face.

My route landed me on the very summit and what I sought
was there, the Orkneys, rising like three hog-backs out of the
sea sixty degrees true north of my position. The whole landscape had that hard, clean look peculiar to showery weather.
The tiny houses, dots of white on the edge of the Kyle, were
most attractive.

Heavy showers were piling over the peaks of Ben Hee to

the south-west, in contrast to the serene skies over Loyal and the blue hills to the east. Quickly I made my way over my next top and got there just in time to shelter. There was a darkness on the peak and sleet came slashing across on the edge of a sudden squall. In the lulls that came as quickly as the storms, I managed the various tops.

Once off the top I was in sunshine and out of the wind. Buckbean growing out of the water of a peat hag on the moor was a pretty sight and I cursed the lack of film that prevented photography. I got to the house as the rain settled in for the evening.

All night it poured, but by the time I had packed my gear in the morning it had cleared to showers. Now I wanted to get to Lock Stack, quite a long way off. [*25 km!*] Nor is there a track till you get to Strath More. I decided to go by the Allt an Achaidh Mhoir. My pack was lighter by a few items of food so I fooled myself that there was little weight in it and swung off.

The going was rough but the foaming burn made for a certain amount of interest. Sooner than I thought I was on top of the pass and traversing west towards the Strath. Here the sun broke through, making silver of the wet rock-slabs on Ben Hee. From below me a cock merlin rose out of the heather, its pointed wings and slate colour showing perfectly.

Strath More was an inviting place to descend to with its wide river reaching up to a most imposing aspect of Ben Hope. Straight ahead of me to the west my pass climbed to a tiny gap high in the ridge. I had a light meal and pushed on by a fine track into a region of wild rocky corries overhung with the inevitable birch. Showers were more frequent now but it was not before I topped the col [*Bealach na Feithe*] and saw a mighty rain-blurred cone, Ben Stack, that I realised I was in for trouble. Cold and stinging, the huge veil whipped across, right in my face. I crouched under my oilskin but there was no sign of a lull so I went on as fast as I could, to keep warm.

67

Suddenly I came to a wonderful place. Through a curtain of rain, beyond an inky loch and in the space between the dim crag of Arkle and the shadowy cone of Ben Stack was a weird jumble of flat-topped mounds, blurred and mysterious, cradling lochans below bulging shoulders, gleams of water that might have been the abiding place of everything supernatural. The whole gaunt and naked landscape was empty of man or any sign of man, a place where the elements could roar and thrash their rains on the tumbled glacier beds belonging to past geological time. All was blotted out in a tremendous rainstorm.

I was grateful for the first sign of civilisation, a house marked on the map, Lone. Unfortunately it was empty and disused but on the map only one and a half miles away was another house marked Airdachchuilinn. I was wet and not too well off for food, so decided to go and ask for lodging.

The house proved to be rather more pretentious than the usual run of keepers' places and in some trepidation I knocked at the door, fully conscious of my tramp-like condition. But here was true Highland hospitality. "You'd better come in," were the kind-faced man's first words. A room was placed at my disposal immediately and a tea of home-made scones and bannocks was ready by the time I had changed my clothes. Mr Scobbie presided in the absence of his wife but the same hearty welcome was extended to me as if I were an old friend of the family. To come to a house like this after a spell of lonely sojourning is like coming home. A stormy sunset had us all shaking our heads as to the weather prospects.

But we were wrong. Morning came with all the glory of early June at its finest. Arkle was my peak, Arkle and its neighbours which had captured my fancy when I had once seen their quartz peaks from the top of Quinag. Now I could get to grips with them. Many rock buttresses invited on Arkle but I had a long day planned and I was anxious to get on to the tops for the uninterrupted views north and west which I knew the peak must give.

1 TOP: Tom Weir, aged three, in Springburn Park, Glasgow
2 BOTTOM: Tom on Doune Hill in the Luss Hills looking down to Loch Lomond

3 TOP: Tom, with Harold Raeburn's ice axe, when president of the SMC, 1984–86
4 BOTTOM: Inspecting the tool chest made by Rev A. E. Robertson (first Munroist) when AER was fifteen years old

5 TOP: Two worthy hill gangrels: Tom Weir and Syd Scroggie
(the latter lost his sight and a leg in the last days of World War Two)
6 BOTTOM: Tom's sister Molly and wife Rhona
at a standing stone on the Island of Jura

7 The world that lured four Scots lads, all self-supporting,
on the first post war Himalayan expedition

8 TOP: Porters in the Rishi Gorge, described in Tom's book,
The Ultimate Mountains
9 BOTTOM: Men and women porters on a Himalayan glacier
as described in *East of Katmandu*

10 TOP: The coastal area described during Sir John Hunt's 1960 expedition to Greenland
11 BOTTOM: Rhona at a camp in the Jotenheim, Norway

12 On a ridge in the Toubkal massif of Morocco's Atlas Mountains

13 TOP: Ringing gannets on the Bass Rock
14 BOTTOM: The view to the mainland from Eilean nan Ron,
Ben Loyal and Ben Hope visible

15 TOP: Stornoway, gateway to the Island of Lewis
16 BOTTOM: A seal pup on Eilean nan Ron, off the Kyle of Tongue

17 TOP: Ready to tackle the Cairngorms in the 'Good old days'
18 BOTTOM: A lass on remote Foula (Shetland) with a pet short-eared owl, which had strayed to the island

19 TOP: George Waterstone, the ornithologist who bought Fair Isle
and did so much for the successful reintroduction of ospreys to Scotland
20 BOTTOM: A crofter woman met in the Outer Hebrides (1975)
who was in her eighties and spoke only Gaelic

21 TOP: Rhona Weir in Glen Lyon, Tom's favourite glen
22 BOTTOM: Part of the one man's epic pick-and-shovel creation on Raasay, the story told in Roger Hutchinson's book *Calum's Road*

23 TOP: The controversial, environmentally misplaced
Coruisk Bridge in Skye, 1968 (storms soon removed it!)
24 BOTTOM: The Edwardian period drawing room in Kinloch Castle
on Rum (may be visited, but the castle is in need of renovation)

25 TOP: The one-time Renfrew Ferry not long after World War Two
26 BOTTOM: Curling stones from Lanark being packed for export to Canada

27 TOP: Colonsay: trying to move cows onto a boat for Oban in the 1960s
28 BOTTOM: Lewis: marking sheep in Ness in the 1950s

29 A waterfall in the Julian Alps (today's Slovenia)

In the vital air and sunshine of that perfect morning, every upward step was a lifting of the heart. I had been looking forward to seeing all my old friends (Quinag, Ben More, Suilven) but even my imagination was outstripped as they rose, purple-blue, bunched and huge over the low moors. How good it was to see them: the unmistakable rock pillars of Suilven; the point of Stac Polly, Cul Mor and Canisp; and west of them the old boys Ben More and Conival. A fainter blue and peering over the arm of Breabag were the Loch Droma peaks of Beinn Dearg and Conival showing as two cones connected by a high shoulder. Left of Stac Polly it gladdened me to identify the edge of An Teallach.

Such a preview spurred me on to the summit, a narrow edge of splintered quartzite almost as dazzling to the eye as snow. Around were the most contrasting colours I have ever seen, snow-like mountains, Mediterranean seas, the green islands of Badcall Bay, and the moorland heaths to Cape Wrath alive with lochans and silvery streams.

I had no realization that my peaks were so bare of vegetation. The whole chain of Fionn Bheinn I could see was composed entirely of quartz blocks strewn to glen level. Down to Loch an Easain Uaine I struck, by the roughest hillside I have ever been on. Every footstep had to be picked with care, and I was glad to take to some delightfully sound rock as a relief. In the hollow between Arkle and Fionn Bheinn I ate with relish some oatcake and an egg, savouring the situation as much as the repast.

Up by Coire a' Chouiteir , over a little pinnacle and another couple of tops and I was on Fionn Bheinn's summit. The view over the dotted lochs and fretted coast was a replica of my memory of the view from Quinag. Mist was creeping over the tops now, and from Gaineamh Mhor and Ceann Garbh I saw nothing at all.

In this mountain fastness there is a celebrated crag by a wild loch, Loch Dionard. It is not an easy place to get to, but I saw a way of including it in my return journey. Down by

69

Cnoc Duail was the way, past the Buachaille Etive Mor-like crags of A' Ch'eir Ghorm (A' Choire Gorm). What a feast of rock exploration is on this remote face!

I came to Loch Dionard. Like another Sron na Ciche the rock rises in a thousand foot sweep. Down its huge face poured a mighty waterfall in spate from the recent rains. Examining the rock, I saw exciting problems awaiting the explorer for the place abounded in grand situations, and it appeared to me as though quite a few rock formations were in its make-up. If only Matt had been with me!

Deep heather that made hard going took me from here to where a path led to An Dubh Loch, a beautiful corrie in the mossy face of Meall Horn. I had been feeling tired climbing the sixteen hundred feet to the top of the bealach but the view from the summit rejuvenated me. The whole of south-west Sutherland was sunlit. On the sea, silvery with sunset, the islands of Badcall Bay were ebony. Above me over the green top of Meall Horn, an eagle was performing diving acrobatics. A line of crags led to the top inviting me to get up there. My tiredness vanished and I scrambled on sound rock into the sunshine.

It was 11pm when I got back to the house but there was no complaint about my late hours or the fact that my dinner had been kept waiting. Fresh trout and potatoes, custard and jelly, and lashings of tea was a fit finish to a memorable day. Bath and bed, and I was ready for both.

I was awakened by Mr Scobbie with the news that a pair of black-throated divers were below my window. Imagine watching a pair of black-throated divers from your bedroom window! Every marking of their velvety plumage was visible. Unfortunately the rain came, and after a visit to a hoodie's nest the weather became impossible. Still we had a good day at 'the conversation', exchanging yarns and ideas. Mr Scobbie's son, Bill, was a keen bird-man so we had plenty to say to each other. I felt I had earned a day off anyhow.

But I was disappointed when the next morning brought

more rain and dense clouds pressing down from the north. It seemed a hopeless sort of day but to my delight it cleared to a breezy day of showers and sun. Round Loch Stack on the hunt for red-throated divers I went by a morass of bog, but all I saw was an excited greenshank. Ben Stack was the natural way to finish and up its steep birch-slopes and rocky ribs I went to the narrow summit ridge to arrive there in sunshine.

Most fascinating for me in the varied view from the summit was the lane of rocky mounds stretching from the mountains to the sea. No doubt that it was worn by ice for the vegetation has been scalped from the harder material leaving smooth rock slabs crowning their flattened tops. Loch Laxford and Inchard are the culminating points of the glacier system as it appeared to me, sitting on top of Ben Stack.

In the light of a marvellous sunset I came down. A fine evening in the Highlands is in my opinion the greatest manifestation of nature. The whole glen was afire, each tree and blade of grass glowing as though lit from within.

The man who said it could be winter any day of the year on the Scottish hills certainly knew his Highlands. Morning brought a howling west wind and a downpour from swirling grey clouds that opened and closed on Arkle. From my window I could see a waterfall high on the mountain smoking like a chimney-stack as the water went up instead of down.

Bill ferried me across the stormy loch which was the end of my leave. He could have let me walk the mile to the road-end to meet the mail car and thus avoid a wetting, but that was not the way of the Scobbies. Climbing means more than just mountains when you meet such people.

HIGHLAND DAYS

EILEAN NAN RON: A VERY FERTILE PLACE

Ever since I saw the white croft houses gleaming on the rocky island of Eilean nan Ron I have wanted to land there, and see how such an unlikely pancake of land at the mouth of the Kyle of Tongue could support a population. Last August I was not only successful, but the lobster fisherman who took me over was the last to leave in 1938. So from him I learned the story of the 'happy island'.

Donald lives in Skerray now, only two miles across the water from where he was born. He still keeps sheep on the island, and at the time of my visit was taking off the lambs to sell at Forsinard.

"It is a very fertile place. You could always get a good return from the croft. With the fishing we were practically self-supporting. With the cows we had plenty of milk and butter and crowdie. The only thing we brought in was flour. There was plenty of peat."

The story of the island folk begins with the Clearances, when people were evicted from the straths and forced to find some sort of living on the coast. In those hard times of 1820, three young couples tried their luck on Eilean nan Ron. I was able to piece the story together from what the lobster fisherman said, and from what another son of Eilean nan Ron, John George Mackay wrote in a thin pamphlet printed in 1962. Mr Mackay said; "I was born on the island and spent my childhood and adolescent years there, and now, with old age creeping over me, and having to spend most of my days alone, I often think of those happy times ... Now that the island is desolate and its surviving natives getting fewer and fewer, I feared that soon there would be no one left to recall the old days. The thought grieved me. Why, I said to myself, why allow the memory of the island to die?"

I had to see the island, and as we bobbed across in a boat strewn with crabs caught that morning, and pincering below our legs, Donald told me of his boyhood, when here were 18 scholars in the school and 11 families on the island. "I had to leave to finish my education at Golspie Academy. There was nothing on the island except fishing and crofting. The girls wouldn't stay. Then one family after another left for America and Canada, some went to Australia.

"We were happy, but look at the landing! Everything coming from the sea had to be carried up these steep rocks. There was no machinery. There was not even a horse." The landing was certainly impressive, a flight of steep steps built up the rocks above a concreted jetty on the edge of a horse-shoe of bay. "I'll pick you up at about six", said Donald as he pulled away and headed back to Skerray to clip some sheep.

Taking possession of a small island is always marvellous, This one, where people had lived for 130 years, starting from scratch, forced the mind back to the first three couples, who would have to build houses for themselves, break in fields, lay a store of fuel and food in for the winter, fish the rocky coast when possible, enter caves to kill Atlantic seals for their blubber, and begin rearing their families, pitting their wits against nature, surviving and building up an independent community. It was all their own work, with the women attending the crofts, mending nets, spinning wool from the sheep for clothing, while the men fished cod and haddock for winter storage in a special cave whose currents of air had a magic property of keeping the fish soft so that it still tasted fresh months after it was caught.

Life was communal. When a new house was needed for a young couple, the menfolk blasted the rocks from the quarry cave and hauled wood, slate, lime and sand from the harbour. But as the population grew bigger they needed a deep-sea boat to fish farther afield, and it was provided by the Duke of Sutherland who got his money back in yearly instalments. A sister boat was added, and as the days of sail passed, the islanders chartered a steam drifter to fish herrings the whole year round from the Minch to Lowestoft.

With the men away most of the time, the women had to work harder, and even manned their own boat between the island and the mainland. Religion played a very important part in their lives. All days began and ended with prayers. The Sabbath was sacred. The only travel was to church across the water, and if this was impossible, a morning and evening service was held in the school, with an islander acting as minister. The language, of course, was Gaelic.

Wandering around the ruins of the village and the green fields sandwiched by heather on both sides, I had a sense of being in a happy place, not too lonely with crofts across the water. And for inspiration there was the silver of the Kyle of Tongue backed by the knobbly peaks of Ben Loyal and Ben Hope. Climb a little and you saw Orkney. From the nearest point on the mainland you could walk to Tongue village in an hour, which school children had to do when the dreaded 'Inspector' was visiting.

The whole island is roughly one mile long by half a mile broad, yet everywhere you are cut off from the sea by rocks. Two pairs of bonxies dived at my head as I strolled across the marshy southern end to look at the kittiwakes on the rock stacks, which are mainly devoid of birds other than shags and fulmars because of lack of ledges.

The north end of the island is much more thrilling, with bigger cliffs of comglomerate, sheering the north-western tip off from the main island. The detached portion is called Eilean Iosal, roofed with smooth emerald turf and much dissected by reefs. It was an impressive wall of rock, pierced by a natural tunnel through which the sea plunged. I was attracted down to investigate. The scrambling was on sandstone conglomerate, compressing in its pink-crush grey stones like large plum puddings. Getting into the tunnel meant climbing over the chunks fallen from the large roof, and creeping along inside was rather eerie, with the water crashing in the semi-darkness along the inclined slabs, not daring to think of the possibility of slipping in.

Back to daylight on the far side was another mass of fallen blocks, offering a 50ft pyramid from which to attack the upper cliff. It looked unlikely because of its steepness but proved straightforward if fairly exposed – a little climbing adventure I would not have missed.

I had time to look at the northern peat banks before crossing the ridge that leads to the houses. A few skeletal remains of gable-ends are the result of houses being dismantled for their materials when the island was abandoned in 1938. Two of them had names written on walls with sprayguns, done most probably by a succession of hippies who took over the island in 1972, one or two of whom stayed through the winter. Unfortunately when they left in March 1973 they left behind a cat which is still living wild, killing the stormy petrels which breed among the stones.

Another strange episode in the island's history was when it was used for three months in 1950 by immigrant volunteers and scientists experimenting to find a cure for the common cold. Possibly a logical use for Eilean nan Ron would be as a bird migration station for it has proved to be good for autumn passage.

The ornithologist who discovered this was a man who is commemorated on the island on a door lintel where an inscription reads, 'In Memory of Ian R. Downhill, Lost on This Island, September 1963'. Ian was a fellow member of the Scottish Ornithologists' Club who disappeared and was presumed drowned, while out in his rubber boat. Ironically there was never a case of an adult drowning or being lost at sea during the whole fishing history of the island. Downhill's bird notes from Eilean nan Ron (which he calls Island Roan) were published in *Scottish Birds*, Vol 2, No 6, 1963, and result from a six-week stay the previous year, from August 3 until September 13.

There is no record on Downhill's notes of the bonxie breeding, which means the birds I saw have colonised since 1963. The peregrine had also bred successfully. Downhill's observations of sooty shearwaters and great shearwaters were the first for Sutherland, and among an interesting variety of visiting waders he recorded spotted redshank. Strangely enough I spotted no seals, yet it is well attested that they breed in caves, and that the islanders killed them for their skins and blubber.

From Donald I heard some more about the decline of the island. He had been born at the peak of its prosperity at the beginning of the century, at a time when newly-wed couples had to leave because of over-population. Then came the 1914 war. Eighteen men left and 17 returned to find the seas had been cleared of fish by trawlers. Let John George Mackay speak, "Education was advancing, and having been all over the world during the war years, the younger generation had been given an insight into what was going on elsewhere, and that sealed the doom of the island. It was the same all round the north and the west coast of Sutherland. The younger people were leaving to make a living elsewhere. Fishing and crofting as their forefathers knew it was reduced to a shadow of what it used to be."

Houses were dismantled and families sailed away to make new lives for themselves, so that by 1938 only 12 people remained, eight of them old. They hesitated on going, but on the stormy night of December 6 they sailed away for the last time, having to delay their departure until the hens went to roost at dark and they could be caught. In imagination I can see the light of the lantern on slippery steps of the rocks, the boat heaving on the dark sea, and the transfer of hens and odd bits of hand luggage before the old women were helped aboard and settled for the stormy crossing of the Kyle of Rannoch to Skerray.

The islander I like best to remember is Betty Macdonald,

the first-born of the original three young couples. She lived to be 95 and never once left the island. Her world was 700 acres, mostly peat and heather, but she must have had a rare sense of 'belonging' in a community that was one big family.

COUNTRY LIFE 1974

ERISKAY

Eriskay is now connected to South Uist by a causeway and an improved ferry service to Barra but the island remains the charming place described thirty years ago.

It was a July morning to cheer the heart, sun shining on a grass brilliant with flowers, and from our tent door a view over rock-speckled knolls, each by a crofthouse above a sea-scape stretching to South Uist. Peat smells vied with the scents of clover and thyme. A corn bunting was an unexpected songster among the twites perched on a nearby fence. Beneath us terns fished in the clear green water, and the rough sail from Oban to Lochboisdale, less than sixteen hours ago, was already a distant memory. [*Tom did not enjoy sea travel*]

Waiting for the kettle to boil for some tea before setting off on a first exploration I read a poem written on 13 February 1889 by Father Allan McDonald, who was the priest on this Island of Eriskay until his death in 1905. Translated from the Gaelic into prose it goes something like this: *Rough, gloomy weather, as is usual in early February, white spindrift of the sand-banks driven everywhere; spray like ashes driven across the sound; sod and slate loosened by the quick blows of the wind. Fierce squalls from the north shaking every gable, hard hailstones which would cut the top off one's ears, men so chilled with the cold that they cannot look outside, huddled indoors at the edge of the ashes. The head of yonder hill above is sheathed in a shroud, since the cold has killed her natural virtue. She has lost her appearance entirely. The*

77

sleep of death has come upon her, and there is no likelihood of her moving until the warmth of spring unbinds her.

Eriskay is only 3 miles long and 1 mile broad, and few people were aware of its existence until Mrs Marjory Kennedy Fraser's *Eriskay Love Lilt*. Miss Amy Murray, an American, took down about 100 airs in Eriskay around 1905 so the world became aware of the marvellous oral tradition of these islands with words and songs going back hundreds of years.

Of all the islands in the Hebrides, Eriskay seems one of the most unlikely for habitation, consisting of little more than two hills whose rocks go right down to the sea. Looking down from the highest I marvelled that it should support a vigorous community of more than 200 people, when so many islands of better soils lie empty, their ageing population having given up.

Eriskay had no more than a miserable hovel or two on it in 1745, when Prince Charles Edward put it on the map by making his Scottish landfall there on his way from France in the ship *Du Teillay* to raise the clans and march upon England. Typically, his arrival on Eriskay was an accident, due to panic at the sight of a ship they took to be an enemy frigate. By dodging among the Barra Isles they managed to give it the slip. So in the wind and rain of 24 July, the Prince was put ashore and taken to a smokey hut where he sat miserably on a pile of peats, waiting impatiently for the Laird of Boisdale, who had been summoned from South Uist for help.

It is unlikely that Eriskay would never have been settled if the Prince had listened to Boisdale who, meeting the Prince, advised him to turn about and go back to France. But while they argued, the hostile-looking ship reappeared off the coast, in company with another. Conversations were cut short. The *Du Teillay* set sail east to Loch nan Uamh. The adventures of the Prince had begun – and he was a beaten man when he came back this way after Culloden, desperate to get a ship to France.

The settlement of Eriskay dates from the Clearances of the

mid19th century and the mass eviction of South Uist and Barra crofters to make way for sheep. To escape being rounded up like cattle and shipped to Canada, some took refuge on Eriskay, and were allowed to stay, because the thin soil was too poor, even for sheep. Wandering around the island in the next few days I could only marvel at what the descendants of the downtrodden settlers had made of their island, as shown by the well-built houses glittering in the neat whitewash and roofed in colourful blue or red. Perched on the bedrock, you had to go looking among the boulders to find their cultivation patches, no more than a few rigs of soil built up with the spade and given treatment of sand and seaweed for growing potatoes.

The islanders say it was the big shoals of herring and mackerel in the seas around them that enabled their forebears to survive. They fished with such vigour that they were better off than South Uist crofters who had been forced off good *machair* land and depended for a living on the burning of kelp. The Crofters Act of 1886 enabled the Eriskay people to rebuild their thatched single-roomed cottages into something better, and today they are among the best-housed people in the Hebrides thanks to the sound financial base of their fishing.

Arriving on a Friday, it was a surprise to find so many motor cars on Eriskay's three miles of narrow road which connects the linear crofts. One of the islanders explained, "It's only weekend traffic. It'll be quiet enough when the men put to sea again on Monday morning and the cars will be in the garage for another week." I learned that a new boat had been added to the fleet of six, fishing for prawns and herrings, while two lobster boats worked the shores.

My visit coincided with a Sale of Work on the island which brought a great traffic there on a Saturday afternoon. Boats came over from Barra and Uist, and the people packed the village hall, filling it with happy Gaelic tongues. Two priests worked the Wheel of Fortune, and a visiting nun won a prize.

79

Eriskay pullovers with a tree-of-life design, and waves and furrows were bargains at £12. Incredibly the amount gathered was £1450 – good going for an island with a population of 200 – raised to pay for chapel repairs.

Sunday was a happy day, as family parties in their Sunday best converged on the chapel for morning Mass. "You should come," said one wee girl, "The Priest will give you a paper to tell you what to do." The chapel perches on a westerly spur above the main settlement on the north tip of the island, and was built by the islanders, who dug the foundations, cut the quarried stones and carried up sand and cement to create something beautiful for their beloved priest, Father Allan MacDonald, who died just two years after the church was opened in 1903.

I saw how well balanced the present population is at a ceilidh held in the hall on the Sunday evening, when the whole entire population turned out in a healthy scattering of ages from young to old. The missing ones were those in the merchant navy or girls away working in mainland hotels for the summer season. The Gaelic singing was a joy, and so was the naturalness of it all, as the audience waited to see who would be called next when the last chorus faded away. None refused their call and my only sorrow was that I had no Gaelic to follow the humour or the pathos of the songs. There were alcoholic refreshments too, and a great sweeping of the floor for a dance which began around midnight and finished only when the fisherman stole away to join their boats and go off for another week.

An islander showed me where to look for the Prince's flower on the shell sand beach known as Coilleag a' Phriennsa. I was advised to search the dunes above it, among the silverweed, ragged robin and lady's bedstraw. It took three hours to find the pinkish trumpet flowers of *Calystegia soldanella*, the sea convolvulus. The islanders believe that the plant grows only on Eriskay, and that it was planted by the Prince to celebrate his arrival on Scottish soil, a romantic notion, upset by the fact that there are twenty post-1930 records from various bits of the Scottish coast, though Eriskay could be its most northerly location in all Europe. Alone, in the rain, I had a strange moment, almost a re-run of history, when an old-fashioned schooner, square sails stretched, hove into view off the bay. It was not second sight but the top-gallant-yard training schooner *Captain Scott*, on one of its island voyages.

From the 609 ft.[186m] top of Ben Scrien, highest point of Eriskay, you get a truly mountain top view, out over Rum, Canna and the Cuillin to the peaks of Ross, while just across the water the dark hulk of Barra stretches southward, with the sands and crofts of North Bay no more than a short sailing distance away. Northward between Eriskay and South Uist is the smudge of a small island called Calvey, enshrined since 1941 in the pure gold of Hebridean memory.

Sir Compton MacKenzie, who lived on Barra at the time, has enshrined for us in his hilarious novel *Whisky Galore* what happened after the cargo ship *Politician* struck a reef off Calvey that February night without loss of life, or too much damage to the 20,000 cases of export whisky which formed her cargo. It certainly was the happiest event in a grim war, all the better for the whisky being of thirty-two different brands. Songs are still sung about it – and it would appear that the oral tradition has handed on more than has been written down – if you have the Gaelic.

Isolation has kept alive old ways and customs on Eriskay, and it has enabled the special Eriskay ponies to retain their purity as a primitive breed. Used for bringing peat in panniers down from the hills, the docile and sure-footed breed is regarded by experts as being closest to the old Celtic horse. At a time when there is so little belief in crofting and fishing among Hebrideans, it is heartening to see one well-stratified and well-balanced community who believe in the old way of life. What Father Allan MacDonald wrote about Eriskay at the beginning of the century may sound romantic but broadly speaking is still strong in right values: *Eriskay . . . of the speckled knolls and the bright white strand; 'tis there one finds strong men who are not afraid when the sea rises, and kindly, tunefully, diligent women who sing more sweetly than the birds on the trees.*

WEIR'S WAY

CONTRASTING ORKNEY ISLANDS

Until recently I had never visited the Old Man of Hoy, though I must admit I felt we were old friends, for in the spectacular film of its ascent by three different routes I was stand-by commentator for BBC Television from the Glasgow studio. Now here was I in Orkney, on the pier at Stromness, in the rain. Of Hoy just across the water nothing could be seen, and I would have put off the visit for another day if the Met. Office at Kirkwall hadn't told me there was no hope of a clear up for some time.

So off we sailed to Linksness pier on Hoy under the highest hills of Orkney, guessed at rather than seen that morning. We took the hill road west until it became a path bending south past the Sandy Loch where great skuas wheeled overhead and fulmar petrels had nests on wee outcrops. Once off the road on a true hill-pass, spirits rose. My wife averred that the rain was refreshing. There was even an illusion of sunshine as we came in sight of green Rackwick and the sandy curve of its bay set between the pillars of pink cliff, the houses perched here and there giving a feeling of life.

Alas, Rackwick is a ghost village of ruins and memories of times past, as talented local artist Ian MacInnes of Stromness explained when he invited us into his holiday cottage for coffee. "The school, (now a hostel for outdoor folk) closed over forty years ago. It's the old story, the young folk left to better themselves, and the old folks remaining died one by one. At last there were only two wee boys in the village. They

82

used to play with my youngster. One morning they drowned while playing with a raft in the burn. It was the end, but the Highlands and Islands Development Board is helping Jack Rendall to restore 'The Glen' and make a go of crofting the place, so maybe the idea will spread. It's such a beautiful place."

Certainly Ian finds inspiration in the setting as does the composer Peter Maxwell Davies who needs complete peace to write his highly acclaimed music. Perched high above the bay and reached only by a steep footpath, his simple cottage has the finest view in all Orkney. I climbed past it on the way to the Old Man of Hoy, interrupting him only for a moment to say hello.

The easiest way to the famous pinnacle is from the school over the flank of Moor Fea among the skuas and the greater blackbacked gulls. Although not marked on the map there is a good footpath, as well as a notice warning climbers that they go at their own risk for there is no rescue service on Hoy. We were in luck when suddenly in front of us the Old Man stuck his head out of the mist, lower parts invisible until we got to the edge of the cliff and we saw his great skeleton.

The story of its first ascent was brilliantly told by the late Tom Patey in the December 1966 issue of *The Scots Magazine*. Patey wrote "As you climb higher there is a unique sense of physical detachment and height ceases to be of any morbid significance. We were higher than St Paul's Cathedral and by the time we reached the top we would be level with the new Post Office tower, London's highest building." Tom had declared after the feat that there wouldn't be a next time. But of course there was, or I would not have been in the television studio watching the antics of Dougal Haston, Joe Brown, Peter Crew, MacNaught Davis, Tom Patey and the other stars.

How has the Old Man fared since he was first conquered thirteen years ago? The answer is that it is now a commonplace climb and done by over a score of parties every summer. I spoke to a quartet of English youngsters who had just done it. I asked if they had found it hard. "Not too hard," they opined. "But it took us quite a time, even though the ironmongery was in place."

While we stood up on the airy headland, looking down on the fulmars on their ledges, the mist swirled clear of St John's head and a gleam of sun warmed the great Orkney cliff a rich red. Plunging in great overhangs and verticalities for over 1,100ft. it too has been climbed, but it took five days, the climbers using mechanical aids and sleeping out on the face. To honour the lifeboatmen of Hoy who died in a wild storm they named their climb The Longhope Route.

The cliffs and moors of Hoy could hardly have been in more contrast to the scenery of the island we had just come from. North Ronaldsay, the most northerly of all the Orkneys, looking to the Fair Isle and the Shetland mainland. Our plan was that we should go there on the once weekly boat. Fate conspired against us.

First the car broke down on the way to Skara Brae and had to be towed back to Stromness, which meant us taking the bus back to Kirkwall and finding digs for the night to be aboard *The Islander* by 7 a.m. the next morning. We were in grand time for the boat but were puzzled when we found no sign of folk or ship. Then we noticed a man in working clothes coming towards us. "I'm looking for *The Islander*," I said, hoping he could help. He pointed out to sea. "She left nearly an hour ago. Were you booked?" I nodded. "It's not the first time it's happened," he grimaced. "The sailing time was changed late yesterday. You didn't give them a telephone number?" We couldn't because we didn't have one. What now?

The harbour official said he would drive us to the airport to be there at 8 a.m. in the hope of getting a Loganair inter-island plane. Placed on standby we were in luck, we each got a seat though on different planes. Waiting to go I had been watching a short-eared owl quartering the grass just beyond the terminal building.

An added bit of luck was that each of us had a pilot seat

position for a superb flight, flying low over the sea to skim Shapinsay and another stretch of sea to Eday. We could hardly have been more intimate with the land, with terns and skuas just below us on the peat moss, and a fine feeling of speed with the hill changing from brown to green as we touched down bumping along on the grass.

Off again following the bays of well-named Sanday [*the 1½ minutes Eday to Sanday flight is the shortest scheduled flight in the world*] and ahead of us was the flat line of North Ronaldsay, blue in the distance but suddenly rich green and yellow with flowers as we pitched down and dismounted into fragrant air. I am all for airstrips without tarmac, and the informality of collecting your own luggage and walking off.

The story of why I had sought out this particular island begins with a Perthshire post box. I had contacted David Dove of the Scottish Postal Board for information about the mail-bus routes serving the glens, and as a result he had asked me if I would act as one of the judges of an essay-writing competition open to school children. The essay had to be in the form of a letter, the subject Places to Visit.

There was no doubt about the winner of the Scottish senior section. The £50 prize went to Mary Elizabeth Muir for the description of her home on North Ronaldsay, and the attraction of mainland Orkney where she attends Kirkwall Grammar School, as do other children of this outlying island once they reach the age of twelve.

We were looking forward to meeting Mary and her family and getting a wee conducted tour of the little island which she had described as being three miles long and one and a half miles wide. Her father was down to meet the plane and soon whisked us to the house in Garso at the north end.

How nice to arrive in a home from home and be made instant members of a family, sharing the normal way of life on the croft. Mary's mother takes everything in her stride, including an Open University degree. Father not only works a croft but runs the school bus and the island taxi service. It was lucky for us to have the two boys and two girls at home before the summer holidays ended and took them to Kirkwall.

First though, a walk with prize winner Mary to the north point of her island, and an exhilarating daunder to the boulder shore through green fields and amongst shingly lochans alive with flying birds, golden plovers and peewits by the score, Arctic terns by the hundred, rock doves in the fields and shelduck on the water. We walked along the famous wall which entirely surrounds the island and is something of a mystery. The length has been stated as fifteen miles following the windings of the shore. It is maintained by the crofters to keep out of the fields the unique breed of sheep which feed on seaweed and are renowned for the quality of their mutton.

I thought them vaguely reminiscent of the goat-like St Kilda sheep, in their agility and dun colour. Ewes are brought to grass inside the wall at lambing time. The earmarks denoting the owners are identical to the type used in the Faroes and Iceland. Mary says the sheep are under the auspices of the sheep court, elected by men of the island, and that is one of the oldest courts in the world. A recent book on Orkney states the wall was built last century. As we watched the sheep eat the seaweed, picking up mouthfuls of juicy ribbon-like morsels, a flock of migrant knots landed beside some turnstones, only a small indication of how good this island is for bird migration, akin to Fair Isle.

In the old days there was a fishing station at Noust and there are still plenty of signs of kelp burning from so long ago. I was to hear about this later. Meantime we were interested in the seals

basking along the shore, wailing to each other but unwilling to forsake the warmth of the sun for the cold water.

Just beyond was the Burrian Broch whose outer face has been incorporated into the wall and the entrance blocked up. Excavations around here have yielded a hut settlement and finds of bone combs and needles, spinning whorls, scrapers and flints. Mary describes in her letter the most exciting thing that has been found, the shoulder blade of an ox, with Pictish symbols and a Christian cross incised on it. This Burrian Cross and Pictish symbols are now used on Orkney Silvercraft jewelry.

Virtually the whole of North Ronaldsay is farmed to rear beef, with the emphasis on silage, hay, pasture, a little barley, turnips and some vegetables. Most crofts are small but mechanisation is widespread. Willie Thomson of Neven, near the Muir's house spoke to me about the changes he had seen in his seventy-seven years, remembering when the population was three times what it is now and cash in your pocket was relatively unimportant. You lived on what you could grow and the fish you could catch. "I remember watching boats going to the Fair Isle fishing grounds, sail after sail. I was told not to count them going out (bad luck) but to wait for them coming back. There were sixty pupils in the school when I was a boy, now it's only five.

"Stronsay was a great fishing station in my day. The boats were 40 to 60 ft. with a lugsail, and we went away for a week at a time. There was a crew of five. It was after the 1914–18 war the island started to go down. Of course there had always been a lot of emigration to Canada and Edinburgh. In Leith there are as many North Ronaldsay men as in North Ronaldsay itself. I'd rather be here than in any city. Look at Kirkwall, people hurry past, never giving you a look. The hard pavements are sore on your feet. The world is full of crime today. You nearly need a lock on your pockets. Here on North Ronaldsay I never knew anybody who locked a door. There is no such thing as crime, thanks be to Providence."

Willie, retired now, and in not too good health, has a hobby which passes the time, painting schooners and sailing ships in full rig on the glass floats which fisherman use on their nets – real works of art produced on a curved surface. He remembers with pleasure the days when he worked as a crofter-fisherman, when the island was well populated and everyone worked at the same task, the kelp gathering, the

---

ploughing with horse and oxen, haymaking, harvesting, sharing a communal life. "I think we were happier," he opines. "Now it's all machines and money. Hardly anybody keeps a milking cow. In the old days there was a lot of fun, and the quality of your work was noticed. You always wanted to be the best at a job. Without the variety of crops the island is not so bonnie as it was. It was lovely in the harvest time with the different colours."

The trend is that farms will get bigger, crofts will be enlarged as population declines, and fewer people will make a better but duller living. Things are fairly healthy at present. Of the 120 or so people who live on North Ronaldsay about 40 per cent are old age pensioners, but there are over a dozen under five years old and about fourteen families between forty and sixty, plus four couples between twenty and forty. In terms of children, a dozen go to Kirkwall Grammar School, as well as five in the village primary school. This does not include lighthouse keepers, the resident doctor, and the schoolteacher who is from England.

Mary Elizabeth Muir will have the last word. She ends: "When I think of home in summer, I think of the smell of clover, wildflowers and warm hay. In winter I think of the glittering constellation of Orion, the Great Bear, the pale iridescent streamers of the Northern Lights. The moon glimmering on the dark waters of the loch where the wintering swans are sleeping. The sound of the sea, in all its moods, is never far from my ears . . ."

TOM WEIR'S SCOTLAND

Rackwick sees many more visitors these days and is a cheerier place. North Ronaldsay is now seeing new developments under a North Ronaldsay Trust set up in 2000, such as accommodation, café and tours involving the lighthouse (at 42m the highest land-based in Britain)In 1987 an observatory was established (with visitor accommodation) for this important migrant spot, something which would have delighted Tom.

IV

DESERT MOUNTAINS AND ARCTIC PEAKS

Tom is perhaps best remembered for the important post-war Hima-
layan expeditions but he ventured to several other, then remote and
scarce-known regions, such as the Atlas, Kurdistan and Greenland,
described here. These were his glory days of exploration, soon cur-
tailed by the hard graft of surviving as a writer but gave us the Tom
Weir who came to know Scotland in such depths and shared his
enthusiasm for decades in The Scots Magazine *and then on T.V.*
He took his chances. He went. He was rewarded. And so are we.

MOROCCO 1955

Tom had read of pre-war climbing in the Atlas and of Bentley Beetham's several seasons there 'discovering a more rewarding field for mountaineering than the Alps, so over-familiar and tame by comparison, with the delights of the unknown', so, with Douglas Scott, headed for Morocco in Spring 1955. Baggage sent by sea was delayed in reaching Tangier but they had superlative birding as migrants poured across the narrows of the Straits of Gibraltar. Vibrant, exotic, heading for Independence, Berber life, mountains; everything fascinated. They began, as many do, with some days skiing up at Oukaïmeden, nearly 9000ft. up in the mountains south of Marrakech where there was, and is, a CAF chalet.

It was packed with young French skiers. In décor and tasteful appointments it stood comparison with any alpine hut that we had ever been in, with a fine choice of meals – at cheap cost. All the beds in the dormitory were taken, but we were invited to feel free and make a bed on the floor.

We were first out into the sparkle of a frosty morn of blue sky echoed in pools of blue water reflecting the snows above. Tiny alpine daffodils of slender form edged the pools and there was a grand singing and chuckling of birds. We saw shorelarks, alpine accentors, wheatears, Mousssier's redstart, jackdaws, choughs and wagtails – before setting off with our skis for the peak – the first to be hauled up on the ski-tow.

We soon found out why, the snow was too icy as yet for enjoyable downhill running: so what we did was climb from the top station to the summit [10,738ft/3273m] and enjoy our first close view of High Atlas peaks thrusting through a white cloud-sea that lapped their lower slopes and cut them off from the valleys. There was no doubt where our first climbing strike should be, by the west buttress of a peak within easy distance of where we stood. The name on the map was Angour.

By the time we got back to our skis, the snow had softened sufficiently to delight the first arrivals and we made the most of it until mid-day, after which the snow became impossibly heavy and slow.

Out of our sleeping bags before others were awake, we were away on a delightful morning to the pass that would take us to Angour. After toiling up to get hands and feet on pink rock, warm in the sun, we came to life, finding steep pitch after steep pitch of high interest, never easy but never too difficult; we graded what was its west buttress as Mild Severe. From the top the peak that commanded our attention was the 6,000-foot north face of Aksoual leading to a pinnacled crest.

A glance at the map identified the pass leading to it, the Tizi n' Ouadi. If we crossed with four days' food we could stay in a simple refuge at the Berber village of Tacheddirt to launch our attempt on the face. It would be quite a heavy back-packing job, so back in Ouka we found a native porter, by name Bourgemaa and it was good next morning to be in roadless country, grateful for the guidance of our fast moving Berber who knew the way and seemed to be enjoying himself.

Tacheddirt was our first close contact with a Berber village, built in giant steps, so that the flat roof of the lowest house was the courtyard of the one above it, and so on to the highest house, narrow alleys leading through. Our refuge stood apart from the village at 7,700 feet [2314m], containing bedsteads, a table, a few chairs and a lockable cupboard. For fuel we gathered a prickly shrub which burns with explosive vigour . . .

At 5 am the fire was lit, eggs boiled in the tea water, a quick breakfast scoffed, and with food in the rucksack, rope and ice axes at the ready, we were away down into the depths of a gorge to ford the river by jumping from boulder to boulder, then climbing over a hill shoulder lying between us and our mountain. In daylight this took only one hour. In darkness, as we were to discover fourteen hours later, it was a very different and heart-breaking story. Everything was frozen hard, the steep snow just above the gorge forcing us to cut steps even at modest angles, then by a gully we reached iced rocks and scrambled steeply out of shadow into sunshine on a silver saddle surrounded by red rock towers projecting against a blue sky. It was good to be alive and faced by a real exploratory problem on virgin ground.

Our reconnaissance of yesterday was paying dividends. We recognised the rock rib which we knew would lead us to a bulging overhang, by-passable by going left on snow. What we had not bargained for, however, was the snow getting soft so quickly, forcing us to stay on the rocks, playing a game of hide-and-seek between the overhang and the snow, enjoying thrilling situations that continued for 3,000 feet, and led us to another of our landmarks, a rock arête which we hoped to climb for 1,500 feet to its top. It proved easier than it looked so we were able to move together, and at 2.30 pm we stepped on to the summit, the climb having taken eight hours with only three halts for food, delightful halts on sunny ledges.

But something ominous was happening to the weather. Our immediate concern was our couloir of descent, and how to get across the rock towers between us and it, for they were more formidable-looking at close range than they had appeared from far below. Wasting no time, we dropped to the foot of the first one, saw there was no direct way up but threading the face like a barrel hoop was a snow tilted ledge, dangerously soft and exposed to a big drop, a tense traverse that took us to the base of the second tower, where the mist was curling. This one had an obvious line of weakness, and in forty feet of difficult rock climbing we were on easy ground leading us to an airy summit crest, with an abrupt drop to the final tower. This one we took direct by its steep arête, Scott vanquishing its overhanging edge as if he were starting the

93

day and not on the exposed top of a remote mountain after long hours of hard climbing.

Now to get off this last one and find the couloir! In mist and snow it is hard to judge distance. We knew we should not proceed too far, so at a likely place started down, slowly at first, then when no rocks interrupted, we decided it would be safe to sit on our backsides and let gravity slide us down. It was exhilarating, we were moving fast and in good control, until suddenly we had to throw ourselves back on our ice axes and brake on the edge of a drop. Nothing for it now but to uncoil the rope, and climb down a series of awkward pitches of rock and ice.

Once down this we were in the true gully and realising that until now we had been in a side branch. Daylight was going fast and we fairly shot down the next 1,000 feet, Darkness was winning the race, however, not only the darkness of night but the darkness of storm. It was time to get out the torch, and while Scott fumbled with the battery I tried to tie a bootlace. I was aware of a flash which I thought was his light, and so did he. A crackle of thunder, followed by stinging hailstones the size of small peas, told us our mistake.

Torch in hand and blinded by frequent stabs of forked lightning, we stumbled down the gully, keeping to the centre as far as possible in order to avoid holes, like miniature crevasses penetrating to the stream running far below. The peaks were clear now, as we could see when each flash of lightning outlined them in quivering purple. There was a nightmarish quality about the remainder of the descent in a wet world of ravines and waterfalls, loose stones and side-gullies which neither of us could remember from the morning. It has been remarked by more than one mountaineer, that electric storms can have an invigorating effect on tired men. The pair of us certainly felt fresher after the storm than we had done before it, but were glad the lightning had not caught us on top of the pinnacles. It was a fine moment when at last the hut loomed ahead, though it had its moment of bitterness when we found we could not unlock the cupboard door, behind which we had hidden our food. We slid into our sleeping bags supperless. After all, has it not been said that to sleep is to eat!

We certainly slept well that night, and once we got the cupboard opened put the eggs in the pan and ate a hearty breakfast before taking a leisurely walk round Tacheddirt to greet the villagers, have a tour around and enjoy the plentiful bird life: shorelarks, black wheatears, lesser kestrels, black redstarts, alpine swifts, rock buntings, choughs, partridges, grey wagtails, dippers and woodpeckers as well as common species.

Being joined by Jim Green they moved round to head to the then road-end at Asni and head for Jbel Toubkal, still seldom climbed until the Seventies boom.

With ten days' supply of food Douglas Scott, Jim and I set off from the Berber village of Asni, where we hired mules and engaged an ancient Berber to guard the car during the time we would be deep in the mountains. Our first base was the Neltner Hut at 10,496 feet [3200m] and to reach it we had to back-pack the last bit as the snow was too deep for mules. Wonderful it was the next day to fix skins to our skis and pole our way to the crest of the pass that looks south to the arid desert. From this pass of the Tizi n' Ouanoums, climbing skins removed from the soles of our skis we swished down on perfect snow after a valuable recce of the peaks we were to climb in the next ten days.

The first of these was Toubkal, 13,670 feet [4167m], the highest peak in North Africa, below which I had my first experience on an earth tremor so strong that not only did the ground heave but so did my stomach in momentary nausea. We realised it was not imagination when stones from the mountain came rattling down. Our route to the top was by the arête [OSO Arête] first climbed by Bentley Beetham, a long

95

mixed route by chimneys and narrow edges to a square-cut tower demanding an abseil. It was snowing on top, and even wearing all our jerseys we were cold.

Following the ascent of Toubkal we went for Afella n' Ouanoukrim trying a line not shown in our guide-book, an arête promising an airy crest if we could keep to its edge. It took us most of the way until it became dangerously loose and we moved east to gain point 4,040 metres on our map, and marked with the word Clochetons (bells) – several pinnacles. They were a joy. Exposed to a drop of 2,000 feet, and with wonderful holds on mostly vertical rock; mountaineering at its best.

The time had come now for us to move back to the Berber village of Imlil, where we had left a cache of food, for entry to a remote valley reached by a 2,500-foot uphill slog, then 1,200 feet down, to enter a ravine of waterfalls above which stands the Lépiney Hut [3000m] below the great rock wall of Tazerhart. The snow gullies seaming this face give winter climbs in mid-summer. Our intention was to go for its Median Arête which was graded *très difficile*.

Jim opted out of this climb for he was less fit and two would be able to move faster than a party of three. That climb extended us, forcing us at one point on to its smooth east wall by a snow ribbon adhering to it like wall-paper, a dangerous traverse on high-angled softish snow where we moved one at a time, looking for any breach that might lead us to the top, now very close. There was only one possible crack-line, which neither of us would have chosen if there had been an alternative. Douglas led it, moving with the utmost caution, each move carefully considered. If he came off he would land on the snow-ledge. My job would be to hold him on the rope before he went over the edge of the precipice. Up and up he moved until there was very little slack left between us. Then came a shout that he was on a belay and it looked OK ahead.

That was a very hard pitch. We had been in mist for much

of the climb. Incredibly, we stepped into sunshine on the top. We were indeed lucky, for Tazerhart's summit is a plateau, and that night it looked like a Greenland ice-cap in miniature. We were privileged indeed to walk over it, and even select a route down before we were enveloped in falling snow. So dim became the visibility that we had difficulty in finding the hut where Jim Green was keeping warm for us a huge pot of soup and spaghetti.

We slept like babies that night, and looking out in the morning saw the snowline had crept right down to the valleys and that we were in for a strenuous traverse back to Imlil. The following morning was perhaps the most sparkling we had in the High Atlas: the Berbers, in their monk-like hooded robes, taking their sheep and goats to the hill; women carrying water from the well; a villager inviting us into his courtyard to drink mint tea with him. It was a morning for a photographic prowl and we made the most of the flowers, the sparkling waterfalls and, at a water-wheel, a Berber grinding barley.

Now it was time to hire mules to transport our skis and luggage back down the valley to where we had left the car in the care of the old Berber who had volunteered to watch it while we were away. He was there, and beaming happily even if his job had come to an end. It had been agreed that we should travel together to Algiers where Jim would drop us off and Douglas and I would make our way home by crossing the Mediterranean to Marseilles, take a train from there to Calais and travel north from Dover.

It was broiling heat all the way on the 2,000-mile journey to Algiers and we didn't envy Jim the country where he was working, while we were going home to the finest month of the year – May – in Scotland, where the cuckoo and swift would be newly arrived and ptarmigan and golden plover would be brooding their eggs on the hilltops. Daffodils would be in bloom, the trees would be in blossom and the bird-song at its best.

We were well content. We had the feeling of having travelled through several centuries in terms of way of life. We had been exploring in mountains where there were no other climbers, and the only guidebook was rudimentary.

WEIR'S WORLD

Tom returned in 1958 with Alf Gregory to make a film they hoped to sell to television showing the Berber life among the always dramatic landscapes of coast, mountains, deserts, gorges; a first sortie into work that would come to dominate his life later on.

Because of Tom's advocacy, and that of Gavin Maxwell, in the mid-sixties I had successive winter months in the Atlas and have been back over fifty times since. One of our first climbs was almost a replay of Tom's with our baggage delayed in Tangier and from Tacheddirt making a first ascent of the next ridge west of their line with a similar outcome, except the refuge was locked and we ended bivouacking on the doorstep.

PEAKS AND PASSES IN KURDISTAN

There is no space to tell of the highlights of our journey from Istanbul across Anatolia to the remotest mountains of Asia Minor which form the wild frontier of Irak, so long closed to European travellers. It is a region where exploration was easier in the nineteenth century than the twentieth, so we felt lucky to have a political permit in our possession, giving us authority to explore wild mountain peaks which have been sacred to the Kurds since the dawn of history.

Thanks to Polunin who had botanised here, we knew we could get public transport to Lake Van in Turkish Armenia, but thereafter we would be dependent on lorries going east towards Persia or into the gorges of the Great Zab which are Himalayan in austerity, where this main tributary of the Tigris roars between sheer rock walls. Thirteen days out from

Glasgow it was a great thrill when the Cilo range burst upon us.

It was the morning of 5th July when we left the village of Hirvata. The local Governor and frontier officials had been more helpful to us than we knew by procuring two Kurdish guides and four horses. We had expected to walk. Now mounted on horseback and feeling like millionaires, we climbed 9,000 feet up a hillside of flowers, great red poppies and multi-coloured vetches at first, until we crossed a ridge and came on to a rolling upland of sparkling snow fields with gurgling streams and meadows of blue and yellow primulas scenting the cool air.

We were on a Cairngorm table-land scarped by a rock wall running along its length and blocking further view. The horses, overjoyed to be on the flat, galloped towards a U cleft which was the only gap in the skyline, Demirkapu, meaning the Iron Gate. We had no hint of the drama of the view that was to meet us. One moment my horse was nodding up a snow slope, the next it was hanging over a sheer drop, and I looked into a canyon walled by red crags and shining glaciers – a mountaineer's dream of towering rock needles falling to velvet green meadows ribboned by streams discharging from the ice. It was the most perfect vision of mountain form we had ever seen.

Three thousand feet down we camped by a spring of clear water on a sward of alpine flowers, conscious that we had never had a more exciting situation for a base, ringed on every side by fantastic pinnacles and Dolomitic walls.

The grass was hoared with frost when we went out to get water for the porridge, and walking was a joy as we headed up the main glacier draining the highest peaks less than two miles away. Primulas were in mauve and yellow profusion, while pink crocus-like flowers actually pushed blooms up through the snow! Ortolan buntings, snowfinches, black redstarts, rock nuthatches, crag martins, sandpipers, red-billed and alpine choughs caused us many a halt, but we were in no hurry since this was a day of reconnaissance.

We had a map with us, made by Dr Bobek's party who made the first survey of these mountains only 20 years ago. Our map was a copy taken from a scientific journal, but it was adequate. The first agreeable surprise of these uncompromising-looking peaks was to find the glacier firm and safe, even where getting hours of sun. This prompted us to consider a snow gully leading up for 2,000 feet to a steep rock ridge, which held possibilities provided we could surmount the steeper sections. The peak corresponded to the Eckpfeiler, 3,700 metres on our map.

The big event of this day was seeing our first snow-bear, to us a legendary animal with about as much foundation as the Abominable Snowman. But here it was, an unmistakable bear loping across the glacier, massive head turning towards us now and then as it climbed at amazing speed on all fours, humpback trusting forward at each push of its thick hairy legs and arms. We were elated at seeing this most exciting beast but had been warned that their natures are unpredictable.

A weird red sky with rain and low clouds banished the thought of climbing next day, so we had a fine alternative by descending the gorge beneath us to a Kurdish encampment of black tents perched 1,500 feet below in the throat of the ravine. With a greeting of "Merhaba," hand touching the breast, they bade us welcome and invited us into their tents, squatting down beside us in their loose colourful clothing and wool boots. They had the open look of frank men, and we looked at them with interest, conscious that we were speaking to semi-nomads of the fiercest and most ancient race in the world, an independent people who have resisted change and survived the passing of all the invaders of this most ancient part of the ancient world.

The Kurds are mainly a pastoral people whose livelihood is in animals: goats, sheep and cows. Right now the yoghourt was being shaken up in a skin bag while a tall, beautifully dressed woman in baggy trousers and white blouse organised a big cooking job. In due course placed before us was a

100

large tray containing delicious new bread and butter, fried meat and yoghourt, round which we all sat and dipped in. No plates here – when you have had enough you withdraw to make room for someone else. A return gift of sugar, some sweets, chocolate and raisins was much appreciated, and no one was forgotten in the share out, even a very small baby who fairly enjoyed its first bite of Cadbury's.

Next morning we set off on another reconnaissance to look over the great wall west of the camp and see what lay on the other side. But it was a Stack Polly ridge called the Seespitze which took our fancy, inviting us to try a complete traverse of its 3,460-metre crest by going up the north ridge and down the south. We soon found that it was a place for cautious route-finding, for the drop beneath was considerable as one bristling pinnacle gave way to another. So we chose the walls rather than the crest, seeing a wall-creeper at one point as it fluttered past with a flash of butterfly wings, my favourite bird of high mountains.

On a peak like this every tower bristling against the sky seems like the summit, so it was a relief to climb one steep pinnacle and see ahead what was positively the last, crowned by a little cairn. We looked 3,800 feet down on our tent from the top, a tiny speck of orange in the green glen. From here the Eckpfeiler south ridge looked much steeper than we expected, but we thought it would go, especially when we were able to force a way down the formidable-looking south wall of our mountain so quickly that we were back in camp by 4 p.m.

Next morning we went for the Eckpfeiler and in one hour reached the glacier, just a little disturbed because of a bear which galloped ahead of us, disappearing behind a rock guarding the entrance to our couloir. Had it or had it not gone up the gully? We looked for traces in the snow, but the surface was so well frozen that it was no reassurance to find none.

We started up and soon forgot the beast in the rhythmic work of kicking and cutting a staircase. Suddenly there was

101

a loud angry growling, and from the rocks rushed a bear, straight towards us. We did not have time to be frightened, for it shot across our path, slithering as it went, not stopping until it was 30 feet away. Then it took a swift look round, pointed ears up and mouth open, and showed us how to climb a gully using claws in lieu of an ice axe. We hoped we had seen the last of it and shouted and blew a whistle to keep it moving, for we had no wish to take it by surprise again.

The couloir took us into a dazzle of flowing snow-fields curtaining a great cirque of rock, so jagged on its crest that nowhere in sight was there a ridge offering an easy traverse. Our reconnaissance paid its dividends in that we were able to choose a line which admitted us to the summit tower in 1,000 feet of rock climbing. We did not play safe now that the top was in sight but took a knife-edged ridge of rock rising 400 feet, where one heel projected over the precipices of the west side and the other over the equally sheer east face. This classic arête was not so sound and we advanced only one at a time to step on to the summit at 1.30 p.m. and laze away a marvellous half hour.

We were above the junction of the two main glaciers with a horse-shoe of peaks on each side of us. In every other direction were grey gorges of Turkey, heat-hazy ridges of Irak frowning down on Mesopotamia, snow peaks of Persia; battle grounds of Biblical races, but now so sparsely inhabited thanks to war and murder between Armenians, Kurds and Nestorians. [*Not much has changed; the Kurds' lands insensitively shared by three countries when lines were drawn on maps by Europeans a century ago.*]

There were plenty of signs of extinct peoples in the mountains, from rock carvings of Stone Age men with bows and arrows to strange hill-top writings and churches of the Christians who lived here when Rome was still pagan. The Kurds destroyed the Nestorian Christian cultivators and sacked their villages, but the terraced fields still grow crops of fruit and vines which in autumn are harvested not by people but by bears.

That afternoon as we descended to camp, after a magnificent glissade down the couloir, the meadow where the tent was situated was a sward of yellow alpine buttercups, and the huge west wall of the Seespitze a luminous shadow with stray sun rays filtering between its pinnacles.

Blocking the whole head of the glen, the 4,000-foot wall of the Geliasin challenged us with the greatest unclimbed rock we had ever seen, but were too faint-hearted to try it. Instead we decided to move our camp around to the east side and look for an easier line up. To do this meant crossing back over the Demirkapu Pass and travelling for two days parallel to the main range by slopes chest-high in flowers, then up a glen to a snow pass leading into the huge defile of the Telgui-Savi ...

A drop of 3,000 feet and we were among the moraines, looking for a site among the stones as heavy rain battered down, continuing into a dismal afternoon. We spent it making pancakes and watching a mother bear with her two cubs rooting amongst the stones, pulling up large boulders as if they were pebbles, to lick beneath them or pick up the stones to lick them as if they were ice-cream wafers. The half-grown cubs bickered continually, biting at each other acrimoniously even when they were scrambling on dangerous rock. This species is the Syrian or brown bear – the same that begs for buns in the zoo.

Our two Kurds were optimistic about the weather. They said it would clear, and sure enough it did, so we made preparations for an early start and were away by 4.30 a.m., attacking the crag immediately above us where it rose as a grey boss tapering to a pinnacle ridge. Straight away we were balance-climbing on polished rock, so scanty of belays and unsound that we did not wear the rope until considerable exposure and a steepening angle forced it on us. Luckily the rock improved with steepness and our spirit went up as we spiralled round a series of gigantic pillars, gaining more confidence as one unlikely place after another was vanquished.

Our fear was that we would find ourselves on top of the next

103

pinnacle and unable to proceed because of some impassable chasm, but always there was an exciting way of by-passing the next spire, until with joy, after four hours of rock climbing, we saw the way ahead to the summit ridge. Ahead loomed a black tooth of rock marked 3,750m. on our map. It gave one hard pitch and there was no cairn on top. Easy ground lay ahead along a twisting ridge flowing without break, dipping down and rising again for a mile to a beautiful ice-cap, then bending north-west to the summit.

The ridge was deceptively innocent, because so many of its ups and downs were hidden, and before we were half-way along it we felt that the grind of putting one foot in front of the other would never cease. Always there was another lump, another bit of snow cornice requiring care above a plunge down pink walls to green ice and crevassed glacier. Then at 1.30 p.m. we were up, over the top, looking down the vast precipice of the North Wall on to our old camp spot below the Iron Gate, thinking how often we had looked up to this most inaccessible point of Asia Minor.

Blissfully we reclined on the snow, trying to take in the vast panorama spread below: rock needles plunging to lonely valleys of terraced fields where houses perched; escarpments of mountains, ridge upon ridge, and savage ravines of rock and ice, many of them unpeopled except by bears, ibex, wolves, marmots, perhaps panthers; deserts, rivers, mountains of the Bible. The overcast sky gave a curious brooding quality to the scene and we reckoned we had never been in a wilder place.

Neither of us felt inclined for the ups and downs of that long ridge again; and the route of descent decided upon was back along the ridge for a kilometre, then south-eastward into a great snow-bowl parallel to the main ridge, where we could strike over at a convenient point to tackle the rock wall above the camp. The route was good until we reached the ridge and took a new line down the face that had cost us four hours in the morning. The new way was chosen because it had much snow on it, but it hung like wall-paper on rotten rock,

104

demanding constant vigilance from us in step cutting, testing the rock, watching for falling stones, always on the alert to check a slip. We tried to banish the thought that somewhere out of sight might lie an unclimbable section, forcing us back the way we had come.

It was a battle with the clock as we moved one at a time in the difficult places. Then as daylight ebbed away we saw that nothing could stop us unless we fell into one of the crevasses and huge holes which were potential traps here. Dusk was drawing to darkness as we got to the foot of the last snow couloir. There was light enough to see two bears scuttle across our path.

Luckily we had a torch with us to help over the moraines and look for the crags which we knew were beneath us. It seemed we should never get to camp, traversing boulders and snow gullies, when suddenly we saw a light and heard a whistle – the tents. Even as we were fumbling, trying to remember the lie of the rocks, a shape materialised out of the night, not a bear but Memhet who had climbed up to our flickering torch to help us down. In minutes we were in camp, where Bahri had the primus going and tea on the boil, seizing our hands in his joy at seeing us safely home.

We thought the world of these Kurds, who endeared themselves to us more and more as time went on. A great quality is their dislike of disappointing you. A good example of it was when we proposed following the gorge of the Rudbare Sin to penetrate the Sat Dag. They knew the gorge would be fly-ridden and uncomfortably hot, that the horses would suffer and that travel would be slow and difficult; but they did not try to put us off . . .

But our money and food was running low. Stupidly we had left our main supply of cash over 200 kilometres away – a course of action prompted by the possibility of being robbed by smugglers known to operate in this border region. All we had time for now was an interesting route into the Reka Gapiri by a pass that proved to be the most exciting of the trip

105

for men and horses, on steep snow and boulder crags cut up by streams churned white in the force of their rapid descent from the highest and shapeliest of the Sat peaks at the head of the corrie.

We spent 53 days away from Glasgow to get 15 days in the mountains, the remainder of the time being occupied by forced delays or travelling. I regard this region as the most rewarding of any in which I have travelled.

SCOTTISH MOUNTAINEERING CLUB JOURNAL 1958

The 1960 Greenland expedition mixed a group of adults and 20 lads, chosen from an initial 150 holders of the Gold Duke of Edinburgh Award scheme, to undertake exploratory, climbing, surveying and natural history projects. Despite a late and wet season the expedition was a great success.

GREENLAND: IN SCORESBY LAND

As members of the Advance Party of Sir John Hunt's 1960 Greenland Expedition one of our jobs was to find a way across this river to fix a base-camp site somewhere on the other side. The Skel is not a single stream like a normal British river but a grey flood of ice-cold water discharging from the snout of a glacier flowing from jagged peaks, tearing its way through boulderfields and raging across the valley in several channels. We had hoped to fix some kind of ropeway using the canoe as an inland ferry. This being impossible we proposed to use the river mouth where the many streams converged in a surging sweep.

It was a grey morning, intensely still and quiet as we lowered ourselves into the three-man foldboat, revolver at the ready in case of polar bears. Where seals lie out on the ice there is danger from this uncertain animal, so we were not taking any chances. Soon the lead of open water we were following was blocked by ice and we put our drill into operation. It was for one of us to hook-in a climbing axe while another squeezed on to the ice to try and set the pack moving. If no gap formed as a result of exerting pressure then we might haul the canoe over the ice to open water or retreat to try another lead. It sounds unorthodox and chancy, but we found it worked, and in a few hours tricky going got to the river mouth and shot over easily.

The thin distribution of wild life and the soggy greyness of the tundra were revelations to my two companions who knew this region at the same period in 1958 when the shores were fringed with mats of alpine flowers with the tundra green as grass. Not that it was completely lifeless now, only you had to look for the little cushions of moss campion and purple saxifrage. It was rewarding to find yellow arctic poppies with alpine mouse-ear chickweed among the stones, or find the erect catkins of dwarf birch among mats of waving dryas. Bees and mosquitos buzzed around through the 24 hours of continuous daylight.

You could hear the soaring dunlin 'reeling' and spiralling squeals of the courting ring plovers. Chestnut striped turnstones gave their sharp triple calls which are so different from the low winter grunts we are accustomed to hear in Britain. But I could find no nests. It was a delight on the 9th July to see our first long tailed ducks, a mixty party of eight twisting up and down leads in the ice in a game of pursuit, giving forth their bagpipe notes. I so frightened a party of six moulting barnacles that they made off into the sea, swimming furiously to get out of range, climbing on to the pack-ice and sprinting over it until they reached another part of the shore, going faster than any man on foot up a steep snowy hillside, leaving only their large footprints behind them.

Pink footed geese had nested in a deep ravine of the river and swam their goslings down to the sea in early July, but I found no evidence of successful breeding among the barnacle geese. The flocks I saw were adults with no juveniles of the year among them. It is possible of course that I was seeing only non-breeders on the coast. My own belief is that barnacle goose, long tailed duck and red throated diver did not breed in the King Oscar's Fjord region of Scoresby Land this year.

Scoresby Land with its narrow fjords and mountain peaks has been described as the most beautiful region of all Greenland. It is known as the Arctic Riviera for its wonderful weather, so it was a shock to Sir John Hunt's large party of 38 to begin their exploration in rain. It rained for a week as they struggled to ford swollen rivers to put high camps on the glacier above the Skeldal. In dismal surroundings of stones and mist they made friends of an arctic fox which became so bold that it took food from the hands of one of the party. More destructively it ate the binding of a pair of skis.

These foxes were well distributed but seemed to be having a lean time this summer owing to the absence of ptarmigan. These usually common arctic birds were so scarce after an exceptionally hard winter than only one pair was seen in all the journeying of our large expedition. Not a lemming was seen either so it was not surprising that the foxes were driven to the tents. In early July when I first saw these beasts they were the colour of Siamese cats as they changed from off-white into their summer brown coats. By the end of August they were pure white again. To watch them dancing over the stones or leaping a stream was to see an animal on springs.

The snow buntings do not trust Mr Fox, and I was led to an interesting sight one day by a cock scolding a fox with darting motions of its face as it tried to lead it away from its nest. Snow bunting cocks were still singing when we arrived in Greenland, and on 11th July I found my first nest under a stone. It contained five blind young. I ringed others later but the birds were remarkably scarce on the whole. It was charming later on to find young ones shivering their wings to be fed. Greenland wheatears were with young at this period too but even scarcer than snow buntings.

It was the arctic terns that most interested Dr Smart and

me. We had seen these birds for the first time on 14th July when five of them were being pursued over the sea ice by skuas. Then on 19th July we carried out an adventurous canoe journey to an island milling with terns. To our joy we found the terns had not begun to lay though many scrapes for nests had been made, so here was a chance to observe their full breeding cycle in an abnormal year.

We returned to the island on 24th July, enduring the same rainy conditions as Sir John Hunt was getting higher up. Four nests contained a single egg so the birds had laid almost as soon as their food supply was uncovered by the ice breaking up. These nests were unusually deep and lined with willow leaves, stalks and catkins, an odd feather and some bent grasses. Eggs were still being laid on the 4th August, especially on the drier tundra becoming exposed as snow melted off it. The noise of these terns went on round the clock as they pursued each other in courtship fish-chases or stood face to face screaming at each other, sometimes joining in communal display, even sharing a sudden silence, as brief as it was welcome. Then the bedlam would break out again as they went off to attack a wandering glaucous gull or an intruding skua.

Meantime we used the incubation period to canoe out to another island at Kap Petersen nine miles up the coast where Dr Smart had found over 50 tern nests in July three years before. There were only two nests this year, but an eider duck was sitting on eggs and on another island we found three more nesting eiders. It was 21st August before I saw any young eiders, two broods of sooty-young at a time when the sea was freezing over at night.

This period of mid-August produced the first hint that the Arctic Riviera was not really a myth in a succession of golden evenings when mountain and sea were stained crimson in the light of the midnight sun, and ice formed thin wafers in the early hours of the morning, a superb time to go canoeing as a light condensation formed, giving ghostly outlines to every feature of the island, transforming tiny pinnacles to aiguilles and changing the flutings of icebergs into Gothic cathedrals or pillared columns of Greek temples.

On such mornings you could hear the seals breathing as they came round the canoe inquisitively, whiskers sprayed out, then, SPLASH, and they were gone. It was in this period that Sir John's party forced a way up the Hjona Spitz, the highest unclimbed peak in the Staunings at over 9,300 feet, a traverse that took them over 26 hours of very severe rock climbing on the upper 3000 feet of the mountain. They were now set to cross over the mountains by difficult glaciers to reach the Schuchart Valley.

On 12th August we thought it was time we went back to tern island. We got there in time to catch the hatch, with eggs chipping and little ones crawling about. One parent bird sat so tightly, only rising off to attack a pencil stub held out to it. We were assaulted by vicious birds wherever we walked on the island at this critical time.

The nests we watched most closely were of course those where we knew to within an hour or two when the eggs had been laid. To our surprise the average incubation period proved to be roughly the same as given for breeding British birds, 21½ days. The cold evidently made little difference. We were not alone in visiting the island to catch the peak of the hatch . I realised this when I awoke in the early hours to a great screeching of terns and the hoarse croaking of ravens.

There were two northern ravens, one of them drawing off the terns as it ran in circles on a snowpatch, head twisting and purple mouth gaping its protest at a snowstorm of terns. It settled into a hole in the rocks, meantime the second raven was infiltrating to a ridge where I knew there were many tiny chicks. I played the part of interloper on these larger than British ravens, throwing stones to make both of them take the air, and it made a thrilling spectacle when both of them took wing, pursued by every tern on the island, the ravens swerving and tumbling as blow after blow was struck. I have heard of a snowy owl being killed by irate terns and

I can quite believe it. They had no chance however with a Greenland falcon which came over one day on an innocent migration flight. It was quite 300 yards off the coast, but the alarm was sounded and every tern responded, leaving off what it was doing to go into the attack. The falcon merely put on a spurt from time to time, its acceleration and streamlined shape marvellous to behold.

Unfortunately our plans for carrying out systematic weighing and measuring the growth of the young terns came to naught as we were asked to abandon the birds and support the climbing parties. Smart was asked to cross the mountains on foot to try and locate a dump of food and take it to Sir John. My job was to go by open boat to Alpefjord 40 miles round the coast to attack some unclimbed peaks here. McNaught Davis was in charge of the open boat and we were to have a share of adventures on this journey.

The craft was an eighteen foot wooden dingy powered by two outboard engines, towing behind it a smaller aluminium boat carrying sixteen boxes of food, petrol, oil and other equipment.

It was calm but bitterly cold when we left at midnight but by 3 am we were compelled to pull for the shore at Kap Petersen. This gave me the chance to visit a pair of arctic skuas which I had found with a nest in late July. One of the birds was still sitting on its solitary egg though the date was 21st August, a time when they should have been ready to migrate. These were light phase arctic skuas, which seems to be an adaption to cold, since dark phase birds have never been found in the High Arctic. I also had opportunity to search for American long tailed skuas which had the habit of coming wailing over the coastal hills morning and evening when I stayed here before.

The absence of lemmings was a disappointment to Dr Smart who had based a research programme on them. However he was now engaged on the vital work of locating a food dump and leading a party of men to a remote spot in the Schuchart

Valley to rendezvous with Sir John. After the coast, he found this valley of dwarf birch and willow a sheer joy for colour. I had the pleasure of flying down this valley in an aircraft, looking down on grazing parties of musk ox, the massive shoulders and black or dun woolly coats showing up well from the air.

My task now was to sail out of King Oscar's Fjord into the recesses of Alpefjord, where the narrowing sea-loch ends among glaciers tumbling their ice into the green water. Weaving our way in and out among floating masses of ice fallen from the ice cliffs hemming us in we speculated on what would happen if a mass were to break off as we chugged within volley shot.

The fjord is shallow here, and over an outcropping rock I could see throngs of terns on the wing, most of them juveniles. I asked Davis to pull in so I could have a closer look in case some might be running around and I might ring them. I found none, but that stop probably saved our lives, for we had hardly started when there was an explosive roar, and down thundered a huge mass of ice like a tall building collapsing, just at the place we should have been. We merely got the backlash of a tidal wave which raced across the fjord to batter the opposite mountain wall in huge columns of spray.

There is no space to tell of our subsequent adventures when one of our two boats was wrecked at its moorings by an onshore gale nor can I describe the sandstorm which raged for most of two days when our tents flapped like the sails of a boat in a gale, only the largest rocks keeping it anchored.

No, Scoresby Land was not the Arctic Riviera this year, but I felt privileged to have seen such an exceptional season where everything was topsy turvy. All generalisations about birds can be wrong.

At this time the geese were gathered into great skeins, flying around in an unsettled manner in preparation for the long flight across to Iceland and eventually to the north of Scotland or the slobs of Ireland. We did manage to ring some sixty terns on Menanders Island, so maybe if another party of explorers goes there in a couple of years or so they will find one of these ringed birds, then we will know that some did indeed get away to make the big flight to Antarctic waters.

Back in base camp I was hearing tale after tale of adventure from the climbing members whom I had not seen for a month or more. Sir John had taken 21 boys with his party of seniors at the behest of the National Association of Mixed Clubs and Girls Clubs. All of them had won the Duke of Edinburgh's Gold Award and all of them were ordinary working lads.

They had enjoyed themselves immensely and many of them had made first ascents of peaks around 7000 feet in previously unexplored territory in the South Stauning Alps. Some had been surveying to ascertain the speed of movement of the glaciers and from their observations we now know that one of these 30 mile-long ice-streams moved over 80 feet in six weeks. The boys had been into the depths of crevasses to take temperature readings, and in a fresh water pool in the ice Stuart Oram caught a fish!

The achievements of the expeditions from the coast to the highest mountains were considerable. In all something like 14 ascents were made, but the biggest disappointment fell to Lady Hunt and her daughter Susan who crossed 100 miles over the mountains to visit an Eskimo settlement only to find that the Greenlanders had not come north this year owing to the ice.

The ladies enjoyed their walk however, just as we enjoyed our days and nights with the birds, watching how they coped with the wintry summer which made the whole nesting period a fight for survival. I would like to visit Scoresby Land in a normal season to sample its days of unending sunshine. Its fantastic beauty will remain forever imprinted on my memory.

Typescript in the National Library of Scotland Collections

V

CLIMBING DAYS IN SCOTLAND

Scotland may be small among the climbing places of the world but with our concentrated variety of landscape and challenging weather, Scottish experience is as valid as any, anywhere. In this section we can only touch on three of our classic areas: the unique rock world of the Cuillin, mighty Ben Nevis and the rolling heights of the Cairngorms, playgrounds for summer and winter adventuring.

In Tom's small book Focus on Mountains, *Sir John Hunt, in the introduction wrote, 'Like all true mountaineers, the big ranges and the Polar regions have not diminished his affection and respect for the smaller mountains nearer home . . . where he began to learn his mountain craft.' That enthusiasm would never slacken and latterly he admitted 'abroad' called less and less due to the endless fascination of Scotland.*

This small book, signed by Tom and Hunt, was awarded to my Braehead pupils on reaching 50 Munros. In one of his TV series he used these lads for a rock climbing programme, using the abandoned Gloom Hill quarry above Dollar — where I'd first hammered in six inch nails as pitons when a boy enthused by books by Weir, Borthwick, Murray et al. (Many years on others claimed first ascents in the quarry). For one scene of a hand groping for a hold round a sharp edge on a climb a boy lay prone on the ground, his fingers simply grasping the edge of a boulder. (The reality of anything on TV would never be viewed in the same way thereafter)The kids brewed up on a primus stove and camped that night on the hillside above at Paradise. They showed Tom a barn owl's nest on the quarry and a roding woodcock passed them in the woods above Castle Campbell.

THIRSTY WORK IN THE CUILLIN

It was 10 p.m. on a superb evening when Iain arrived at our rendezvous point in Pitlochry. "Look how they're grinning at the prospect of being free of their wives," said Iain's wife as she drove off.

We drove the car north and deferred decision of what we should do until Dalwhinnie. Iain was thinking of Sutherland, but I was oriented towards the Cuillin. We agreed to sleep on it, camp somewhere on Loch Lagganside and decide in the morning.

Midges in hordes resulted in the tent going up in record time and ourselves into the sleeping bags without so much as a cup of tea. A breeze in the morning made breakfast a delight and since it came from the north-east with sunshine and crisp visibility, we headed for Skye, determined to be climbing by lunchtime.

I thought it was almost too good to be true, for on dozens of summer days on these finest rock peaks in Scotland I have invariably been unlucky for weather. I had never known what it was to be thirsty on the Cuillin, though I had heard plenty of the sufferings of other climbers in heat wave conditions. I was to learn.

Only the cool breeze saved us from being broiled as we plodded over the moor at midday, enjoying the sight of a greenshank piping agitatedly from a boulder, telling it's young to keep down among the white tufts of waving bog cotton. Glimpses of twites and wheatears were other excuses for stopping, and soon Iain was suggesting a five-minute snooze and a sandwich in preparation for the Sgurr nan Gillean pinnacles which had gradually strung themselves out in profile.

117

On the move again, his stride had a new swing as he exclaimed on the marvel of the rock. "A hold wherever you put your hand. I had forgotten it was so rough." Each taking a different line, we met on top of the third pinnacle to look down the vertical line of descent, and Iain was so impressed that he began uncoiling the rope.

As is the way with gabbro, it is easier than it looks, but there is an awkward step on the steepest bit here where any unroped man must take great care. The best climbing lies ahead now, straight up the fourth pinnacle and down into the gap for the top of the Sgurr itself, rising in a bristling wall. Then came the great moment when we stepped over the top and the view burst upon us.

What bliss to peel an orange, slake our thirst and look along the grey rock spine rising and falling above shadowy corries in ten miles of sinuosities with thousands of feet of ups and downs between. Across the glen in amazing contrast to the gabbro, the smooth crowns of the Red Hills were glaring pink, becoming abruptly purple in the splinter of Clach Glas and the elephantine bulk of Blaven. In a glance we could look from the white houses of Portree beneath The Storr, to Harris and the Uists.

Our route now lay along the Western Ridge, over the 'gendarme' where you have the fun of swinging from his head above a mighty big drop and enjoying it all the more because of the size of the holds. [*the gendarme has since disappeared*] The rocky way continues with a delightful scramble leading you to the top of Am Bhasteir, beyond which is the Bhasteir Tooth, first climbed in 1889 by Norman Collie.

The tooth is below but to get to it means overcoming the beetling wall. We chose different routes. Iain eased his way down the awkward bulge nearest to the Tooth on the edge of a big drop. I chose the Lota Corrie side, which involves delicate traversing of a steep wall. By the time we arrived on top the bronze light of evening was setting in. The Outer Isles were silhouettes and the lochs at our feet pale blue. We would have lingered for the full glory of sunset, but for thirst. Saturated with sun, our thoughts turned to water with lemonade powder in it. So we hared over the tops to come down under the pinnacles of Sgurr na Gillean, to slake our thirst below the gorge.

The marvellous breeze was till blowing when we awoke to another perfect morning. We knew where we were going, to the Glen Brittle side for Coire Lagan and its superlative rocks. This is where Iain had done his first climbing in the Cuillin, as a medical student, living frugally in the Youth Hostel and brashing Forestry Commission trees to get to get money for what he did eat. His main memory of the Cuillin is hunger!

We gravitated to the Western Buttress of Sron na Ciche, for its shade and also because this is the face where two of my most memorable climbing adventures occurred. The first was on Mallory's Slab and Groove, when I had to abseil for the first time in my life as a matter of life or death. The second was a war-time climb with an officer of the Scottish Horse named Ramsay, when we embarked on the 1,000ft. face on a day when wise men would have stayed by the fire.

The date was mid-September 1943, and the wind was thundering on the crags and the rain battering as we roped up for the Median Route. Heaven knows what we did climb, but benumbed and battered we each led our pitches until a line of overhanging chimneys blocked the way and Ramsay took over. This fine cragsman was killed in the war. His lead was certainly heroic that day, and even to follow stretched me to the limit. Yet we went over Sgumain and Alasdair after that climb. We were indeed in the act of going for Thearlaich when an even more violent gust of wind than we had so far experienced hit us with the equivalent of several pails of icy water. At which even this hard man blinked and said, "Perhaps we should go down."

So, now that Iain and I were here on a perfect day, why not for old times' sake, get into the cool by having a wander on that face and trying to find the Median Route. The extraordinary depth of shadow made it impossible to pick out features on the dark gabbro, so we followed our noses and after a few hundred feet knew we were well off line.

Iain had led to an overhanging impasse, and now called me up to see what I thought of the way ahead. It was a Captain Ramsay sort of situation, black roofs and clefts blocking upwards views. Unwilling to commit myself until I had explored other ways, I tried a line I had noticed on the way up to join Iain, an airy, slanting crack.

It was the open kind of climbing I love, exposed, steep and interesting without being too difficult. Moreover, there was a continuation, with a choice of ways opening up, and the last rope lengths were up a splendid basalt arête, delicate balance climbing offering food for thought in places. Iain had the pleasure of the last pitch, and as I looked up the rope I saw his body become a halo of gold as he moved out of shadow into sun and gave a yell of delight at what he saw as he came over the top.

No wonder. The little harbours of Soay were immediately below us, edged by birchwoods, a pancake of greenery. Beyond it over the blue sea, were the near peaks of Rum above the white sands of Kilmory, with blue-grey Canna on one side and Eigg on the other.

I thought of the lucky men who were first to climb these peaks, and were immortalised by having tops named after them; of Sheriff Alexander Nicolson, the Skyeman who, at the age of forty-six, in 1873, worked his way to the top of what is now called Sgurr Alasdair, of Charles Pilkington, who made the first ascent of the Inaccessible Pinnacle and for whom the peak upon which we were sitting – Thearlaich – was named; of John MacKenzie of Sconser, the first British mountain guide and native-born rock climber, who climbed the Cioch with Collie in 1894 and is forever remembered in Sgurr Mhic Coinnich.

What a discovery for the Alpinists to make, long after the Matterhorn had been climbed – a range of difficult and unexplored mountains in Britain. Sgurr Thormaid is called after Professor Norman Collie, an outstanding mountain explorer of the biggest mountain ranges, who so loved the Cuillin that he settled permanently in Sligachan in 1939 and is buried beside John MacKenzie in the little cemetery at Struan. To come back to the present. Never did a man see a bonnier evening than that in the Cuillin as we leapt and slid down the Great Stone Chute to celebrate in lemonade the quenching of a noble thirst.

Morning saw us off again, this time into Coire Tairneilear for some fun on the face of Sgurr a' Mhadaidh. What makes this corrie so superb are the little alpine meadows of flowers and fern amidst such a cliff-walled cirque. Now and again we sat down just to enjoy the scent of thyme and drink from the numerous springs. Mhadaidh's four peaks stretching from Bidean Druim nan Ramh give perhaps the most sustained bits of up and down rock climbing in the Cuillin, with some route finding problems. Striking along to the southerly peak, we met two climbers just about to leave its top. Their first question was about the next bit of ridge, and what lay beyond to Sgurr nan Gillean.

Then they told us a remarkable story. Leaving home in Yorkshire at 6 p.m., they had motored all night, crossed over to Skye by 9 a.m., dumped their car at Elgol and walked to Coruisk by the Bad Step, arriving at 4 p.m. A two hour halt for a meal, then off they went with bivouac kit to the top of Gars-bheinn to snatch a few hours' sleep before setting off to do the whole ridge at 5 a.m.

When we met them they had been going for thirteen hours, were saturated with sun and suffering agonies of thirst. Their thoughts were fastened on a high spring of cool water in the Fionn Choire, alas, still several hours distant. I thought they were too heavily laden with gear for a push involving 10,000 feet of clambering and, indeed, they themselves voiced the thought as we went along the ridge together.

At least we could do them a certain amount of good by

121

saving them time on route finding. Also, since our thirst was less than on other days, we still had two oranges which we passed to them, and it was better than eating them to see how much these were enjoyed by two men who desperately needed them. I regret now that we did not stay with this couple, for it was after the main peak of the Bidean their route finding went wrong. Time was lost, and it was 11 p.m. before they could ease their sore throats at the Fionn Choire spring.

Not surprisingly, they decided to bivouac there, setting off again at 3 a.m. down Lota Corrie, intending to climb Collie's route on the Bhasteir Tooth which Iain and I had descended two days before. But they failed to find the way, and after an hour's searching came back to the col, missed out the Tooth by climbing Am Bhasteir from its easier side, then set off for Sgurr nan Gillean.

But things went wrong here too. They failed to find the route along the Western Ridge, and after various intimidating verticalities, bailed out with an abseil, retreated to the Bealach na Lice and abandoned the tops by Lota Corrie for the weary trudge down Glen Sligachan and over the pass to Coruisk to arrive at noon. They had been on the go for thirty-one hours. Nor could they sit back, for Frank Milner had business appointments in Yorkshire the next day. So they had to pack up immediately and see about getting back to their car at Elgol. Luckily they got a lift across Loch Scavaig in a tourist boat, and motoring all night arrived home at 6 a.m. not having been in bed since they left four nights and three days before.

Not many men in their prime could survive that pace and output of nervous energy. But reflect that one of the pair was sixty-two years old, and he told me he did not climb his first peak until he was forty owing to a seven days a week job. Moreover he has done very little rock climbing, though he and Frank have been winter climbing in Scotland every year for the past ten years. Stan Bradshaw, the veteran from Padiham in Lancashire and Frank Milner who is just over half his age, are keen to have another go. In a letter to me Stan says, 'How about joining us? It would be so much easier, I think, with someone who knew the route intimately. We lost such a lot of time route-finding.'

I think the secret of doing the main ridge is to keep your equipment down so as to be able to move swiftly over the long sections of moderately difficult rocks. What I would do is leave a rucksack of spare clothing etc., at Sligachan Hotel, book a room there, and get driven round to Glen Brittle, timing my plod up Gars-bheinn to arrive there about daybreak. The boots I would wear would be light. In addition to food, I would carry a plastic bottle holding about two pints of water, and I would carry climbing line rather than rope for it would be used double only for abseiling. I would expect to be out for about fifteen hours between Glen Brittle and Sligachan. For me the ideal weather would be breezy with shifting mist and sun

Footnote 1: Stan and his friend Frank achieved their ambition by doing the main ridge of the Cuillin in just a day a year later. Beginning in Glen Brittle at 3.30 a.m. they were in Sligachan at 11 p.m. in a joyous 19½hour day. In a letter to me immediately after it Stan wrote: 'We had a cache of food planted at the Inaccessible Pinnacle, and once we got it we felt nothing could stop us. We were tired when we got to the Bhasteir Tooth, and once again we couldn't find the route, although we had made a reconnaissance in advance. We wasted a bit of time and energy, but once we were up we could relax, for we knew nothing could stop us getting to Sgurr nan Gillean. It was beautiful! Everything about us was grand – the colours, the sea and, swinging away from us the marvellous ridge and the corries we had traversed.'

At sixty-three years of age the jaunty wee man had done it, and he is busy ticking off the Scottish Munros as I write this. And I'm sure he'll do them before he's seventy. He's the youngest old man I know.

Footnote 2: The astonishing Eric Beard at the age of thirty-

123

one ran the Cuillin Ridge from Gars-Bheinn to Gillean in 1963 in 4 hours 9 minutes. At the time he did it he was holder of English, Irish, Scottish and Welsh fell-running records. He we killed in a car crash in 1969. In the last letter I had received from him he had cycled from Yorkshire all the way to the Alps to climb there.

Footnote 3: As this book goes to print (Sept. 1980) I hear that Stan Bradshaw has climbed all the Munros.

[*Footnote 4: The current Cuillin Ridge record, set in 2007 by Ed Tresidder, is 3 hours, 17 minutes, 20 seconds.*]

TOM WEIR'S SCOTLAND

THE BIG BEN

Here I was on Ben Nevis with two young folk who knew as little about the mountain as I did on my first ascent. I was going to the top by the pony track on a promising morning of crisp visibility though a full thousand feet of mist still capped the summit.

Of the half-way hut that was used by the roadmen who maintained the track in Observatory days, there is nothing left. When we dossed down in it all those years ago I didn't know that this was one of the places where you paid your one shilling toll fee to be allowed to walk up the track, four shilling if you rode a pony. To build the track cost £800 in 1883, and until it was opened on that date only a few eccentrics had climbed Ben Nevis. Of these the most extraordinary was Clement Wragge, a gangling red-haired Englishman nick-named the Inclement Wragge by the Fort William folk because he climbed the mountain every day regardless of the weather. Leaving at five in the morning he aimed to be at the summit by nine and back down in the town at three in the afternoon, having obtained in that time a scientific record of the weather differences between sea-level and 4,406 feet.

It was the astonishing weather variations between sea and summit which decided the Scottish Meteorological Society to build the first mountain-top observatory on Ben Nevis, lying in the direct path of Atlantic storms. What Wragge had been doing was a feasibility study over a period of two summers, climbing the Ben from June to October inclusive. The £4,000 required to build the Observatory was raised in Scotland, as was the money for the pony track.

Suddenly everyone wanted to climb Ben Nevis – over 4000 within a year. Many of them would arrive in Fort William by the West Highland Railway which opened in 1894 bringing the mountain within easy range of the mass of the Scottish population. Trade in the town was brisk. A hotel was built on top to provide bed and breakfast for those wanting to stay for sunrise, and there was serious talk of extending the railway from the town to the summit.

Talking about these things my young friends and I overtook the first climbers of the morning, a family in yellow oilskins, father and mother with a bright-faced wee girl roped between them. In foreign accent the man asked if I thought the weather would remain fine. "We turned back from here yesterday. We would like to climb up the highest peak in Scotland but perhaps it is too much for this little girl?" She was not quite six. "She'll do it if you can keep her interested," I told him. "Tell her about the wee house there used to be on the top – the highest in the whole country. Give her something to look forward to." They were from the flat lands of Holland.

We broke off from the path after crossing the Red Burn to see what we could find in the way of mountain plants among the boulders: fir club and other mosses, alpine ladies mantle, starry saxifrages and the tiny least willow. No snow buntings singing as I had hoped, but I have a feeling they nest here. We were well in the mist at 3,500ft. and at 4,000ft. were on the unbroken snowfield between Carn Dearg and Ben Nevis which Wragge called the Plateau of Storms.

I used the compass now in this dimensionless world of

125

white mist on snow, to keep on parallel course with the big cliffs which sheer away from the plateau edge for roughly a mile between here and the top of Nevis. Then suddenly came the proof that all was well: the summit suddenly bulged in front of us, the mist pouring off north-eastwards revealing the black thrust of crags soaring to thick lips of snow cornice.

Our spirits soared as colour flooded around us and below us. There was green-shored Loch Linnhe, a ribbon of soft grey winding to the blue hills of Mull. The Pulp Mill on its peninsula looked like a toy. Highland topography at a glance. Behind the deep cut of the Great Glen jumbled ridges stretched from Knoydart to Kintail to Glen Affric.

Our first delightful surprise when arriving was to find the Dutch family already there. The wee girl said she wasn't even tired and proved it by grabbing my ice axe and digging furiously into the snow while we talked. They were amused when I told them about the Fort William man who claimed the first wheeled victory on Ben Nevis by pushing a wheelbarrow to the summit, followed in 1911 by a Model T Ford which took three days to reach the Observatory, but a mere 2 ½ hours to return after a night cooling down. At the news of the victory of the internal combustion engine over the steeps of the mountain, a public holiday was declared in Fort William and a pipe band played to greet the entry of the motor car into the town. The man with the wheelbarrow was there trundling along in the procession. It was to be another thirteen years before the motor car could equal the wheelbarrow and go up and down in a day. That came in 1928 when a Model A Ford achieved the feat.

We took a walk along the cliffs to identify the peaks stretching from Ben Wyvis to Ben Lawers, Schiehallion, Ben Alder and the high mass of the Cairngorms, the nearest approach to true Arctic terrain we have in Scotland and still very white after an exceptionally long winter and cold spring.

Sheltered by the modern survival hut which perches on what used to be the Observatory conning tower, I thought

126

about the disappointment Wragge must have felt when the Observatory was built and he was refused the post of Super-intendent which he wanted. But you can't suppress a man's pioneering spirit. He had been in Australia, and he went back there, getting his due as Government meteorologist and set-ting up mountain-top observatories on Mount Wellington and Mount Koscuiszko. The world remembers him as the first long-range weather forecaster. He died in 1922.

The staff at the Observatory was normally four and they seem to have got on comfortably together with little friction. Visiting students came to stay. One was C.T.R. Wilson, a Nobel Prize winner to be from Glencorse whose work played an important part in the development of nuclear physics. It was the optical phenomena shown when the sun shone on the clouds that surrounded the hilltop that turned his thoughts to imitating them in the laboratory which led to forty years of tracking atoms.

Life on the highest mountain had its share of fun. The team enjoyed the snow, tobogganing from the observatory to the Plateau of Storms – a thrilling half-mile course with a 20ft. drop and a sensational bit known as MacLean's Steep. For skating they made a pond on a big tarpaulin stretched on the flat roof; and for curling matches they would descend 2,000ft. to the half-way lochan. In summer they played quoits and amused themselves hurtling rocks over the cliffs to see them bounce and smash with sulphurous smell.

Later, in 1892, they had to warn tourists not to hurl rocks down the cliff. An incredible thing had happened: a family from the north of England had scaled the 2,000 ft. cliffs. In four days the Hopkinson brothers pioneered two of the great clas-sics of Scottish climbing, Tower Ridge and Observatory Ridge. Strangely they wrote not a word in any journal about it.

In March, two years later, a noted Scottish Mountaineer-ing Club alpinist came with a strong party and made the first winter ascent of Tower Ridge which Collie described as being comparable with the Italian Ridge of the Matterhorn –

powerful praise and not over-stated. These great crags are a volcanic cauldron of lava which did not erupt but subsided inside a mass of softer material, its heat changing the nature of the surrounding rocks. It was erosion by moving masses of ice scraping away the softer material which uncovered the inside of the mountain and made its lava the north-eastern outside we see today, a superb architectural form of ridge and spire, buttress and arête, gully and chimney. From below they look even more daunting than from above, so all praise to the Hopkinson brothers in finding two of the best natural lines.

Among the early pioneers was Dr W. Charles Inglis Clark, Scottish Mountaineering Club President from 1913-19. His name is remembered in the only true alpine cabin in Britain, situated below Tower Ridge. Dr Clark built it to commemorate his son Charles, who died of wounds in Mesopotamia. It was opened in 1929.

I've been looking back at the record of the official opening of the hut on 1 April five decades ago. The time was 7 p.m. They had just cooked a splendid meal on the club stove. It was snowing hard outside when the door was thrust open and in lurched two climbers. They had fallen from Gardyloo Gully, lost their ice axes, slid 600ft. and were fumbling their way down when they saw the light beside them. Clark wrote, 'Thus early our hut had justified itself in time of danger.'

Time of danger – in fact mountaineering accidents were very few on Ben Nevis until the sudden popularisation of the sport in the late 1950's when the climbing revolution took place and streams converged in all seasons on both sides of the mountain. Death became commonplace, over fifty in two decades, many of the victims totally lacking any idea of what to expect on this most savage of Scottish peaks. There is less excuse for ignorance today than when Richie and I went up on our first visit.

TOM WEIR'S SCOTLAND (c. 1979)

A CAMP ON RUM

It was the most perfect of May evenings when we sailed into Loch Scresort, the kind of evening when you should have no care in the world and bags of grub for a long stay. We had the grub, but no reassuring letter of permission had answered our request to land so we were a bit anxious as we watched the little island boat pull alongside the steamer. As Harris was the next port of call and we had no intention of going there, some positive action was called for.

Our strategy was simple. The biggest man in the party, Matt, leapt into the boat as it bumped alongside. The luggage followed him as quickly as we could pile it on, so quickly that he could give neither explanation nor hear the protesting voices demanding them. When Arthur MacPherson and I arrived we just waved our hands ashore and muttered something about a letter and the Estate Agent. At once the sun shone more brightly, and the mountains towered higher and finer than our most vivid dreams as the little boat swung in the direction we wanted.

Now for the head keeper. The walk to his house was the perfect introduction to the island, for his house is in the bonniest part of this well-wooded little bay. Through the birches at their brightest green, on a path that wound amongst turf gay with wild hyacinth, sorrel, violets, orchis and clustering primroses, we were led to a little clearing. Then we heard something. As one man we stopped and listened. It was repeated for us, a shivering exultant little song, the song of a wood warbler, a bird none of us would have associated with a sterile island like Rum. No refusal could come on top of this touch of pure charm.

And the omen was good. The keeper, instead of giving us a swearing as we had been led to expect, proved to be a friendly man who told us we could camp where we liked, and to call on him if we needed anything. The boat would be at our disposal when we wanted to leave, too. On a grassy flat at the edge of the bay, within sight of the peak of Hallival and an oyster-catcher brooding its eggs, we pitched our two tents door to door . . .

Showers drove us quickly back to camp when we essayed a walk, but in that short outing we had seen a peregrine stoop in a headlong dive over a wood, and watched seals playing inshore. Good to lie in the tent and listen to the flighting sounds of roding woodcock.

To waken to the steady patter of rain on canvas was a disappointment. On such a day the landscape was bleak and barren, and into the cloud we climbed, intent on finding rock. We found it, but the climbing proved cold, wet work, more difficult than we wanted in the conditions. We were thankful when the crag eased to a boulder-strewn summit which we thought must be Askival. Lunch was called for.

During the halt the mists began to flicker, revealing fragments of sunlit ocean; and just as the optimists were predicting wonders a bristling summit was revealed, a mighty shoulder where no shoulder should be if we were on the highest peak of the island. We headed for it while it was there, for it was evident that we were well south of the top.

To our delight – for we carried no guide-book – a fine rock rib barred the way to the top. It gave a sparkler of a climb, steep and rather severe on the line we chose, but glorious fun, for the conditions had changed as though by magic. The wind had dropped and the steep rocks dried quickly in the hot sun.

More fascinating to us was the near view of the Island of Eigg, the crofts on the Bay of the Singing Sands facing us across a narrow strip of sea and the miniature mountainland of rocky tops and lochans around the Scuir showing to perfection. Only eight months previously we had spent a week there and been charmed completely by the amazing fertility and rich variety of its scenery and bird life. The Scuir had given us some really sporting rock climbing and views most memorable. I recommend Eigg to any lover of mountains.

130

Hallival was next, a pleasant scramble leading on to Bark-eval by a stony ridge where cushion pink, purple and starry saxifrage, and even violets and primroses were blooming. After such a splendid day it was good to leave the tops for the run down to our bay, where birds were singing and the old primus beckoned.

Another of the joys of camping in this place was to awaken to the soft voices of the eider mingling with the dawn chorus of the waders and woodland birds. One could hear the songs of warblers, wrens, blackbirds, chaffinches, meadow pipits and skylarks mingling with the sounds of ravens, hoodie crows, grouse, curlews, golden plovers, oyster-catchers and sandpipers.

Dibidil at the foot of Sgurr nan Gillean was a place on which we had set our hearts, so, when we saw the sky shaping itself for one of those days that come but once or twice each spring, we made ready to go.

That walk was a sheer joy, not only for its splendid views over the sparkling sea to Eigg and the dim chain of mainland hills, but for the grand fun we had on the sea cliffs, where large colonies of gulls were nesting amongst the sea pinks. The best find was in a recess on a difficult little traverse. This was a large, wool-lined nest containing two red-mouthed, black, naked youngsters which none of us could identify. Nor did we get a clue from any hovering bird. We had to tear ourselves away from these great sea cliffs, for outside mountains there is nothing so fascinating as this combination of rock scrambling and bird hunting.

What a sight was the oasis of Dibidil Bay and the sheer sweep of Sgurr nan Gillean as it came into view round the headland. It was agreed that we had never see a Scottish hill look higher or any bay more attractive. Sun-bathing, our backs comfortably against a warm rock just shaped for the cult, we lazed away a happy half-hour. [*Dibidil now has an MBA bothy*]

Nor did that half-hour in the sun cause Sgurr nan Gillean to grow any shorter. Indeed, the grass slope had not only lengthened but steepened alarmingly. It was a relief to get it over and touch down on rock for the scramble up the last few hundred feet to the summit. That grass slope is worthy of Very Severe classification. But the reward was more than worth it. All Scotland was washed with blues that day, each wave of distance distinguished in its own subtle shade, from the Outer Islands round past Torridon and Ardnamurchan Point to Ben More of Mull. Most splendid of all though, were the Cuillin rising straight out of the sea and dappled with the pattern of the drifting clouds.

Ainshval was the next peak on the ridge, a grassy walk with a real edge of rock providing a good scramble down to Bealach an Fhuarain. We were now ready for serious rock work, for above us rose a fine buttress to the west of the ridge on the main face of the mountain. It looked formidable, but our grim visages relaxed when we found it to be liberally supplied with holds for all its steepness. This peak, Trallval, with two sharp tops, is easily the finest in the island and most Cuillin-like in appearance.

Over the ridge of Barkeval by a long traverse, and we raced down to the tents for a first-class meal. All of us were feeling the effects of too much sun, but we weren't complaining. We agreed we might have had as good a day in the west before but never better.

Heavy rain and thunder in the night was a surprise, to say the least, particularly as my tent was leaking badly. However, some first aid with a groundsheet and all was well. It was nice to get a good long sleep and eat a leisurely breakfast. Also, it gave us the chance to explore the woods for birds. We were astonished to see some turtle doves – birds one associates with the South of England but not with the Hebrides. We learned that they do not breed here, but occur for a few days each spring, obviously a passage movement between their winter and summer quarters. The long-tailed tit was another enterprising species colonising the woods of Scresort.

We knew it would be a good day for our last climb on the

132

island, and so it was. Blue sky was breaking through the low mists when I looked out, and soon the sun was shining brightly. Enjoying the curling clouds and glorious scents, we stepped it out over a fine hill pass to Bloodstone Hill. The approach by a green glen of short turf was good, but on top was even better.

There is enough shading on the map to indicate a gigantic cliff on the north-west side, and we were hoping to descend for a climb, but alas, these Ordnance Survey men are not to be trusted: the cliff is a mixture of grass and rotten rock. The spectacular drop to the sea gave an airy feeling, and from an eyrie up there we looked down on Canna and its crofts and across to the Skye coast.

Disturbing hundreds of deer, we crossed Sron nan Saigh-dean to Orval, to where there is a tremendous pinnacle. [*which has been climbed*] Unfortunately the strata here, like those of the Storr of Skye, are most unsound; after pulling out hand-fuls we had to abandon the idea in favour of rock at an easier angle.

On top the visibility was hard and sharp in the low light before rain. The panorama was impressive, from the snowy hump of Nevis past Moidart to the lochs of Hourn and Nevis, then round past Applecross to Skye and the Outer Islands, then the Dutchman's cap, and the hills of Mull fronted by the ridge of Ardnamurchan. The sea was grey like steel and the hills in tones of grey and black.

In showers we came down to the softer country of the glen, and at last to the woods of the bay and the scents of lime and mountain ash, a contrast to the barren, upper world where we had been for the last ten hours. The sun was shining now, and across the brilliant sea was Knoydart, every peak of its Rough Bounds as if shaped in glistening amber.

A present of three eggs was the perfect finish to this, our last climb in this grand little island where the folks and the weather had treated us so kindly.

SCOTTISH MOUNTAINEERING CLUB JOURNAL, 1948

AVALANCHE

I am writing this with my injured leg propped up on a couch, and every now and then I have to wriggle my posterior to avoid too much pressure on a large raw scar on that place. This continual wriggling causes pain on my bruised thighs, and if I cough or sneeze, a pain shoots from my lower ribs to my chest. But I shall start from the beginning.

It was a day in February and four of us were keen on a difficult climb. The preceding week had been glorious with sun and frost, and eagerly we awaited the weekend for an attempt on a classic Scottish mountaineering route, the Upper Couloir of Stob Ghabhar. We knew it would be in superb condition for an exacting climb on steep frozen snow and ice. The stars on Saturday night as we motored up towards the Blackmount had a frosty sparkle. But overnight there was a dramatic change. Raw winter had returned with a clamping down of visibility and snow falling out of low yellow mists. There was no wind and we saw no reason to call off our climb. Our intention was to park the car on the south side of the mountain, contour round to the north-east face, climb the couloir, and descend southwards down easy slopes to the car.

The walk up the glen that leads over was uneventful, but in the hour taken to cross the shoulder to the north-east side we could feel a change brewing. The snow fell thicker and the wind became unpleasant. Black crags were hung with icefalls and whitened where snow could lie. We sank deeply at every step. This was not quite what I had expected. The ice, yes, but not this depth of new snow. Obviously there must have been heavy snow up here for some hours. I was beginning to have misgivings about the couloir. We kept a careful compass check and at last we were faced by a steep gully.

The Upper Couloir of Stob Ghabhar is a narrow 300ft. cleft enclosed by two rock buttresses abutting directly on to the summit. We were 600ft. below, at the foot of the Lower Couloir, and it is usual to combine the two couloirs by making one long climb.

We tied on the rope and I led the straightforward steep slope, but at once noticed that the exceptionally dry and deep surface snow did not seem to be adhering to the mountain. I cut through with my ice-axe to the underlying strata and found a substance as hard as ice. The sun and frost of the past week on the thin cover of old snow had made the hillsides so icy that this new snow was merely resting on it. There was danger here, avalanche danger, and I proved it when I slapped the adjacent slope with my ice-axe and caused a large mass to split off. The couloir was out for today, obviously. But unwilling to abandon the mountain we agreed to try a route to the left on what looked to be safer snow. This was indeed safer, and we climbed swiftly in deteriorating conditions of rising wind and blowing snow.

Had we chosen the easiest route to the summit all might have turned out well. Instead of that I broke off at an ice-fall flowing over rocks. I said, "This will give a sporting climb and should be every bit as good as the couloir." I got to it and was soon balanced on a steep wall of ice chipping hand and foot-holds.

This is probably the most truly satisfying branch of the climber's craft. Ice climbing calls for delicate balance, judgement in spacing the holds, and ability in shaping them to give secure foot and hand-hold. Now and then I had to hang on and try to glue myself to the mountain as fierce blasts of wind and spume struck. The ice-fall gave eighty feet of exacting climbing with an exit on to steep and difficult ground. I lost no time in finding a belay and bringing up my second. The other two followed. We were now on a slope of new snow lying ten inches deep on a hard frozen undersurface of ice covering rock. The danger was evident, and I cut every step through to the underlying strata, and several times had to desist to avoid being swept off by the now ferocious gale with accompanying blasts of spume.

In three 100ft. rope lengths I found myself above the lowest rocks of the upper couloir and knew I must be close to the summit. But I was faced with a worrying problem. The bank of snow in front of me was so steep that I could almost touch it with my nose, and it looked avalanchy.

I warned my second to find himself a good anchorage by digging the shaft of his axe up to the head in hard frozen snow, and tying himself to it. The others were eighty feet lower down and were joined to us by the rope. I prodded the snow with my axe and found it so deep that it was impossible to get through to the old underlying snow. This was serious, but such a depth of snow might be reasonably consolidated. I decided to shovel out a groove and tramp it down as I wriggled up. This is a laborious technique as I knew, but as the summit was so close I began shovelling with the head of my axe. I climbed up a couple of steps and was quite pleased with my work. This was going to work out all right after all. As a further test of consolidation I plunged my axe up to its head and gave the shaft a tug. Quite silently and with irresistible force the whole slope heeled over on me, hurtling me downwards.

My second man was torn from his ice axe so firmly planted in the hard snow. The other two members of the party saw a great snow-tide advancing on them and tried to hold. They were lifted bodily and hurled down with us.

I was below the avalanche and my first reaction was that we were going to be smothered by the pressing weight of the snow. At such times a swimming motion is supposed to bring one to the surface and I began swimming. I need not have bothered. The next moment I was in the air turning over and over. Things hit me and jarred my bones, terrific jerks tore at my ribs (the rope joining us). I was a detached spectator who sees himself in a dream hurtling to death and wakes in nightmare.

"No human being could survive this," I remember thinking. And I blamed myself for causing it. Four people were going to die and I was responsible for not turning back when I should. The mind is strangely calm in such moments of crisis. The others told me they, too, were resigned to death. Then suddenly I felt myself begin to slow up, and at once I started swimming to get to the surface. To be buried and suffocate would be worse than sudden death. I came to rest beside my second and I feared he was dead. His face was covered in blood, but he answered my question and thought he was all right.

My leg was numb from my thigh downwards and I felt it trembling with shock. My gloves had been torn off and my hands were swollen and lifeless with cold. "I better get something on my hands," I said. I had a spare pair of gloves in my pocket and as I tried to get them blood spurted over my jacket and hands and I realised that my own face was covered in blood.

At that moment there was a shout from above. Neither myself nor my second were yet capable of rising. The other two joined us. The nylon rope had snapped between us like a piece of string, hence the reason that they had stopped at a different point. All were concerned about my eyebrow which was split open and was the source of so much blood, but there was no pain.

We reviewed the damage. One man was almost unscathed. The other two were badly bruised and in considerable pain. My second had taken a battering on his face and thighs and his legs hurt. The third had two badly twisted ankles and various bruises, but he thought he could walk. I felt that any man left out on that hillside that night would die of exposure in the blizzard which was now raging, and consequently delayed not a moment in starting off on the long traverse back round the mountain.

For three of us each step was an effort of will. Our footsteps of the morning had filled in, and the going was now much harder in the considerable depth of snow. One man had to lie down and pull himself over such obstacles as he could not

137

climb. We did not take any chances in nil visibility. A compass course was maintained on the complicated traverse round the mountain and we struck the hill track that takes such a good line down the broken ground between Beinn Toaig and Stob Ghabhar. It was nearly 6 p.m. when three of us reached the little school-house of Clash Ghabhar [*now the JMCS hut*] so we made about one mile per hour. We were now a couple of miles from the car. The missing man with the twisted ankles was not far behind, we knew, so the two injured members went on for help, the sound man could climb back uphill and help the fourth member.

We were lucky. The keeper at Forest Lodge had a van, and after plying us with tea he ran the vehicle up the rough track to the schoolhouse. His arrival was well timed, for our two companions had just reached the schoolhouse as the van drove up. The injured man could not have gone further for the snow was balling up on his boots, causing his twisted ankles to turn at every step. Soon we were assembled in the keeper's warm kitchen and assisted into our spare clothes from the car, for we were soaked to the skin. These fine people were kindness itself.

There is always a fortunate side to any unlucky event. We still had a driver for our car and we had friends only twenty miles away. We went there, had baths, a hot dinner, bathed our wounds and one man went to bed. We motored to Glasgow, arriving in at 2 a.m., and next day had expert attention at the Western Infirmary.

Will it stop us climbing? I doubt it. Mountaineering is no more dangerous than many another sport. A combination of events had led us on that day, first the windless morning, then the sound condition of the snow on the earlier part of our climb. Our nearness to the summit and thought of a speedy descent out of the blizzard to the more sheltered south side of the mountain made me reluctant to abandon our climb until I had first tested the safety of the bank that was our undoing. So much of mountaineering is a matter of judgement. In

138

this case my judgement was wrong, and the descent rather speedier than any of us expected. All of us should be well to climb again in a matter of a few weeks. Fluid and blood on my swollen knee and a fractured patella may retard my own progress a bit longer, but that is just retribution.

I wrote this to beguile the time, not for publication. Since then we have visited the scene of the accident, mainly to look for our ice axes. We found them and were shocked to see what we had fallen over. The average angle of the slope was around fifty degrees, with one drop of over 100ft. and sundry smaller drops. One of the ice axes was broken, the one used to belay me on the last part of the climb. It was a new and modern Swiss axe. We had come down a good 600ft. and more. If this had been an Alpine climb I would not have dreamed of forcing it under such doubtful conditions and certainly not attempted it under conditions of storm. The moral must be that no matter how keen one is to climb, there is a time for turning back. Scottish hills in winter must, in fact, be treated as Alpine peaks.

TOM WEIR'S SCOTLAND

Tom had one other serious fall (in 1970) while rock climbing with Len Lovat on Ben A'an in the Trossachs. Leading, he came off and flew forty feet, crashing and rolling to squash his spine, crack a hip and damage ribs. "The hospital time was useful for getting some writing done". Before the more settled years in Gartocharn he would scribble in tent or bothy or train, anywhere as "to write you must write".

CROSSING THE CAIRNGORMS BY SKI

After the eleventh day of sunshine in Aviemore I knew the time had come to put into operation a plan I had to ski across the great plateau that rises over 4,000ft. between Spey and Dee. The conditions were perfect, with long snow tongues shooting like gigantic waterfalls from glittering cornices, which overhung the edges of snow-smoothed summits. The hard frosty sky held not a cloud, and robins and hedge sparrows were singing round the houses as I wheeled out my bicycle to tie my skis along the cross-bar, taking care that my handlebars would not jam.

I was not fooled by the spring-like weather, however. I knew I was going to climb into winter, so into my rucksack went a light groundsheet, four candles, a little shovel, a supply of concentrated food and a solid fuel cooking stove in case I were caught in a sudden storm.

With these necessities and my ice-axe to dig a trench in a snow drift, I was equipped to make a bivouac and survive a blizzard. The candles were carried as a source of warmth to raise the temperature inside my igloo once the drifting snow had sealed the cracks.

That was the theory, but I was not expecting to use the survival kit. I hoped to be sleeping that night in the keeper's house at Luibeg twenty miles across the mountains if all went well. So off I went on the bicycle, pedalling up the stony track that leads into Glen Einich. Soon I had to walk, and I was glad to rest my binoculars on the handlebars to watch crested tits raising and lowering their barred head-feathers as they gave out the sharp vibrating trills that distinguish them anywhere. Louder, more metallic sounds came from the crossbills feeding on the top-most pine cones.

Where the pines thin out I was in a different world of snow drifts on the road, but I could ride for much of the way to Coire Ruadh of Braeriach, below which I dumped the bicycle and set off up the steep slope that leads to a narrow ridge between two horseshoe corries. It was a mountaineer's choice rather than the easiest line, and I paid for it by having to hang my skis on my rucksack while I hacked my way up a glassy section, before the ice gave way to more easily-cut hard snow leading to the open summit.

What a wonderful reward it was to be up here, with miles

of sparkling snowfields before me, none of it below 4,000ft. "This is worth all the hard work," I thought as my eye ranged from the top of Braeriach round to Cairntoul where I was going. I was in a world of utter silence – a polar waste but for the warm reds and pinks of the Lairig Ghru pass far below.

The River Dee rises close to the summit of Braeriach near the sweeping precipices of Garbh Coire. There was no sign of the 'Wells' that day as I swooped past the place, enjoying my wild situation on the lip of the great cornices plunging into space. Down there I could see frozen Lochain Uaine hemmed by Ice Age bulges. I was moving fast over the ups and downs of the Garbh Coire edge but so was a subtle change in the weather. Visibility was closing in, and the distant sky was grey, not blue. But I was still in a brilliant world, tinged with gold snow, the snow appearing almost warm against a violet sky. It was also a sign of approaching night and time I was down off the top of Angel's Peak.

Which way should I go? I could shoot down towards the Devil's Point and drop to Corrour Bothy; or choose the longer and steeper slope, which plunges directly to Glen Geusachen, I chose the latter and felt almost dizzy with the succession of linked turns that brought me helter-skelter to the last tongue of snow fanning into the heather. I abandoned my skis by sticking them upright in the snow and fixing in my mind the various landmarks that would take me back to them. All I had to do now was follow the glen down to the Lairig Ghru path, but it was dusk by the time I leapt across the Dee and my last three miles to Lui Beg cottage were in starlight.

"It's yourself," said Bob cheerily when he opened the door. "You'll be ready for your dinner." I was, and I was soon sitting down to it in borrowed clothes. Although they did not know on which day I would make the crossing, they were ready for me. I had of course written explaining my intentions if the weather held. "I must go back in the morning in case a change comes," I said to Bob. I had a shock coming when I looked out the next morning at seven. Mist swirled round the house and the air was mild. However, I had risen with the object of making back to my bicycle, so I decided to try. Unfortunately the mist did not thin out as I had hoped, and it was snowing on the plateau as I steered a compass course, pausing every few moments to take a bearing in the white-out.

Far out on the Monadh Mor I was forced into a decision: whether to risk being overtaken by darkness before I was off the plateau, or ski back along my tracks to Bob's cottage. I chose safety first and was glad I had done so when at the edge of the snow line I met a fox walking slowly in my direction. The lolling gait and grey mask almost touching the ground showed that he had no clue of danger. I stood quite still, and on he came, closer and closer, the sheen on his red coat and long brush tail showing he was in fine condition. Then with a foot in the air he froze, ears up, nostrils twitching. We were eye to eye, and I swear I saw his expression change as he noticed me and spun round, diving behind a heathery knoll to disappear into the mist.

What was he doing up here? After the speckled ptarmigan, no doubt, since these birds are unable to fly safely when the world is opaque. I had seen a pack of twenty or so sitting in neat little holes in the lee of a cornice. The cunning fellow was no doubt going up to take a look. The only other birds I had heard that day were snow buntings, tinkling out of the mist, veritable sprites of the blizzard.

It was black darkness by the time I pushed open the door of Bob's house. "Well, well. I'm glad to see you back, I can tell you. We've been worried for it's been wild here." Bob was to give me hospitality for the best part of a week, as the temperature shot up and the Dee rose to a brown flood impossible to cross.

It was no hardship – not with this keeper who lives in the highest and most isolated house in the Cairngorms. With the Labrador we went visiting fox traps, and watched the hungry deer foraging in hundreds among the newly uncovered heather. We saw the return of the golden plover to the moor and the oyster-catcher to the river – happy sights and cheering sounds. More unexpected was the sight of three yellowhammers outside the bedroom window: strange birds up here, as strange as the robin I was to find perched beside my skis later in the day. The partial migrants were on the move, and so was I – back to my bicycle.

The thaw had changed the face of the Cairngorms in the week since I had crossed them. The great plateau was now at the rags-and-tatters stage, but there was still more snow than bare ground, as I saw from the top of Cairn Toul, enjoying a mighty view of peaks stretching from the North Sea to the Atlantic. This time I intended to go back to the head of Loch Einich by way of the Monadh Mor, so I left the top in a long traversing line, taking Carn Ban Mor as my guide, then striking out towards the dip that marked Coire Dhondail – a long, long way, and an ample opportunity to watch the many pairs of courting ptarmigan crowing their creaky cries from many a snow patch. But gradually the brown crags of Sgoran Dubh were drawing close, and soon I was on the lip of the plateau, looking down at what at first glance appeared to be a sheer drop.

Getting down posed an interesting problem. The drop was not sheer: the illusion was due to the snow cornice that overhung the steep face between me and the corrie. The cornice itself had been split by the thaw all along the plateau edge, but it was still managing to defy gravity. I could not risk climbing down anywhere here. There was one place, however, where it was uncracked, where the angle was less than vertical, and down it I lowered myself, ice-axe driven in to the shaft as I kicked steps downward, hanging on to my axe. I took it carefully for 200ft. then I considered it safe to relax.

Below me now was Loch Einich, with no obstacle between me and it. Indeed, there was a magic highway in a ribbon of silver ending in the blue water, and soon I was swinging down there on snow as smooth as silk. The ski-ing was over, but looking back to the great bowl of the corrie shining against

143

the blue sky I could hardly believe that only half an hour ago I had been up there. But the evidence was there, in the flowing curves left by my turning skis.

"It's not really so far," I thought, as I visualised the way I had come since morning: the pines of Glen Derry, the traverse round Carn a' Mhaim, then over the Dee to Glen Geusachen and the plod to the top of Cairn Toul, peppered with rocks where everything had been smooth snow the week before. Then out over the Monadh Mor, alone in the great depression between Bheinn Bhrotain and Carn Ban, a strange place at over 3,000ft., where I once met a dipper. Here, too, is a nesting-ground of the dotterel, my favourite bird.

Now I was down in the glen, with only two miles of walking to reach my bike. After twenty miles on foot and ski I was in no hurry, especially when a merlin rose from a heathery moraine and with squealing cries skimmed low over me. And before I reached my bicycle there was a sight of a goosander, white-breasted and streamlined, followed by its mate. All too soon I was twisting down the stony track to Speyside, enjoying the effortless travel of a downhill run. In the evening light, the green of the Caledonian pines shone with a golden light, and the bark glowed with an extra touch of pink. Down here was a rich overlapping of bird sounds, the echoing of curlews, drumming snipe and swooping lapwings, while from the trees came the staccato songs of chaffinches, mistle thrushes, blackbirds, coal tits and goldcrests. Coming from the arctic heights of the tundra country to the fullness of spring down here gave me feeling of having encompassed two worlds.

WEIR'S WAY

VI

NORWAY TO CORSICA

*In the immediate post-war years when Tom began to roam moun-
tains, he found worlds where climbing was hardly known, equipment was rudimentary and techniques hardly changed from decades
earlier. This often gave his writings a freshness, tinged with wonder,
which cannot be recaptured today. He soon went to the Alps and
would return to climb and ski there till well into his eighties but,
at the same time, the hankering for less known mountain regions
would lure him to ranges like the Juliun Alps or Corsica. The first
visit to Norway was in 1951.*

NORTHLAND MOUNTAINEERING

Back from India with some £50 still in the kitty we studied the map, estimated the fares, decided to risk the trip, and lost no time in packing. We carried food because we knew that many items are rationed in Norway, and we meant to stay up there just as long as our money lasted.

Our first lucky break came with the offer of a lift from Bergen to Trondheim – a journey that would take us through the famed Hardanger Fjord, over the highest road in Norway by the glaciers of the Jotunheim, and then across the tundra country of the Dovre Fjell. This was indeed a gift from the gods!

A boat leaves Trondhim daily for the North Cape, calling at the remote fjords, and continuing by the Lofoten Islands, Tromso, and finally Kirkenes on the Russian border. Since the sea is the only highway in Arctic Norway these little craft are packed to Cup-Tie capacity. But the travelling is good fun, the passengers providing the entertainment.

We were regaled with exciting stories of the late war and the burning of Arctic towns and villages by the Germans; told of the 1940 Commando raids which we had forgotten, and about the naval actions that sunk German destroyers and battleships. On this distant coast these raids maintained the morale of the people. Otherwise, they said, life would have become unbearable.

The first day's sailing was pleasant, creeping past rocky headlands where little villages clustered below ice-covered peaks. Crossing the Arctic Circle we ran into rain, which continued all the way to the grim crags of Lofoten and Svolvaer, our destination.

147

The capital treated us decidedly roughly. Camping a mile from the town, we fought against the wind to get the tent up, but the gale became so fierce that we were compelled to pull the flapping canvas down again before the poles gave way. Luckily for us there was a little ski-hut close by. The windows had been blown in, but it offered shelter. At 2 a.m. we fell on the floor and didn't stir for twelve hours.

The outstanding feature that attracted us to Svolvaer is the Goat, a great pinnacle crowned by a couple of horns, which rises sheer above the town. Taking the rope, we set off to climb it, scrambling through boulders, ferns, and dwarf birch to face the formidable granite wall.

We climbed to a little neck where the crags rose steeper, and here Scott tried an overhang while I investigated a vertical crack. After some juggling on small holds, and a cautious crawl up a smooth slab, I found a place to stand some thirty-five feet above. The vertical face beyond was split for a hundred feet by wide cracks which enabled us to reach an airy perch.

The rest of the party took anchorage and I set off, hanging outwards for the first lift. The situation was incredible – like being on the wall of a skyscraper. I got a sort of aeroplane view of the pigmy town, before hauling myself over the bulge and realizing with a shock that a difficult bit of climbing lay ahead. For fifty feet I followed a diminishing crack splitting the huge wall of this soaring slab, each awkwardly-placed hand- and foothold demanding careful thought. One last shuffle on toe-holds, and I reached a ledge under the highest horn, where I could help the others to join me. They were suitably impressed by that wonderful downward view.

A short horizontal groove assisted me to swarm up the edge of the loftier horn. Now for the second horn! This lay a few feet below, across a gap of perhaps five feet which would have to be jumped. Even as I balanced myself for the take-off the sound of solemn brass-band music drifted up to my ears.

I recognised the tune as The Dead March, and I jumped with its full implication in my mind. I landed safely.

Comfortably ensconced on this rock-splinter, we looked down through fifteen hundred feet of space to the local cemetery, where a funeral procession proved to be the source of the music. Beyond lay the sunlit sea and chain upon chain of fantastic peaks.

The town, with its houses dotted about on rocky islands, was spread out like a map, with fish-drying frames gleaming in the sun and the little harbour busy with boats. Near at hand, the clustering peaks rising sheer from the sea filled us with anticipatory excitement, and we started the descent with the knowledge that high adventure waited all around us. Looping the doubled rope round a spike, we slid the difficult upper section and climbed down the remainder. We all agreed that the day had proved a first-rate appetizer. [*An attempt on the Vaagekallentind was defeated by the weather.*]

That night, like the days that followed, was wild with wind and rain. We moved into the Raftsund, where the rock spires rise from the sea like Chamonix aiguilles, During the ensuing week we managed only two climbs, but during that time we penetrated into the Trollfjordvand, which is a glacier offshoot of the wildest sea-fjord in Norway – an ice-covered loch lying between dark rock walls. The climbing was difficult, but we found the lovely islands deeply satisfying. Bread was baked for us by the good lady of a nearby croft, and we were allowed to use the family boat to catch cod and saithe – the mainstay of our diet. Milk and eggs were also forthcoming, but not the weather we needed to climb. An old truism in the Arctic is that the farther north you go the better the weather becomes, and accordingly we decided to head north.

Moving from one place to another is no problem at all in Lofoten. The Vestfjord, east of the islands, is one of the richest fishing banks in the world, and if you want to go north or south you simply hail the first fishing boat going your way.

We went north to Narvik and over the mountains to Lyngen Fjord where, according to Slingsby, 'nature has developed her wildest and most eerie forms.' This is the remotest and loftiest group of mountains in Arctic Norway.

I haven't the space to describe all our doings at Lyngen – our ascent of Jaeggevarre, the 'Mont Blanc of the North,' which took twenty-three hours of exacting mountaineering during the longest day in our experience. But I must tell you about the Jagervandstind which gave us the finest type of climbing adventure.

[*They set off with provisions for three days of adventurous climbing, till . . .*]

. . . No more than fifty feet above us was the narrow summit, but it was too cold to linger between these soaring ridges. We followed the snow-corniced ridge south-westwards, climbing down a thousand feet to a col, whence rose another jagged ridge. Such a challenge could not be ignored, and we started up it.

The climbing was steep and interesting – over ribbons of snow clinging to the knife-edge rock, and broad slabs hanging out over space. Then, suddenly, the ridge ended; there was a great notch in it. Below our feet beetling rocks prevented us peering into the gap, and the wall on the far side appeared unclimbable. Twenty feet down we could see a rusted iron spike projecting from a crack, showing that some climber had been here before.

The question was; if we went down, could we get up the other side? If not, was there the possibility of return? Scott went down, protected by the rope, climbing neatly out of sight, but taking such a long time that I knew the task must be exacting.

Fifty feet down, he started up the other side. Climbing with infinite caution, he moved leftwards, following a narrow crack till he overhung the main sweep of the mountainside. At this fearfully-exposed point he halted awhile; then, reaching down with his right hand as though to tie a shoe-lace, he stooped to a position that looked as if he must eventually fall. His right hand and right foot pulled him into the wall, where he squeezed his face hard against the rock. His left leg and left leg moved slowly forward, groping for holds. But he eventually straightened up, still moving leftward and climbed on to a platform.

Watson went next, descending on the spare rope, our first hundred feet having now been used up. Twenty feet down I asked him to put a sling round the rusted spike so that my own rope could be threaded through it. From the scuffle that ensued I knew the climbing must be hard. This wasn't a cheery thought, for – owing to lack of rope – I should be only partially protected in the event of a slip. All went well, however, and very soon we joined Scott.

Nothing could stop us now! Climbing along an airy crest, we passed several pinnacles to find the spear-like summit immediately ahead. Sensational to the last, it forced us out on to a narrow ledge where our bootnails had nothing below them for over a thousand feet but fresh air. Above this the rock actually overhung, but it was no more than a test of nerve, for the holds were like jug-handles. Finally an exciting forty-foot scramble brought us to the very summit.

During the climb a beautiful sun-glow had suffused the peaks, and far to the south we saw snow-mountains receiving the first rays. The time was 4 a.m. All round us mist streamed over the scattered ridges, which only permitted the sunlight to penetrate at intervals, making fascinating patterns on the great mountains all around . . .

It was 9 a.m. when we got to our bivvy, and already the first spots of rain were falling from an overcast sky. Watson wakened me after four hours' interrupted sleep. It was raining heavily. Scott hotly rejected the idea of evacuation and forthwith turned over and returned to a state of coma. There was nothing to do but lie there and get wet. We stuck it out patiently until a half-gale struck us, whipping the protective sheet like a sail and hurling torrents of icy rain over us.

Clutching sleeping-bags and other gear, we made for some boulders and hurriedly improvised a shelter. Under this we got the primus going, a perfect fury of rain meanwhile battering down on the sheet as we fried our ham and eggs and swilled tea.

Our return down the glen was a rout. Spurts of water were pouring down my neck made the thought of dry clothes really alluring. Boulder-hopping and stumbling through birches, we eventually reached our objective only to meet disaster. The base-tent had been blown down, and every stitch of my clothing had been scattered and saturated. Films, books, maps etc, were in a similar state . . .

Gathering this merry flotsam together, we dejectedly made for the nearest house. The kindly people there took one look at us and immediately understood our plight. What we needed was a room and a fire and both were speedily forthcoming. With no dry clothes available, all I could do was wrap my damp sleeping-bag round me like a kilt and accept Scott's offer of a pullover. Rain beating on the windows made us glad indeed to be inside, cheered by the thought that directly our sleeping bags were dry we could snuggle down.

Morning brought a wonderful change. The fjord was flat calm and sunlight sparkled on the wet fields and snow mountains. Hanging our sodden garments out to dry, we seized needle and thread and started to repair sundry tears in the tent. It was a good thing we did, for before another twenty-four hours had elapsed we were at action stations. The over-taxed tent tore away at the guys, ripping the pegs out of the ground and bringing the whole affair down on top of us.

I must pass over our return to Lofoten and the happy days we spent on the great crags of the Raftsund. We also spent many pleasant hours fishing in the clear green of the Vestfjord and jolly evenings when the kindly crofter-fishermen of these parts allowed us to share hospitable firesides while they entertained us with songs and music. We had picked a bad summer, but during forty-five memorable days we packed in a full measure of adventure to add to our Himalayan memories. Taking everything into consideration, it was an excellent way of spending that last £50!

WIDE WORLD, 1952

TO THE ALPS

I had no experience of mountains other than those of Britain, and I knew that if I was to achieve my ambition of being a mountain explorer I should go to the Alps, learn about glaciers and hazards of crevasses and ice-falls, subject myself to the rarefied air of the heights and learn to read avalanche dangers associated with permanent snow, affected by frost and sun. So in early 1948, off I flew to Geneva with two others in the direction of Arolla. As I had only a fortnight they introduced me to the chief mountain guide of Evolena, Pierre Maurys.

I wanted his advice, since with currency restrictions then in force, I had a mere £35 of an allowance. He smiled and nodded his head comfortingly when I told him that I wasn't trying to engage him, but wondered if he could direct me where best to go to find peaks suitable for me to climb on my own. The date was 11th July and none of the highest summits had been climbed that season because of unsettled weather and heavy snowfall.

I told him something about my background, and learned that he had been to the Lake District as guest of John Sugden, a member of the Fell and Rock Club, his visit to gain some conversational practice in speaking English. The hotel in Les Hauderes where we talked was managed by his wife, and the pair were joint owners. As he ordered morning coffee, he excused himself to make a telephone call. When he came back he said, 'I have been talking to Madam Berens in Chamonix. She is a Dutch Lady who has engaged me for the whole

153

season, but is playing golf till the weather gets better. I can go with you to the Dent Blanche if you wish, and climb with you as a friend. But first I must go to church, then at 2 o'clock we shall set off to the Cabane Rossier. You stay here for family lunch. My wife will attend to the food we need for the climb.'

I could hardly believe my good fortune as we waved goodbye to his wife and two wee girls for the stony path zig-zagging ever upwards. Past alpine meadows bright with flowers for grey moraines giving way to glacier ice where we were in shrouding mist and sinking into deeper and deeper snow. The plod seemed never-ending but at 8 pm we were at the cabane, and soon bedded down 7,000 feet above our starting point.

At 4 am I heard the ring of Pierre's alarm watch. A meagre breakfast and by 5.30 we were tying on the rope and embarking on the shadowed ridge, while all around us summits of peaks glowed in the red light of sunrise. Below us the glaciers had the soft sheen of satin. Technical climbing began almost immediately on iced rocks and frozen snow. Gaining height we were in a world of mountains for level cloud filled all the deep valleys.

We could see now that the ridge ahead was in fierce condition, hung with cornices, the rock face hidden in new snow. It was the place from which a French party had retired the previous day because of avalanche danger. Pierre, who knew the face well, chose a rightward traverse, to the edge of the Grand Gendarme, whose pinnacle it was his intention to climb as being the safest way. Anchored to a good rock spike, I could take in the view around me: the Matterhorn, Obergabelhorn, Zinal Rothorn, Weisshorn, Mishabel, the Oberland peaks and the Mont Blanc range.

I had read that of all the mountains in the world, none surpasses the European Alps in form or variety, and that no other mountains can provide better training for the aspiring alpinist, or offer sterner tests in difficulty for the experienced. As yet I had no yardstick to judge the truth of this for this was my very first encounter with glaciated peaks rising so high above deep valleys. Looking back, I realise how lucky I was to be climbing with such a man as Pierre Maurys and to have the whole mountain to ourselves.

Most parties avoid the Grand Gendarme. Watching Pierre on its airy crest, his position would have satisfied the most earnest seeker of the sensational. Exposed above a great void, he had to remove a glove with his teeth at one point and, hanging on by one hand, tuck his ice-axe through the strap of his rucksack to leave his hands free to surmount the vertical crest of ice-veneered holds. He was smiling when I joined him and, pointing out the way ahead, said he was sure we would make the top.

Snow cornices and ice-plastered rocks, some rock climbing on clean stuff, more snow cornices, and at last, ahead of us, a fragile leaf of snow projecting into space – the summit.

We shook hands on top: "I congratulate you on the ascent of Dent Blanche," said Pierre, but it should have been the other way around. Pierre was the man to be congratulated after that bold lead. The half-hour spent on top was delightful. We had tea, beautiful stuff out of the flask, bread and raw bacon, and an orange, while all the time Pierre pointed out mountains, naming them until I could take in no more. One could only sit and let the awe of such an Alpine experience sink into one's being.

So ended my first ascent of a 14,000-foot [4000m] Alpine peak.

WEIR' WORLD

Sadly, as Tom noted, Maurys and a client were killed by a lightning strike on the Innominata Ridge of Mont Blanc in 1964.

THE ALPS ON SKI

Two nights without sleep, and the discomforts of third-class travel, could not diminish that impression of 1949 when I was on two week's leave from the Ordnance Survey. Other members of our ski-mountaineering party were already in Grindelwald, and I soon located them and set to assemble fourteen days' food for four in preparation for an early departure the following morning to the Jungfraujoch. Our loads felt alarmingly heavy, but meantime we needed sleep. All too soon we were cramming skis and rucksacks aboard a train that climbs higher than any other in the world, via a vein hacked out of the interior of the Eiger, but with passages for passengers to view the 6,000 feet of its infamous North Wall.

How strange to emerge at last on a railway station like any normal one, except that this one has a magic exit at 11,400 feet [3475m], an ice tunnel that leads horizontally to open on nothing but uncompromising steep mountain side falling abruptly to the Aletsch Glacier, the largest ice-stream in Europe. It was our route down to a cross-roads of glaciers called Concordia. But between us and its gentle gradient was the formidably steep drop from the tunnel which would require careful control on the descent with heavy rucksacks. We slid off, keeping speed down by gentle turns, then it was bliss to coast happily for seven effortless kilometres, until above us we saw our goal, the alpine hut perched on a rock, reached by steep ladders. We could lighten our loads by making a depot of half our food.

Rucksacks lightened, we turned our faces south-west towards another hut, the Hollandia, a 2,000- foot climb above, and a hard push for bodies just out from Britain, with ahead of us the bulging ice-falls and hanging seracs of the Aletschhorn. It was a welcome moment when we topped the final rise and saw the cabin perched on the lip of a rock ridge as the peaks flushed in the alpenglow.

Soup was uppermost in our minds as we entered the hut at 10,000 feet [3050m]. It was packed with Easter weekend Swiss skiers, and all were up before dawn to climb a peak and descend on frosty powder snow before the hot sun slowed ski-ing down. Skins fastened to the soles of our skis for climbing, we went for the Mittaghorn, by an ice-fall, to reach a crest of powder so dry that it squeaked below our skis. It was bliss up there, looking down on the soft blues of the Lauterbrunnen Valley, and letting the eyes range round the panorama of summits: Dent Blanche, Matterhorn, Weisshorn, MontBlanc and its neighbours. Then off with the skins for the descent, a swoop on light powder, showering like diamonds at every swinging turn of the skis. All too soon we were at the hut, eyeing with pleasure the route we had taken down from the 3,890-metre [12762ft] peak. We had the same conditions next day for the Ebnefluh.

We were away at 5 am, the peaks clear-cut in the starry sky, an alpenglow suffusing the tops with pink as we climbed the great expanse of the glacier narrowing to our pass, the Grunhornluke. My diary records: 'No morning since the world began can have been more perfect for the view that lay before us from its crest, snow sparkle underfoot; above us red rocks warm with colour, and the great face of our peak, the Finsteraarhorn, 14,022ft [4274m], highest in the Bernese Alps, in rock, snow and ice, shadowed against a blue-green sky.'

To reach it entailed a run down we had been looking forward to, a smooth descent on frozen snow with a surface of the lightest powder that made turning silent and effortless, and all too soon we were at the Finstreraar Hut, one of the remotest in the Oberland.

We wasted no time dumping our gear. Skins on our skis, we climbed steadily upwards, and made for the Hugisattel to the North Ridge. The climb was of the kind that Scottish mountaineers are familiar with in Glencoe and Ben Nevis. Step-cutting on frozen snow and clearing rock holds of ice we made height quickly, conscious that clouds were beginning to drop down on the mountain, and we were going to need all our time to get down before dark.

We made it but kept the rope on for descent on skis to the hut, moving cautiously in a heavily crevassed area, and at 7 pm we entered the hut conscious of our good fortune in having had such a rich reward from first light till last. We had snatched it just in time, for snow fell all that night and all of next day and the following night. We had the hut to ourselves, until on the second day the door was thrown open and in came a Swiss guide with two of his clients. Then just before dark a party of four Swiss railwaymen arrived worried because they were due back at work the next day, but the bad weather had forced them here when they failed to find the pass they were making for.

All we could do was sit out the bad weather, and it was still snowing when we left the freezing cold Finsteraar Hut for the climb back out, all linked to one rope, each taking a turn at trail breaking in exhaustingly deep snow. Not till we had pushed our way to the welcome of Concordia was there any respite from the gruelling hard work. We even had to push our way downhill so deeply did skis sink in the snow. But how good to get in where we had food, and ransack it for a communal meal with chance companions who were now friends.

Next day we said our goodbyes, the railway party skiing down the glacier which would take them to the Rhône Valley, while ours went exhaustingly uphill to the Jungfraujoch which we had descended so joyfully ten days before. With relief, after an hour we saw the black dots of people moving down towards us, and looked forward to reaching the trail they would have broken. They were a search party looking for the railwaymen, so were delighted to hear our news that they were safe and well.

WEIR'S WORLD

1 At the Shelter Stone in the Cairngorms: Tom Weir,
George Roger, Matt Marshall, Percy McFarlane

2 TOP: Tom inspecting the 'Viking' watermill at Dounby, Orkney
3 BOTTOM: The Guizer Jarl preparing for Shetland's Up Helly Aa winter festival

4 TOP: Shepherd Alex MacKenzie and his dogs
5 BOTTOM: An idyllic haymaking scene on the Island of Raasay

6 TOP: Hamish McInnes, mountaineer and inventor extraordinary
7 BOTTOM: John Ridgway, who set up an adventure school in Sutherland
after rowing the Atlantic with Chay Blyth

8 TOP: Adam Watson, long-time companion,
from the Cairngorms to Arctic Norway
9 BOTTOM: Cdr Victor Clark, DSC, inspirational captain
of the training schooner, *Captain Scott*

10 TOP: Heading for the Cobbler in the years when we had snow
11 BOTTOM: On the Braeriach plateau

12 TOP: Following the one-time Oban railway line in Glen Ogle
which closed in 1965
13 BOTTOM: Two skiers facing the Lairig Ghru in the Cairngorms

14 TOP: Dick Balharrie with nosey ponies inspecting a hind
and her calf at the Beinn Eighe Nature Reserve Centre
15 BOTTOM: Before the bridge: the Kylesku ferry in the 1960s,
looking to the Stack of Glencoul

16 Decorative fungus on a tree in Glen Lyon

17 TOP: Gulfoss, typical of the powerful waterfalls in Iceland
18 BOTTOM: A scientist catching puffins in the Faroe Islands,
where they formed part of the local diet

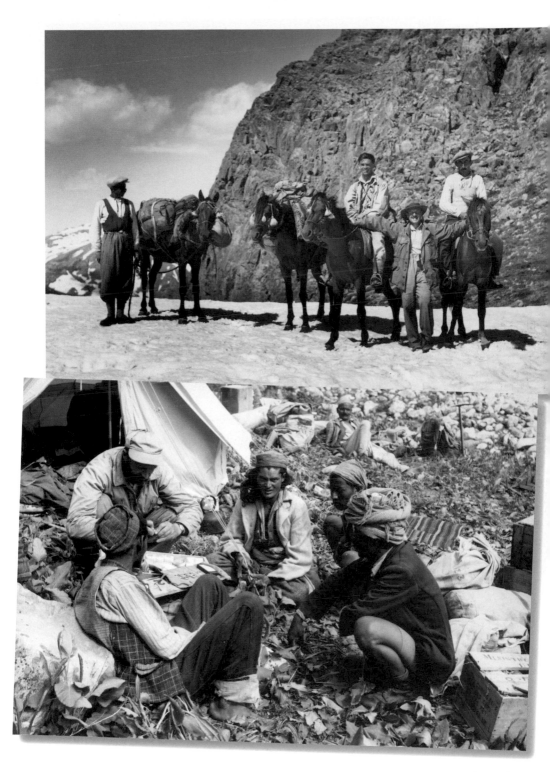

19 TOP: Douglas Scott and Tom Weir with guides
Memhet and Bahri in Turkish Kurdistan
20 BOTTOM: Tom Mackinnon (the team's medic)
with porters in the Garhwal Himalaya

21 TOP: Milking time: a Kurdish woman and children
with their flock of sheep and goats
22 BOTTOM: Young schoolboys in a remote Himalayan village

23 TOP: Stags and hinds in the Reay Forest, Sutherland
24 BOTTOM: The Great Stack of Handa, first reached in 1876
by a raiding party from Lewis

25 TOP: Construction work on the Garry Hydro-Electric Scheme: somewhat
pre Health and Safety days with the airborne worker
26 BOTTOM: Enlarging the Corpach basin on the Caledonian Canal

27 TOP: Stac Lee, one of the spectacular gannetries of the St Kilda group
28 BOTTOM: Tom Weir, Douglas Scott and Adam Watson and local lassies
on a Norwegian farm where they camped

29 TOP: 'The last train' as Aberfeldy Station was closed, 1965
30 BOTTOM: Clearing points and passing the tablet at Balquidder Station
(closed 1951)

THE JULIAN ALPS

Some words from Dr Longstaff led me to the Julian Alps of Yugoslavia [*now Slovenia*]. This is what the author of *This My Voyage* answered when he was asked what he thought of them: 'They have become, after 40 years' devotion to mountain scenery, the most desirable of all mountains. I want to visit them more than I desire to see again any other region of the Alps, more than I desire to see again the frosty Caucasus, Himalaya . . .'

Imagination is never so stirred as when it is quickened by anticipation, so the first sight of the Julians, grape-blue against the glow of a fiery sunset, held me spellbound. They stood above the clouds, an incredible vision above near, rain-blurred slopes, round which thunder rumbled.

As the train climbed through forests, chugging past lonely outposts of strip-cultivation, where tiny fields of wheat were yellowing, my impression was of a wild, almost primaeval land. Here among the pines, I was told, roamed bears, wild pigs, wolves and deer: a contrasting country to the neat fields and orchards of the fertile plain around Ljubljana – for limestone marks its frontiers dramatically; the Julians, springing north of the university town, make a dramatic boundary with Italy and Austria.

Everything is telescoped in the Julians, rock buttresses, razor edges, wooded bluffs, so that there is virtually no Alpine zone with chalets as in Switzerland. As Longstaff puts it 'The month's approach in the Himalayas is magically traversed in a day.' Only chamois can find footing on the middle slopes for these are of rock, and this is the finest chamois country in Europe. From the railway line in Ratece (approximately 3,000 feet above sea level) the walk through a forest of magnificent pine trees to an Alpine zone of dwarf conifers and red alpenrose occupies only an hour and a half. Red-backed shrikes and black redstarts were the commonest birds.

159

Never having seen a chamois before, it was a pleasure when going down to the river for a bathe to meet one poised on a rock, slender antlers raised and with every muscle of its fawn body, tipped with ebony along its spine, alert. Yet it didn't bolt, but merely sprang to a more inaccessible ledge to take another look before disappearing.

Girdling these mountains is a splendid chain of mountain huts, and that night I had my introduction to my first one with three Slovene alpinists who had befriended me in Ljubljana. We shared a little bedroom and had a simple meal of macaroni soup and a large plate of plain macaroni, with tea to follow; plain fare, at a cheap price, but my new found friends had come prepared and supplemented these scanty rations with sausage, bread and cheese. One can go anywhere in the Julians and be sure of food and shelter at a very moderate cost for climbing is the national sport of the Slovenes, and out of a population of less than 2,000,000, no fewer than 65,000 are members of the Alpine Association.

Triglav is the highest peak in the Julians, a fantastic mountain, the Ben Nevis of Yugoslavia, and everyone wants to know if you have climbed it. Legends cluster round it and dreamy-eyed climbers sing songs to it in every hut. Red paint-splashes cross the passes to it; it is situated in the midst of what Longstafff describes as '. . . a typically Tibetan desert; huge rounded slopes and hollow basins leading to the naked cliffs of a lunar landscape; not a tree; hardly a plant; lifeless.'

We went to it from the green fertility of the Trenta Valley beloved of Dr Julius Kugy, who wrote of the Julians in one of the best books of Alpine literature, *Alpine Pilgrimage*. From this beautiful glen we swung into a cirque of peaks blocking the head of the valley like a battlemented wall, wondering as we climbed how we were going to breach this face defending our peak.

There was a choice of two ways: by a rock climb up the wall and over the battlements, or by an amazing path blasted and engineered out of an easier part of the mountain. Bomb-

and bullet-holes and coils of rusty wire told the story of that path. We were on the old frontier between Italy and Slovenia, and the track led to an abandoned military post round which there had been much fighting. The Trenta valley where we had come from was under Austrian domination for many centuries except for a period between the two World Wars when it was ceded to Italy. Beloved Triglav and all its environs is now Slovene territory.

That night we stayed in a new mountain hut perched 7000 feet up, commanding a wide sweep of range on range of saw-toothed peaks and ridges, changing colour from steel-grey to blue-black, as high masses of clouds from the Adriatic drifted round them, investing them with mystery and a huge bulk out of all proportion to their 9000-foot size. Our hut had been rebuilt because a winter avalanche had destroyed the old one, and I had a chat with one of the young joiners working on it. He spoke not only English but Russian, German and Italian as well; and his intention when his day's work was over was to go up to the top of Triglav for the sake of the view. His ambition was to visit the high Alps of Switzerland.

We were somewhat unlucky with weather on Triglav and its associate peaks, but the impression of the fantastic wildness of this glaciated desert was perhaps heightened thereby. Rain and mist swept the tops, but there were sudden clearings and astonishing revelations of mountain edges set above the green ice of Triglav's 5000-foot north face which gives the longest rock climbs in Yugoslavia, and boasts its only glacier.

Every peak we climbed brought its own reward. Triglav is only 9395 feet [2864m] high, but in getting to it we had moved through scenery of astonishing contrasts, from fertility to desert. We were to see an even more amazing change when we crossed the bare Hribarice Pass plunging down slope after slope of desert rubble to find ourselves suddenly on a shelf of spreading pine trees, stolen, as Longstaff so nicely puts it, from the Canadian Rockies. 'A waste,' he says, 'but how beautiful, of rolling limestone levels covered with open forest pine. How could one expect such a piece of Western America in Europe?'

This is the Valley of the Seven Lakes – tiny lakes, each of which nestles on its own shelf of pine trees, for this landscape is a series of great and complex steps, and I found it hard to appreciate that by merely crossing its enclosing edge I could exchange my present surroundings for the Alpine pastures of the Trenta valley.

Scotch mist and rain had dogged us on the descent, but we were to see what Julian rain was like in the next twenty-four hours when it fell in monsoon torrents, and the hut filled up with Slavs driven from all parts to shelter. Soon we were all friends together, and with songs and stories the time quickly passed. All were eager to hear about life in Britain and to give their views on Yugoslavia. German proved the most useful common language among us.

A bright morning followed the rain, and in the space of an hour or two from leaving the hut we were to have our greatest surprise of the trip, when suddenly we stepped round a corner and found ourselves looking, not into another hidden shelf, but down a sheer mountain wall to a large lake cradled 2000 feet down – Bohinj Lake. The surprise of this left one almost breathless with astonishment.

Down the mountain face goes a zig-zag path, safeguarded by wooden steps and handrails, twisting down to a ravine formed by the waters of the Savica river where they thunder out of a hole in the cliff and plunge in a mighty waterfall after a long subterranean course.

Here the 'Tibetan desert' of Triglav and its lack of rivers is explained. All the waters on the heights percolate deep into the limestone to form an underground torrent which travels for miles before it suddenly bursts forth in this fierce jet. We followed the course of the river to its end in Bohinj Lake where we bathed – a perfect finish to a memorable day.

There was one other place we wanted to see and that was Martuljek. Longstaff had said of it: 'Is there anything else in all the Alps, including the whole range of the Julians, comparable to the hidden mystery of Martuljek?'

A short railway journey by Lake Bled and northward from Jesenice and we were there, on a sparkling morning, among meadows which wound to pine trees enclosing a gorge: beyond this was a fierce pinnacle called Speke. By tumbling waterfalls and broken rocks edged with pines we climbed, losing the path and finding it again; side-stepping to avoid coiled adders asleep on stones; or stopping to watch a sparrow-hawk describe a rapid loop in pursuit of a small bird. In the cool of the forest we brewed coffee on a wood fire.

Then came a moment when suddenly there were no more obscuring trees and ahead of us rose walls of rock 3000 feet sheer, splintered grey against a blue sky.

This was where Longstaff had made his bivouac, feeling himself '. . . as cut off from the world as any anchorite'. We had no bivouac and had simply to treasure the few hours spent among the dwarf scrub and the flowers, with the forest and gorges below, and above us peaks, secret and brooding, almost overwhelming in their steepness.

It was a vision of the Julians we left behind, for this region has been kept as a wild national park. There is one little log cabin for climbers but nothing in the way of equipped huts. Here are no fixed ropes or splashes of paint as in other parts of the Julians. A man is alone with the mountains, and the rock climbs here must be amongst the finest in Europe.

WIDE WORLD

CORSICA

Corsica was visited twice, in 1962 with Rhona, in 1969 with Len Lovat. Considering this, when I mentioned Corsica wasn't the Alps, a friend's response was, "No, it's better", which I think Tom would agree with, for Corsica, like the Julians, is part of the wilder, remoter, uncrowded, very beautiful mountains Tom most loved. I've certainly followed his dictum that 'Corsica was a place to come back to'. He flew each time; anything to avoid being on the sea.

We made plans to leave early by hired taxi, to the limit of the driving road, at 3,000 feet, in a canyon booming with the sound of water. This gorge forms a natural pass through the mountains by the Lac de Melo, but the road above our camping platform had been swept away by an avalanche whose cone of snow still blocked the river, and huge boulders lay above the place we would have to cross in order to climb Monte Rotondo, 8,400 feet.

After reconnaissance, and a pleasant day exploring the forest in company with ring ouzels and alpine choughs, we were away early next morning. Down we went to the snow-bridge, then walked on a grassy track zig-zagging up a pine-clad shoulder for 2,000 feet, until quite suddenly we were faced by an icy corrie where the step-cutting began. Ahead of us the black tooth of our peak looked tantalisingly close, flanked by rows of pinnacles each side, but as rope length followed rope length, it never seemed to get nearer. Meantime an advancing sea of grey-black clouds was swallowing up the valleys, and flakes of snow began to fall.

I had no intention of turning back now, not with the best bit of the climb before us – a steep gully in the final crag. We were on top by 4 pm so the climb had taken eight hours, all of it full of interest. Among the splendid Corsican pines, 150 feet and 200 feet high, mistle thrushes had been singing, greater spotted woodpeckers were distributed almost to the snow-line, and I'd seen my first wheatears of 1962 just below the snow, among dwarf birch and alders.

Now there was no time to linger, but push down the steps we had cut in the icy snow until it was possible to glissade on open slopes free of rocks, to cross the snow-bridge over the river at dusk, climb up to the tent and get the Primus on for welcome soup and tea. What a night of rain followed! Water-

164

falls became noisier, and now and again there was the crash of rock-falls. We feared we might be flooded out, camped on such thin soil, but the ground held firm and I suspect was the only dry spot in the Restonica Gorge. We lifted our camp in the morning and pushed down to Corte.

Corsica was the place to come back to, and seven years later, in the month of May, Len Lovat and I camped below the Punta di Ferro in the range known as the Aiguilles di Bavella, and every day for a week looked out from our tent at 4,000 feet on the red ball of the sun rising above the Mediterranean. Generally we were awake by 4.30 am and away as soon as possible so as to avoid being fried on the granite. The mornings were so beautiful, wandering through alpine meadows and gullies spiked with Corsican pines, to rocky places that could be described as hanging gardens. Also, without guidebooks, there was the joy of exploration, finding our own ways. We hired a Renault and after a week on this range drove north to the corkscrew roads for the highest peaks on the island, for mixed climbing on rock and snow. Paglia Orba is the Matterhorn of Corsica and, restocked with food, we camped below it a few days later. Pine trees, a roaring river, green-sward for our tent, no-one but ourselves in the glen, Paglia Orba before us, we were away at six in the morning to storm the bastion. Instead of a mixed climb we were surprised , once we had negotiated two red-rock towers, to find its upper part very like the snow-plastered crags of Ben Nevis in April, when Scotland's highest summit is still in part-winter condition.

Soon we were hacking a way up the frozen snow covering the rocks, and gradually, from the cold blue shadow, we crept into warm sunshine and took to the clean rocks to reach the summit at mid-day. One peak in particular held our eyes, the famous Tafonato, a narrow pinnacled blade whose perpendicularity is pierced by a window through which we could see daylight. We visited it two days later, after a technically hard rock climb on the Cinque Fratti, and a traverse of its five pinnacles. From up there we had the sight of two golden

165

eagles being mobbed by an attacking force of squealing alpine choughs and a croaking raven.

Now for the Tafonato. Everything about it had a special aura, even the take-off point on the narrow col – a veritable neck of snow cornice between red pinnacles. The beginning was, in fact, a bergschrund – a miniature crevasse formed by the snow-ice shrinking away from the rock wall. We had one anxious moment here when a boulder whizzed past us from above. We waited, listening, then feeling that this was just a one-off rock-fall, we stepped across the gap between snow tongue and rock, moved up unroped, and were soon whooping with delight, so sound and bristling with holds was the steep rock.

We went straight for the great hole gashing the upper mountain and arrival on its sill was an exciting moment, looking down on a new valley, vertically below. What a situation, on a rock peak so thin that from the window to the summit we wound right round the mountain, finishing on a superb wall that was airy rock climbing at its best, near vertical, and with small perfectly shaped holds for toes and hands.

There was an unexpected moment of magic on the way down, when at the window, I heard an absent-minded whistle which I thought was from Len and he thought was from me. It was a glissando of four notes – whee-oowhee ooo' – then the maker flew past in a flash of lavender and crimson, and like a butterfly landed near us, to be joined by two others – wall creepers, birds I had last seen in Nepal. What a delight they were to watch in this setting, dove-grey on chest and back, wings red edged with black, white spotted on the primaries, short black tails and longish curved bills, and black throats. Constantly as they climbed they flicked their wings to show their red flashes.

Our last climbs involved a bivouac in a corrie of high crags and snow-fields. I slept little, because the night was too perfect, with the brightness of the stars and the Milky Way like lace. Also there was a half moon poised on the crest of a jagged ridge, and as it dropped, the pinnacles were edged in halo. With only a light sleeping bag, I was glad of my quilted jacket. We got the eggs on the boil at 4 am to be away at five.

Above us was Punta Minuta, 8,800 feet, no more than four hours away, up rock ribs and frozen snow. From its summit we looked down on Calvi and across the glen at Paglia Orba and Tafonato, which gave a feeling of intimacy with this wild country where we were the only climbers. In all, we climbed ten peaks and failed one.

WEIR'S WORLD

VII

A VARIETY OF INTERESTS

'The spirit of enquiry leads up a lane that has no ending' wrote Beatrix Potter in her diary and Tom exemplified this in his long career. Tom had a wide range of interests and was fascinated by places, their people and histories and the readable features he wrote were always well-researched, often first appearing in the Scots Magazine.

THE TROSSACHS

The word Trossachs is said to derive from *bristly* which is a good description of what is perhaps the finest bit of small-scale country in Scotland. Here Sir Walter Scott got his inspiration for *The lady of the Lake* and *Rob Roy*. And it was the publication of these books 150 years ago which brought the first tourist boom to the Highlands.

Earlier travellers did not write so ecstatically of the Bens and Glens. The usual impression they brought back was of a disagreeable country of ugly scenery, where roads were bad and the accommodation worse. As for the Trossachs, despite its proximity to the Forth and Clyde valleys, it was one of the last bits of the Highlands to be civilised, thanks to the warring MacGregors, whose most infamous son, Rob Roy, was a legend even in Scott's time.

Rob Roy had died an old man, peacefully, with his boots off, in Balquhidder in 1734. Living in a Scotland weakly governed from England, Rob began imposing his own discipline of law by guaranteeing protection for those who could pay for it. In that time money was scarce and cattle was the true currency of the Highlands, so Rob, having set himself up as a cattle dealer, could ensure that a drove could get to market if protection money was paid. If not, then the cattle would mysteriously disappear.

Many tales exist about Rob's exploits, and although Sir Walter Scott was not born until thirty-seven years after the death of Rob, the outlaw was still very much alive in folk memory when Scott first came to the Highlands as a lawyer's clerk to superintend an eviction. Rob would have hated life in the Highlands that Scott was seeing, with the clans disinte-

171

grating and the Highlanders being forcibly evicted from their lands to provide sheep grazing.

Law and order was on the march. Thomas Telford was building the Caledonian Canal and a road network of nearly 1,000 miles, and Clydeside had become the centre of the new steamship building industry, thanks to James Watt's revolutionary discovery of the principle of the separate condenser. Sir Walter Scott was living during a time of industrial revolution, and though his mind dwelt on the romance of the past, new discoveries were opening up the Trossachs.

The subsequent tourist traffic provided a business opportunity for the Loch Katrine MacGregors who plied boats for hire between Stronachlachar and the Trossachs. In 1843 they showed that they were still the wild MacGregors when a small iron steamer was launched on the loch threatening their livelihood. They responded by towing it away during the night and sinking it.

By this time however, Glasgow Corporation had plans to raise the level of Loch Katrine and bring its Highland water to Glasgow. To do this meant building the biggest aqueduct in Britain, and when the soft water flowed at the turn of a tap in 1859, the consumption of soap was halved in Glasgow. At the same time a slate quarry was opened above Aberfoyle which was the third largest in Scotland and continued to function until 1951.

I wonder what Sir Walter would make of the changes if he came back today? One thing I am fairly sure about is that he would find the Trossachs just as beautiful as when he wrote his poetry. At the time when Scott was writing of this territory, trees were mainly used to provide charcoal for iron smelting, while the bark of the oaks was utilised to tan leather. For these purposes the Duke of Montrose planted 1,200 acres of timber in twenty years. He also built the toll road from Aberfoyle, still known today as the Duke's pass, though it was rebuilt in the thirties and has been free to the public ever since.

On that high road from Aberfoyle to Loch Katrine you

travel through some of the best modern forestry in Scotland, now part of the Queen Elizabeth Forest Park. Here you can appreciate how nature and man manages to mix natural oaks and birches with American spruces and European larches. To see it at its best, leave your car at the little parking place near the summit and take a walk up to the indicator viewpoint. In autumn there are very few more colourful places in all Scotland when the deer grass is crimson and rock peaks and lochs are patterned with the gold of larches and birches.

I have a particular affection for this bit of country because I grew up with its spruce trees. Indeed I knew my way over Rob Roy's territory even before the Forestry Commission began their work in 1940. Today the woods are so vast that I think even Rob would have a hard job to sort out all the trails, with something like 170 miles of forest track. My own feeling is that the Trossachs is a much more interesting place than when I first got to know it.

The wild life is so much richer today especially for the birds of prey: hen harriers, short eared owls, sparrow hawks and buzzards which hunt the woodland fringes while, in the clearings, you can listen to the liquid bubbling of blackcock at dawn, and at dusk, listen to the churring of nightjars. There are also crags where peregrine falcons nest, and a familiar sound on a still evening is the thin reeling of grasshopper warblers.

It is fortunate that this forest with a highly scenic road passing through its middle has never suffered a serious fire. "The public are the best vigilantes," says the Commission. Early alarm, quick communications and a dependable regular fire service has taken away much of the worry. Most of the timber is now beyond the first vulnerable ten years, so the fire risk is less. The park has its own Roving Ranger who patrols constantly in his vehicle. The Ranger is employed to help people enjoy themselves, and he does his best to encourage them to make full use of the opportunities for fishing the lochs, walking the hills, learning about the trees, or hiring a pony to go

173

trekking the trails. The Commission take a lot of trouble to provide the maximum recreational facilities. On the timber production side, they expect to harvest something like 70,000 tons by 1992. The present Labour force is about sixty-five.

Loch Katrine is eight miles long with an average width of one mile, and half its total length is over 400 feet deep, with a maximum depth of 500 feet. One of the best places to see it is to sail from the Trossachs pier in the *Sir Walter Scott*. The first part, under the crags and knolls of Ben Venue is especially fine, but there is never a dull moment on the 1¾ hr. trip. The big pylons you see striking across the hills of the upper reaches of the loch are those of the Cruachan Pumped Storage Scheme. Incidentally, the sail is very cheap due to the fact that the *Sir Walter Scott* has been plying the loch since the beginning of the century and has long since paid her way.

Ben Venue throws down a bouldery north-eastern spur, forming a narrow pass peppered with boulders high above the loch, the *Bealach nam Bo*, the Pass of the Cattle, which Rob Roy used to drive stolen cattle to secret hide-outs. When I visited Rob's grave at Balquhidder one day and heard that thieves had stolen the bronze railing and the chains from around his grave, I could almost see in my mind's eye the image of Rob looking up at me, the powerful, red-headed man, slightly bow-legged, with abnormally long arms, shaking his head at such a mean action, unthinkable for one like himself who was of noble blood. And true enough, the real story of Rob Roy is one of generosity. He shared his bounty with the poor, and never killed a man although he dearly loved a fight.

Perhaps this is what appealed to Scott, himself a highly civilised man with forebears who were Border reivers. As an adventurer with the pen, Scott has no equal. When he built Abbotsford, his mansion on the river Tweed near Melrose, it was worthy of the man he was. He earned more money from the pen than anyone had ever done before, but he died in debt, and he probably killed himself by overwork trying to pay off his creditors. The debt was due to the failure of his publishers. If there is life after death then I know two red-headed men who should be great company for each other.

TOM WEIR'S SCOTLAND

150 YEARS OF THE CALEDONIAN CANAL (1972)

To trace the beginning of the Caledonian Canal we have to back to 1773 when James Watt reported on the practicability of a shipping canal through the Great Glen. Studying the full sixty miles separating the Atlantic from the North Sea, Watt had seen that the watershed was a mere 115ft., and that nature had already provided a waterway of ribbon lochs for all but a third of the distance. He estimated that for a cost of £165,000 coastal ships would be able to avoid the unfavourable winds and strong currents of the Pentland Firth and fishing smacks would have east and west coast waters open to them, and the Baltic and West Indian trade would be stimulated.

But the Government did not act, not even when John Rennie had drawn up another scheme in consultation with Watt in 1793. Then in 1801 it commissioned Thomas Telford to visit the Highlands and report on what public works would be most likely to benefit the natives and teach them the habits of industry. Telford was asked to look into every aspect of communications and trade, suggest where roads, harbours and fishing stations might be built, and advise on the possibility of a canal along the route surveyed by Watt and Rennie.

The energetic Telford – the son of a Border shepherd and a time-served stone mason – was forty-four years of age, and behind him the solid achievement of connecting the Severn, Dee and Mersey by the Ellesmere Canal. He had fought his way to the top, moving from Eskdale to Edinburgh, then to London, learning dock and wharf construction in Portsmouth to become surveyor of public works in Shropshire by the time he was thirty. In his Highland survey for the Government, Telford saw that the various aspects of his remit were 'not only practicable but are capable of being formed into one intimately connected system, which would evidently have a striking effect upon the welfare and prosperity of the British Empire'.

This resulted in him being sent back to the Highlands the following year to report more fully and extend his survey. Exhausted by his travels, he spent the winter writing up a staggeringly detailed plan, for a 20ft.-wide Caledonian Canal linked to a road programme covering 920 miles of new construction, together with harbours and churches. The Government acted with unusual decision, agreeing to pay the full cost of the canal and accepting half the cost of other works.

The canal had taken on a new importance to the government because of the danger to naval and coastal ships from attacking French privateers. This, and the road programme, would also help to stem the tide of emigration from the Highlands. Asked to report on the emigrant situation, Telford had stated that 3,000 were in the process of leaving, and thrice as many preparing to leave the following year. The Government feared that if too many Highlandmen emigrated they would lose their finest source of military recruits.

Telford was appointed as principal engineer of road and canal works at 3gns. a day plus travelling expenses. William Jessup was the consulting engineer, a man with whom Telford was to associate happily during the next twenty-five years. And from the Ellesmere Canal he brought another two outstanding superintendents, Matthew Davidson and John Telford, who began work before the end of that year on the Caledonian Canal's eastern and western terminals.

But even as Telford collected his gangs of stonemasons from the shores of the Moray Firth, and gathered his labourers from Lochaber, Lismore, Kintyre, Skye, the braes of Morar and elsewhere, an event was taking place on the Forth and

Clyde Canal that was to have world-wide significance in altering the course of shipping history.

That event was the trial of the first steamship, using James Watt's revolutionary discovery of the principle of the separate condenser, which is still regarded as being 'perhaps the most basic invention of modern times'. Telford was being pressed to make more building speed, but the canal that he thought he could build in seven years was to take nineteen, by which time ninety-five steamships had been built in Scotland, and Clydeside had become the world centre of a new industry.

Government interest lapsed owing to the ending of the French wars and the continual expense. Yet even in the urgent days when Telford was being pushed to make more speed, he was having to pay off some of his badly-needed workforce because the Government was alarmed at the cost of his labour bills. It was a false economy, because wages and costs of materials were to escalate all too soon.

It took five years to build the three lowest locks of the Fort Augustus flight, with steam pumps going – James Watt again – to get rid of the water and allow the work to go on. In fact the lowest lock had to be 20ft. below the level of Loch Ness because of the loose gravel. But the most difficult piece of engineering was at the Clachnaharry sea lock on the Beauly Firth where the mud was 55ft. thick and the entrance had to be carried 440yds. beyond the shore line. The eastern section from the Beauly Firth to Fort Augustus had been open to traffic for four years before the first passage from sea to sea was made. Henry Bell established his steamship business in 1820, taking six hours to Fort Augustus, where a diligence took passengers down the military road to Fort William to board another ship and sail for the Clyde through the Crinan Canal.

In the end the canal was opened before it was ready, and the depth of 20ft. envisaged by Telford had dropped to 12ft. owing to the costs of getting greater depth by dredging and tearing a way through a tangle of giant oaks embedded in

177

the entrance of Loch Oich where they had been carried down river in distant times.

The violent criticisms of the costly canal died down as 800 vessels passed from sea to sea in the first eighteen months and a new service of steam boats plied between Glasgow and Inverness. And at the same time as the Caledonian Canal was opened Telford had completed his great Highland road-building programme, achieving more for his country than any other single man before him.

Telford died in 1834, disappointed in his outmoded canal, but it was being brilliantly successful in one of its main aims, as a source of employment for destitute Highlanders as its banks and walls kept collapsing. Also it needed deepening and after being closed for three years it was reopened in 1847 with a depth of 17ft. by which time it had cost the Government £1.4 million – nearly three times as much as Telford had estimated.

The deepened canal did not attract more revenue, though it was popular with the visitors to the Highlands, and 15,000 passed through it by steamer in 1863, just two years before the Perth-Inverness road opened, ushering in an era of increasing speed. By 1909 a Royal Commission dismissed the canal as antiquated, yet it could pass ships 150ft. long and 35ft. beam, drawing 13ft. 6in. of water, whereas the successful Forth and Clyde canal could accommodate ships no more than 68ft. 6in. long by 19ft. 8 in. beam. The difference was that the Forth and Clyde canal was serving an industrial area.

The Government had to act to save the canal, no longer important to coastal shipping, when Laggan Lock collapsed and banks at Corpach, Bananvie and Fort Augustus crumbled. The reconstruction proved its value in 1914 when war broke out and vast quantities of explosive mines and military stores had safe passage by avoiding the Pentland Firth. Not so much use of the canal was made in the Second World War.

Mechanisation of all locks was completed in 1969, and the building of a Pulp Mill at Corpach resulted in the basin having to be enlarged to accommodate timber ships. During this period of renovation the canal was closed for ten months between 1964 and 1965, when drainage revealed some of the original Telford workmanship. The bigger basin has resulted in a good turn-round of ships and a general increase in trade. The passage time has been reduced an hour or two by mechanisation, and the general future of the canal seems more assured.

The most heartening aspect of the Caledonian Canal traffic is that it had greatly increased over the Fifties and Sixties, with a steadily mounting number of yachts and cabin cruisers adding to the fishing boats who are its main users. It seems certain that the recreational use of the canal will increase with more leisure, since the broad waters of the canal provide sporting travel against a background of peaks rising as high as Ben Nevis. [*Recreational use now dominates.*] No pleasure ship operates the full length of the Caledonian Canal, but there is a daily sailing from Inverness in summer to Loch Ness by the converted ice-breaker *Scott II*, which has accommodation for sixty-five passengers.

The northern approach was a route long before there was a canal with naval vessels victualling the garrison at Fort Augustus. In 1651 Cromwell's forces used Loch Ness as a waterway. No doubt the first users were the early men using dug-out canoes to penetrate the hostile forests. The paradoxical thing is that Telford's great engineering work would have been in vain but for the steamship, for navigation proved too difficult for an age of sail.

WEIR'S WAY

179

LARGO REMEMBERS SELKIRK

The folk who have the good luck to live in the auld Seatoun o Largo declare their village to be the Riviera of Fife's East Neuk. It felt like it in the few days I spent there recently. My guide was Allan Jardine, a descendant of Alexander Selkirk's brother, so the first stop had to be the famous statue erected by Allan's grandfather David Gillies, 100 years ago.

We approached it by way of a narrow street of traditional cottages. The life size statue looks down from the second storey of one of these and the plaque reads: 'In Memory of Alexander Selkirk, Mariner, the original of Robinson Crusoe, who lived on the Island of Juan Fernandez in complete solitude for four years and four months. He died in 1723, [1721] Lieutenant of HMS Weymouth. This statue was erected by David Gillies, net manufacturer, on the site of the cottage where Selkirk was born'.

It shows a rugged, bearded figure dressed in goatskins, sewn into knee-length trousers and tunic, his right hand shading his eyes, the left gripping his gun. It was the work of T. Stuart Burnett, and was cast in bronze at Leith by Sir John Steele, R.A. When the Countess of Aberdeen unveiled the statue on 11 December 1885, 500 railway excursionists travelled from Dundee to witness the ceremony.

Allan Jardine's wife, Ivy, has researched the life of Alexander Selkirk, even travelling to Chile and flying from Santiago over the Pacific for 2½hours to make the dramatic landing on the island where Selkirk watched every day for a ship to take him off. She went with her son, also Allan, and two friends from Largo to meet the people who live on the island. She looks back on the trip as a wonderful adventure, and recalled for me the thrill of dropping out of the clouds on to the tiny airstrip perched sensationally on the edge of 800 foot sea cliffs. Waiting for them were fishermen with mules to take them and their luggage down arid slopes to the seashore, and into a fishing boat for a thrilling two-hour sail to the inhabited part of the island. On the way they passed sea lions basking on the rocks and admired the changing colours of the water, alive with fish. As they sailed, two lobsters were cooking over a fire in the centre of the boat. These were later served to the passengers along with the local white wine.

The islanders came out to greet them with shouts of welcome and the first thing Ivy did was plant the heather she had brought from beside the Crusoe Hotel. Ahead of them were six days of exploring the 12 by 5 mile island, including a climb up to 2,800 feet to the look-out point which Selkirk visited every day in the hope of seeing a sail. Once he had to run for his life when pursued by crew from enemy ships, and only his fleetness of foot saved him.

Up there, Ivy's son, Allan, placed a commemorative plaque, beside another placed by Commodore Powell and the officers of *HMS Topaz* in 1868. It records that Alexander Selkirk '... was landed from the *Cinque Ports* galley, 12th February, 1709.'

A privateer is a ship owned and officered by private persons authorised to capture enemy merchant vessels. The *Cinque Ports*, on which Selkirk was the navigator, was such a ship. As a result of gun battles it was in a dangerous condition, and the death of the Captain had placed in command an officer he disliked intensely. Selkirk had pleaded that the ship should dock for repair. This was refused, so he demanded to be put ashore on Juan Fernandez with his belongings and some food.

He knew that there was water and some firewood on the island, that there were goats and sea-lions and turtles, and he could survive as other people had done, notably an Indian, marooned by accident, who had spent three years there before being rescued. English sailors had also been marooned there in the late 17th century. It was well known as a good anchorage for buccaneers.

What Selkirk didn't know though was how he would cope with loneliness, for his life had been spent on crowded ships where living space was at a premium. He was 28, and soon became depressed and melancholy. At first, he lived in a cave and ate only when he was driven by hunger. Later he moved into the hills where he built two huts. Rats nibbled his bare feet, so he made friends with cats descended from domestic animals which had abandoned ships for life ashore.

He might have settled down happily to island life if he had known that *Cinque Ports* had foundered shortly after leaving and that the eight who survived were taken prisoner by the Spaniards and held in Lima jail for seven years – among them the hated Captain. As it was, it took him eight months to find contentment in solitude. Reading, praying and singing psalms had brought comfort and ease of mind. In later life, he claimed his Christianity had been a great comfort to him.

The Largo party were taken to Selkirk's cave, and found two families living in it and some women outside cooking, as children played nearby. They saw the wild goats whose flesh and hairy skins had been lifesavers for Selkirk. The islanders live mainly by fishing, and there is an abundance of wild vegetables and fruits. Without cars, newspapers and television they lead a simple life and entertained their visitors with flutes and guitars. They had never seen or heard the bag-pipes. Allan, who had been pipe-major at Fettes college, put that right by playing them selections and two special pieces: one a lament in memory of the period of melancholy during Selkirk's first year of loneliness, then a reel as the navigator found joy in his desert island life.

When Britain claimed the island from illegal possession by Spain in the 18th century, the Chilean Government installed a garrison on Juan Fernandez in case of a takeover by Britain. About 120 years ago, the island became a penal settlement. The islanders today are mostly descended from these prisoners.

Ivy has never been able to forget the beautiful island and its tranquil way of life. She would love to go back and spend at least a year there and do something for the people, perhaps teach traditional Scottish dancing, Fair Isle knitting and handicrafts.

However, she has been researching the history of Largo and working on a volume to complement her *Seatoun of Largo*, a collection of Victorian photographs. Under a picture of the fishing harbour as it used to be, are the words: 'He that will view the Kingdom of Fife must go round the coast, and no coast in all Britain has so many quaint, charming old sea-side towns with histories so interesting.'

The quotation is from Daniel Defoe (1660 – 1731) who was a political agent as well as a prolific author. He was deeply interested in promoting British trade with the South Seas, and there is no doubt he was intrigued by the rescue of Alexander Selkirk.

Finding Selkirk was a stroke of luck for Captain Woodes Rogers, for about 50 of his men were in a bad way with scurvy and required fresh food and vegetables to cure them. They were taken ashore to camp and a party went with Selkirk to collect all the food they needed. He amazed them by outrunning the ship's bulldog to catch a goat. He knew where succulent greens grew, and the sick men were soon on the mend. When it came to leaving the island, his knowledge of local winds and currents was of immense value.

Within a short time he was given command of a ship with a crew of 100 that had been taken as a prize, and he was to go round the world before returning home with £800 in his pocket, his share of the loot. It was a voyage with plenty of risks, raiding along the Pacific coast from Chile to Panama, dominions of Spain at the time. The most rewarding booty was gold and silver being taken from Mexico and Peru to the Spanish Treasury in Europe.

Rich in plunder as the voyage was, it was high on hardship, in ships holed by gunfire, with much fever and dysentery on board. In hungry times men ate rats and paid as much as sixpence for them. It was October 1711 when Selkirk arrived back in England via the Hebrides. The full story of the first circumnavigation of the world for 123 years can be read in *A Cruising Voyage Round the World* by Captain Woodes Rogers.

It doesn't tell though, of the return home to Largo of Selkirk, arrayed in splendid finery, when he was thought to be long dead. Even his mother didn't recognise him for it appears that his face had become much more thoughtful looking. Indeed, it was remembered by his shipmates privateering with Woodes Rogers that he was never rough with captives but kindly, especially with the women. Happiness, however, he seems to have left behind on the island for he is quoted as saying, 'I am now worth £800, but shall never be so happy as when I was not worth a farthing.'

He was restless and couldn't settle to an idle life. Sometimes he would take a boat to Kincraig Point and would stay there for a time because it reminded him of his island. He took solitary walks, a favourite one being to Keil's Den where a burn ran close beside the ruin of an ancient keep. It was hereabouts that he met a 16-year-old girl milking a cow. Her name was Sophie Bruce and he ran off with her to London. About a year later we hear of him going to sea as a naval lieutenant. Before his departure he made a will consigning all his worldly goods to Sophie.

In 1719, he was aboard *HMS Enterprise* in Loch Alsh in a flotilla of three frigates intent on bombarding Eilean Donan Castle, then occupied by a force of Jacobites reinforced by 300 Spaniards. The castle was reduced to ruins, and a land battle between Government forces and the Jacobites took place in Glen Shiel, the defeated Jacobites retreating over the top of a Kintail peak now known by the name of Sgurr nan Spainteach, *the peak of the Spaniards*.

When next we hear of Alexander Selkirk, he is in Plymouth, married to a merry widow by the name of Frances Candice who kept a public house much frequented by sailors. On his wedding day, he made a new will leaving all his worldly goods to his wife. Then he went to sea, contracted a fatal fever, and was buried at sea somewhere off the coast of West Africa. Sophie contested the claim of Alexander's widow to his effects, but because of the differences between Scottish and English law, she lost.

184

Selkirk had left Largo to avoid being called before the congregation following his behaviour with the lassies. Nothing is known of his career till taken on to the Cinque Ports *as navigator – which might suggest he was already acquainted with Pacific waters. There is no evidence of Defoe having met Selkirk.*

EXPLORING SCOTLAND

Tom's interest in trains started early; living in Springburn it could hardly have been otherwise for most of the population worked in the locomotive-building industry which dated back to 1842. His mother worked in the yards, his father (killed in World War One) had been an electrical engineer, his mother's father an engine driver, his mother's mother an engine fitter and wagon painter. In the Seventies he researched and took photographs for a series of four booklets on the Kyle, Mallaig, Oban and Highland lines, still valued by railway aficionados, full of concentrated information. Sadly, only one, much abbreviated, can be given here as an example.

One of the few times I have seen Tom abashed was following his mentioning, in a 'Scots Magazine' article, how he had been given a lift across Rannoch Moor in a goods train, an indiscretion that saw an admonitory memo being circulated to all drivers.

If Tom's railway books are much sought after then so are his books on the Scottish Lochs mentioned in the bibliography. They are packed with facts and figures, history and folklore, and illustrated with his own pictures. Lochs or trains, these books are treasured so are difficult to find.

THE RAILWAY WINDING NORTH

At Dunkeld you have the feeling of having entered the High-lands, with the Tay compressed between prickly hills for the first time and wooded slopes replacing fields. The bridge over the river, connecting Birnam on this side with Dunkeld on the far bank, was a ferry point across the Tay until Thomas

Telford built his bridge in 1809 and the first stage coach in history ran the 117 miles of road between Inverness and Perth. The journey took ten hours.

The train comes in through Birnam Wood, made famous by Shakespeare's Macbeth, when MacDuff's men took down branches from the trees and, hiding behind them, moved against the murderer of King Duncan, fulfilling the prophecy: 'Macbeth shall never vanquished be until Great Birnam wood to high Dunsinane Hill shall come against him'. (Shakespeare was in Dunkeld in 1601 on his way north with his dramatic company to play in Aberdeen. The tradition has it that he heard the bones of the story here.)

The train runs parallel to the A9 along the green flats of Strath Tay, on natural terraces of alluvium, steep wooded hills on each side. The Duke of Atholl's cannons fired canisters loaded with seeds of pine, larch and spruce onto Craigie Barns and Craig Bhinnein and the exploding canisters scattered the seeds from which sprang seedling trees which grew into a forest. Under Craigie Barns, below the A9, is a fragment of General Wade's military road, built from Inverness to Dunkeld by Drumochter between 1728 and 1734. In the space of two decades Telford gave us 920 miles of new roads, including the A9. And it was one of his assistants, Joseph Mitchell who built the original Perth-Inverness line.

Of the stone Garry viaduct of ten arches Mitchell merely says they are 35 feet high. Their total length is 508 feet and the cost was £10,000. In fact it is a work of art in stone, built on a graceful curve in a river gorge of natural beauty. The Soldier's Leap is down on the river below, marking the spot where a sentry of the defeated army leapt 17 feet across the rocky River Garry to escape the victorious Highlanders under Viscount Dundee in 1689.

Out of Killiecrankie the valley widens and the train sweeps over the River Tilt into Blair Atholl station. In 1974 the staff was one porter and three signalmen, where there used to be 59, including stationmaster, two clerks, two porters, three

186

guards, three signalmen and three carriage-and- wagon examiners.

Porter Jimmy McBain, who has been here for 25 years and has seen the Highland Railway become the LMS and finally British Railways, works from 13.00 hours until 21.30 hours six days a week. On his day off he doesn't want to go anywhere because he'd rather be here! He showed me the mark against the station building wall where the Duke of Atholl's private waiting room used to be. The Duke, an early opponent on the coming of the railway soon became one of its advocates.

* * * *

In this wilder stretch of Glen Garry the train runs for much of its course above 1000 feet. When Joseph Mitchell stayed as guest of the Duke to show him the proposed line of the railway and win over his favour he mentioned to him that 36 years earlier he had breakfasted in that room with the Duke's grandfather. The Duke replied: "Ah! How odd! Your father built the Tilt Bridge and made the new road below the castle and now you are come to make the railway".

Mitchell had inherited his father's job of Inspector of Highland Roads and bridges before becoming a railway engineer, and inherited much goodwill from landed proprietors. He had staked out the route of the line for miles with white flags to indicate his proposals to the Duke of Atholl, and objections were quickly overcome. Suffering from cancer of the throat and very ill, the Duke had the pleasure of travelling from the summit of the line to Pitlochry on the eve of its opening. Mitchell records: "He seemed to enjoy the rapid motion in descending from the County March at the rate of 50 miles an hour – rather a dangerous speed on a new-made line".

Dalnaspidal is the highest railway halt in Britain, at around 1400 feet. Closed to passengers in 1965, the station is opened when the A9 over Drumochter is blocked by snow. And storms can be sharp and deadly here. The trench-like loch

187

lying south of the station is Loch Garry, whose waters are tapped into Loch Ericht by a five mile tunnel running north west to a power house operated by remote control.

The County March cottages (on the Perth side of the boundary) are uninhabited now; they were built for surfacemen in telephonic communication with signal boxes and stations. Food was delivered by goods train and when the lady of one of these houses took an acute attack of appendicitis during a snowstorm a passenger train picked her up for the quick run to Perth.

Lillian McLagan who was brought up in these cottages has written: 'We lay in bed at night listening as the great engines toiled up to the summit, sometimes having to stop to build up steam, then having reached the top, the heavy wagons bucked and jolted and rattled helter-skelter down the other side'. The great geologist Sir Archibald Geikie wrote of Drumochter, 'Even the comforts of a railway carriage and a good locomotive do not wholly deprive one of its terrors, for trains are snowed up there almost every winter, but no one who cursorily makes its acquaintance can realise what the Pass Drumochter was in the old coaching days'.

General Wade in 1728 was the first to tackle its bould and burns with a road squad, working in straight lines where possible, building to a standard width of 16 feet. Ordinary rankers, from 500 to 600 of them, got 6d a day extra in pay working a season from May to October on the road. Neil Munro's The New Road we get a picture of the pass facing the troops: 'a bleaker prospect was difficult to save that the innumerable streams, loudly bickering on hillsides, took in pools the colour of the sky or glint of sun, the landscape had one universal hue of dull grey and purple, wearisome beyond endurance; . . . Even cursed that barren hinterland on which they were imprisoned by gloomy mountain walls'.

Lillian McLagan again; 'No one without knowing weather conditions can envisage the speed at . . .

of a blizzard. Once when a goods train was snowed up in the Pass my father walked past it without even seeing it'.

Mitchell knew something would have to be done to combat high wind and sudden drifting so he built timber screen fences on each side of the exposed cuttings and had light snow ploughs in reserve. Over 40 years of using the line in winter I have found the service reliable, despite the fact that 73 miles of the line between Inverness and Perth are above 500 feet and 27 miles above 1000 feet. Trains manage to run reasonably to time when road travel is impossible.

* * * *

The Carr Bridge railway station is inconveniently half a mile west of the village where the River Dulnain permits a crossing by viaduct. Just out of the station beyond the Findhorn the cuttings are through boulder clay and the line passes over the Baddengorm Burn, once the scene of a serious accident in 1914 after torrential rain made a waterspout of the burn and undermined the foundations of the bridge. The train running on the subsiding track was thrown down the bank. One of the coaches dropped into 20 feet of water and was submerged. Five passengers were killed and nine injured. Trains were switched to the Forres route until a new bridge was completed – three weeks later. Another cloudburst in 1923 did even more structural damage, though fortunately no traffic was involved. From 1863 until 1894 the Inverness line had a marvellous safety record, with no loss of life until the latter date, when a collision at Newtonmore killed one man and injured another.

Road and rail are gradually forced together here on the Slochd, at 1315 feet the second highest summit on the line. This pass had to be forced to make a direct route to Inverness and cut out the Moray Firth detour to Forres, where Mitchell's line had struck across the hills, which had been a considerable commercial success for 35 years. The new

189

direct way was built to forestall competitors seeking to reach Inverness by Fort William and the banks of the Caledonian Canal. Authorisation for the Slochd was granted in 1884, one year after Mitchell's death. The engineer in charge was one of Mitchell's former partners, Murdoch Paterson. It shortened the Inverness-Perth journey from 144 to 118 miles.

West of the Slochd the line had to cross one of Scotland's most dangerous rivers, the Findhorn. This entailed a quarter mile long viaduct on the form of a graceful curve. The granite towers carry nine 130 foot spans of steel lattice work 143 feet above the river. The danger comes from the sudden floods in the hills beyond Tomatin, where the river has its source. Fishermen have been swept away by walls of water big enough to knock men off their feet. The sun can be shining where they are fishing but up in the hills there can be a cloudburst and the first hint can be a wave of cloudy water.

The most impressive viaduct of all is the sweep of 29 arches across the River Nairn at Culloden. Here the line makes a broad horseshoe, skirting the moor where Highland hopes were dashed in the last battle of the Jacobite army, fought on April 16, 1746. Built of red sandstone, the arches span 600 yards and carry the train 128 feet above the river. The broad middle arch is a 100 foot span, the others are 50 feet – a perfection of geometry, Murdoch Paterson's monument, for this fine engineer, who had master-minded the building of the direct line from Aviemore, died while superintending its construction. Trained by Joseph Mitchell and afterwards his partner, Paterson had seen the line through to Wick and Thurso.

* * * *

Tain, capital of Easter Ross is an important station and in pre-rail times was the site of the important Meikle Ferry. A prominent spit projecting into the waters of the Dornoch Firth was where cattle were swum across in droving days.

The line from Invergordon to Bonar Bridge was opened in

1864 and Joseph Mitchell was still pressing forward with it despite being stricken with paralysis on the last stages of the Perth – Inverness line in 1863; yet here he was surveying and building 26 ½ miles of new line and having it in the service by October 1864. He reported, 'the cuttings amount to 550, 000 cubic yards (20,000 of rock), there are 27 bridges over streams from 40-50 foot span and 26 public and accommodation road bridges'. The building cost was only £5180 per mile.

At Carbisdale Castle the line crosses the River Oykel with an iron girder bridge of 220 foot span, carried 55 feet above ordinary tides on five stone side arches. There is a station at each end of the bridge: Culrain on the west, Invershin to the east. The passenger fare used to be ½d – a bargain when there was no crossing nearer than Bonar Bridge. That half mile between stations (and over a river) could be done for the halfpenny until 1917.

The student of topography might wonder why the line took to the hills here into such sparsely inhabited country when an easier way presented itself from Tain, crossing the Dornoch Firth at the Meikle Ferry, serving Dornoch and north along the coast. The Duke of Sutherland, coming forward with £30,000, and adding another £12,500 when the route was in doubt, clinched the decision to go to Lairg. He wanted it to go to Lairg to open up the interiror of his own remote lands. No doubt the Duke had more than the welfare of the remnant populations on his mind for the people had been largely replaced by sheep, which meant a considerable traffic for the railway. Even today the autumn sheep sale in Lairg is the biggest in Scotland, with 30,000 and more on offer – though none are carried by rail today. The Highland Railway actually mooted the possibility of a branch line from Lairg along Loch Shin to Laxford Bridge, as was another to take a line from the Kyle of Sutherland along the River Oykel through the wilds of Assynt under Suilven and the River Kirkaig to Lochinver!

* * * *

Authorisation had been given to carry the line from Golspie on to Brora, but the difficulties of going by Lairg had absorbed the available cash – so the Duke of Sutherland, whose castle was at Dunrobin, only two miles beyond Golspie decided to make railway history by building his own line northward. Obtaining Parliamentary consent in June 1870 for 17 miles of line along the coast to Helmsdale, he had already jumped the gun and the line was open in November that same year and the Duke's little locomotive and rolling stock were running a service.

Brora has always been noted for its coal mine, the oldest in Scotland, producing the youngest coal – Jurassic coal as distinct from the usual Carboniferous, which at 260 million years old belongs to a period twice as distant as the Brora coal. Alas, the little mine, worked by crofters on a profit-sharing basis, ran up against difficult times and had to close. It could one day become viable since there is still plenty of coal underground. The 'black stones' had been mined since 1529, when used for fires to extract salt from sea water. In all its years it never knew a serious labour dispute.

In Brora we are also brought up against the Clearances; here, on the links, on land unfit for cultivation, crofters evicted from better holdings were expected to make a new life or emigrate.

At Helmsdale lies a sheltered harbour, one of the fishing stations set up by the Sutherland Estate in their 'improvement' programme of clearing the straths of people and re-settling the evicted crofters on the coast to make a better living for themselves. But the fishing villages were too remote and it did not pay to make textiles in the north when the mills of the south could produce them so much more cheaply. Instead of curing the poverty the First Duke of Sutherland created more.

Turning away from Helmsdale and the coast into the hills by the Strath of Kildonan, the railway traverses some of the classic country of the Clearances. The distance from here to

Wick along the coast is about 35 miles, but the distance by the rail is 60 miles by the inland route via the Sutherland border and across the breadth of Caithness.

This strath is historic for more than the Clearances, for it was the scene of a gold rush, with strikes being made in the Kildonan and Suisgill Burns and in burns at Kinbrace, further up the line. The Kildonan Burn site where the big rush began is marked today by a signpost, Baile-an-Oir, *City of Gold*, and in 1869 it cost £1 per month to stake a 40 square foot claim. Excisemen were there to ensure that one tenth of any find went to the Crown. Helmsdale became a boom town, with 500 miners hard at work and getting enough gold to pay them the equivalent of 50 pence a day. The Duke of Sutherland organised a dinner for them and Robert Gilchrist, who had sparked off the strike, was allowed to carve the joint. Gilchrist had prospected in Australia and knew something about gold. But the goodwill of the Duke did not last. The sheep farmers, sportsmen and gamekeepers prevented the miners from extending their explorations and winter saw the end of the rush. But £11,000 worth of gold was panned, according to the official Excise statistics. It is to be hoped that there was a lot more which the Crown never heard about.

From Kinbrace a road goes off across the moors to Strath Naver, where some of the most inhuman Clearances took place. The first hint of it came in 1818, when a crofter paying his rent was told to tell his neighbours that the rent for the half-year ending in May 1819 would not be demanded as it was determined to lay the districts of Strath Naver and Upper Kildonan under sheep. Then came summonses, delivered to 1000 houses. Just over 60 years before the coming of the railway a parish of over 2000 people was uprooted and their homes burned. Now that the people had gone the main benefit of the railway would be to the Sutherland Estate. Kildonan and Kinbrace stations (now unstaffed) were built to serve shooting lodges, as were the private platforms of Salzcraggie and Borrobol, now closed.

Forsinard is where the main line breaks away north-east, climbing in four miles to leave the Duke of Sutherland's territory and enter Caithness in roadless country at 708 feet above sea level. Joseph Mitchell has surveyed this route for the Duke. But that gentleman, suspicious by nature and careful of his money, wasn't satisfied that Mitchell was being economical enough. He engaged English surveyors to find a better way. Murdoch Paterson, Mitchell's old partner, engineered the line at a cost of £5077 per mile, over £1400 per mile less than the English estimate.

Georgemas is the most northerly junction in Britain and 45 ¾ miles from Helmsdale. This is where the Wick portion detaches, to go off east to reach its terminus in 14 ¾ miles. Thurso lies 6¾ miles to the north west. The characteristic dun moorland on the traverse from the County March to Altnabreac was notorious in severe winters for snow blockage, though little trouble has been experienced since the sever winters of 1955 and 1963. [*In this latter British Rail made the startling announcement that they had 'lost a train'.*]

Readers may wonder why the line went inland from Helmsdale and across largely uninhabited country when the populations who stood to benefit most lived on the coast. The problem was the Ord of Caithness, where the mountains, dropping steeply, end in sea-cliffs. Joseph Mitchell did not think the Ord practicable, nor did the engineers who followed. [*It has been and still is a challenge for the A9 road.*] Before surveying the railway line from Inverness through Ross-shire into Sutherland and finally to Wick and Thurso, Joseph Mitchell had maintained the Caithness roads for 22 years.

Mitchell was in Wick in 1852 when James Loch, factor of the Sutherland Estate was canvassing for the election. As Loch walked round, behind him went four men carrying half-burned croft timbers and others followed baa-ing like sheep. Three years later, in Sutherland, Mitchell was constantly stopped and told: 'Did you hear the news? Loch's dead'.

To end on a more cheerful note Tom concludes his railway stories with what an old man's grand uncle recalled of the first train to arrive.

He used to laugh at the reaction of a startled woman when she saw the puffing monster squealing to a halt, breaths of smoke belching from it, and dripping with water where escaping steam was condensing. She exclaimed angrily, 'They're working that poor beast ower sair. Look how it's blowing and sweating!'

THE HIGHLAND LINE

VIII

TOM'S PEOPLE

Tom had a gift of putting people at their ease which made him such a good TV presenter. Over the years he met and wrote about hundreds of people from all walks of life. Following are features on a much loved figure from the world of climbing, on a pioneering naturalist, on two men who influenced him in many ways when young and an inspirational sea captain, all special people. The last recalls a brief serendipitous encounter.

REMEMBERING TOM PATEY

On the jacket of the book in front of me there is a colour photograph of a climber swathed in awkward bundles of climbing rope. One hand on an ice-axe is plunged into dangerous looking powder snow, the other is clutching a short second axe. From the body rope hang ice-screws and pitons, and the straps on the boots show he is wearing crampons. The strong face below the shock of snow-rimed hair is not smiling. The mouth is open in an interrogatory glance, elongating the lines on his cheeks almost to lantern jaws. The man is Tom Patey, who sadly crashed to his death on 25 May, 1970.

One Man's Mountains is a collection of his best essays and verses, and they catch the spirit of the 50s and 60s as surely as Alastair Borthwick caught the 30s in his classic *Always a Little Further*. I discussed this book with Tom when we climbed the Cioch Nose on Applecross together only a few days before he parted from his rope while abseiling from a sea stack called The Maiden at Whiten Head, on the remote north coast. The day Tom died he was due to meet Livia Gollancz, publisher of his book. They were going to discuss his work and he intended to resist any rewriting of it. "Because I've worked damned hard on these pieces, and I need the money now." Tom, the unashamed television climber, willing to take part in any B.B.C. circus for the fun as much as the reward, wrote the best of his work for sheer pleasure. And when he did write for money it was often to satirise the 'Professionals.'

The book shows the evolution of the climber from days of innocence when he was a shy and retiring schoolboy, to his extrovert singing and piano accordion playing on Aberdeen Climbing Club meets, when the bar room jollity was as important as the climbing.

It was on Lochnagar that I first climbed with Tom Patey and his able partner Mike Taylor. Bill Brooker led a separate rope, and we all went to Eagle Ridge, narrowest and steepest of the ridges. As an introduction to rock climbing on Lochnagar it was a test of adhesion for me on holdless slippery granite, hands half frozen in the falling sleet. But Tom was exuberant as he scraped, lunged, grunted, drawing breath only to extol some feature of the elegant route I might be missing. By contrast Taylor looked meticulously controlled and demanded his right to lead some of the choicest pitches.

Tom put our ascent to good use by doing the climb again the following week-end when it was submerged in eight inches of powder snow. His companion was Tom Bourdillon, who happened to be giving a lecture on Everest in Aberdeen and found that a by-product of it was to be doing the hardest climb of his life with the reigning Tiger.

I remember on the Bealach nam Bo, as we sat in the car listening to the rain, asking Tom if he had regrets about being a doctor when he might have become a professional climber. His reply was vehement, "I'd rather be a good doctor any day. Climbing is not a reason for living.

Providing a good medical service to a remote region like Ullapool and the North West is as important to me as any climbing. I've worked hard to build up that practice, and I've enjoyed it, though I'd like more time for climbing."

Then he confided to me his remarkable intention to solo the North Face of the Eiger that August. He reckoned from his past attempts with others that he needed only one good day to top the 'greatest mixed route in Europe' – his words. His intention was to prepare the way so as to be able to go up in the dark when conditions were right, using his exceptional speed to forge up the dangerous upper part at break of day, before the stonefall barrage could begin.

Why did he want to do a route that had been done over a

hundred times before, when he was such a pioneer of new ways? "Because it has every problem in climbing heaped on top of each other. The big objection to it is the time it takes – so you are liable to be caught out by the weather. Get up it before the stuff starts to fall and you have only gravity to contend with. Every day you are up there lessens your chance of staying alive. And I want to live." Six days later Tom was dead and Ullapool had lost a good doctor. Winner of the Gold Medal for Physiology in his second year at university, he could have gone very far in medicine had he given free reign to his academic abilities. Good G.P. though he was, Patey had in him a tough, almost a callous streak, a demand that his friends be as hard as he was. Before he graduated I was due to give a lecture in Aberdeen, but collapsed with flu on the eve of departure from Glasgow. The doctor was called and pronounced me unfit to travel. "Under no circumstances must you go."

I phoned Adam Watson with the bad news. He was sympathetic. Somebody else would have to be found to take my place. An hour later the ebullient Patey was on the line, assuring me that most doctors were fools, that a man like myself shouldn't be stopped by anything so trivial as flu ... So I arrived in Aberdeen, gave my talk, was whisked about from one house to another afterwards, and finally whisked to Ellon in a snowstorm to arrive in the early hours of the morning at a stone-cold house – his parents were away and the house had been lying empty for three weeks. Yet I enjoyed myself, watching him sit down at the piano the moment we came into the house and, between songs, hearing him enthuse either about climbs he had done or was going to do. The fact is that Patey had a way of expanding you with his presence. Our eighteen years of age difference disappeared.

The University Lairig Club flourished then as never before or since with upwards of seventy members attending climbing meets. Many came for the jollity, though nearly all enjoyed a little fresh air prior to the evening's entertainment. I have never been a lover of big parties, so I was rather shaken when Tom joined us one New Year, with what looked like one of these meets of lads and lasses. And they brought with them a potent concoction of spirits, and as Tom took liberal swigs between dance numbers, his agile fingers became livelier and livelier on the accordion. He was still playing when most of the dancers had collapsed.

I don't know when we went to bed. But he was with us in the morning for a climb which he declared to be a new route. True, he looked terrible, as pale as a ghost and racked by a cough. But this was not abnormal. The cough came from smoking, the face belied a man with so much stamina that when alone in the Cairngorms, he frequently ran to the crags, punched a few hard routes and jogged back again.

'How does he climb, solo and so briskly?

On twenty fags a day, and Scotland's good malt whisky?'

Tom's own satirical songs published in the book are subtly delightful. Listen to the *Hamish MacInnes's Mountain Patrol Song*.

> Gillies and shepherds are shouting Bravo
> For Hamish MacInnes, the Pride of Glencoe.
> There'll be no mercy mission, no marathon slog
> Just lift your receiver and ask for DOG.
> They came from their kennels to answer the call,
> Cool, calm and courageous, the Canine Patrol.
> Sniffing the boulders and scratching the snow,
> They've left their mark on each crag in the Coe . . .

All sorts of characters are mirrored in the verses with an economy that any writer would envy: Bill Murray of the 30s, Chris Bonington and Joe Brown of the 60s, the stuffier members of the Cairngorm Club; none with wickedness, for Tom was essentially a kind man, however hard his exterior. He was a son of the manse. But I never heard him talk about God until our last day in Applecross. He opened his heart on many things as we talked in the car. Tom had no conventional religion, but he believed that the good in man lived on after he was dead, therefore there must be an all-seeing God. We talked about the Himalaya, the Mustagh Tower, Rakaposhi, and the Norwegian routes he had been doing with Joe Brown. None of them shone for him so much as his early days with his Aberdeen friends.

He did not think it was sentiment. In these early years all of them were true mountain explorers, opening up new corners of Scotland for the very first time. With the rapid sophistication of climbing and its organisation in the 60s something simple and joyous had vanished. There was too much emphasis on reputation, too much talk about character-building.

Freddy Malcolm and his friend Sticker are recalled in the book. They were the leaders of a tiny group of working lads who called themselves the Kincorth Club. As Tom says, they came to regard Beinn a' Bhuird as club property and built a subterranean howff on its flank.

These boys had a quiet style, so quiet that 'night after night their torchlit safaris trod stealthily past the Laird's very door, shouldering mighty beams of timber, sections of stove piping and sheets of corrugated iron.' The Howff records the opening ceremony: 'This howff was constructed in the Year of our Lord 1954, by the Kincorth Club, for the Kincorth Club. All climbers please leave names, and location of intended route; female climbers please leave names, addresses and telephone numbers.'

No outdoor centre could turn out lads like these. They developed their own characters and became first-class performers in any Cairngorm climbing situation, and most of their winter pioneering of hard routes was done in the remotest corries. They knew what they were doing. This is how Patey sums up his companions of his Cairngorms days: 'The North-East climbers of the early 50s were all individualists. But never rock fanatics. There are no crags in the Cairngorms within easy reach of a motorable road and a typical climbing

203

week-end savoured more of an expedition than of acrobatics. If the weather turned unfavourable, then a long hill walk took the place of the planned climb. All the bothies were well patronised – Luibeg, Lochend, Gelder Shiel, Bynack, the Geldie bothies, Altanour, Corrour and, of course, the Shelter Stone. At one and all you would be assured of friendly company round the fire in the evenings. Everybody knew everybody.'

But even the more halcyon days had their shadows as Tom recounts, 'when in August 1953 Bill Stewart fell to his death on Parallel Gully B. Although his initial slip was a mere six feet, the rope sliced through a sharp flake of rock and he fell all the way to the corrie floor. It was a cruel twist of fate to overtake such a brilliant young climber, and for many of the "faithful" it soured the love of the hills they had shared with him.'

But the impetus to make new routes, though by a smaller number of climbers, went on, and rich harvests were reaped. The Aberdeen boys broke new ground in Applecross and Skye, laying siege to Alpine peaks of increasing difficulty season by season. Serving in the Royal Navy from 1957 to 1961, Tom was attached to Royal Marine Commando, thus had plenty of scope in a unit practising mountain warfare at home and abroad. Marriage could not have been very easy for his wife Betty, for a climbing genius is not the most restful man to live with.

Just look at his record over his last half-dozen years, with his assaults on Atlantic rock stacks, and forays into every corner of the North West, including the first winter traverse of the Cuillin of Skye, with a night out on the ridge. Then in 1970 he did what I think is probably the boldest piece of solo climbing in the history of Scottish climbing by crossing the great wall of Creag Meaghaidh, in 8,500ft. of traversing in bold situations 'unrivalled in Scottish winter climbing.' I know of no one who thought it could be done in a single day, yet Tom, starting around a normal lunchtime, finished it in five hours in conditions which were ' . . . far from ideal – an unusual amount of black ice and heavy aprons of unstable wind-slab.'

But as he says in his book, it was one of these days when a climber is caught up in his own impetus. One description made my stomach turn over in the sheer horror of the situation. He had made a false move and was trying to rectify it when a wind-slab ledge 'suddenly heeled off into space and I was left in the position of a praying mantis, crampon points digging into verglassed slabs. It was a moment of high drama – and horror – best contemplated in retrospect. Hanging on by one gloved fist jammed behind frozen heather roots, I had to extract a small ring spike from my pocket and batter it into the only visible crack. It went in hesitantly for an inch then the crack went blind. Time was running out, as my supporting hand was rapidly losing sensation.'

That piton simply had to hold him, and it did, as he used his teeth and free hand to thread the rope through it, then tested it by hanging free on it to try to pendulum on to a lower ledge from where he might continue the traverse.

Perhaps you have dismissed Tom in your mind as a fool for exposing himself to such extremes of danger when he had a wife, three children and the responsibilities of a scattered medical practice. Yet as Christopher Brasher so well expressed it in his Foreward to the book: "... What is a man if he does not explore himself; if he does not challenge the impossible?"

WEIR'S WAY

TWO LUCKY PEOPLE

"I'm the luckiest chap in the world," said George Waterston "Even when taken prisoner after the battle of Crete in 1941 I landed on my feet amongst a fine bunch of naturalists in a prison camp in Bavaria in 1943. Purchon was studying swallows and field crickets, John Buxton wrote a book on

205

redstarts as a result of his work, Peter Condor, now Director of the R.S.P.B., was studying goldfinches, and I was busy on wrynecks. In fact, some of my wrynecks were driving out the redstarts from nest boxes we had made for them."

I prodded George to tell me some more. "Well, it was there that Ian Pitman and I began thinking about Fair Isle, and how marvellous it would be if we could get a bird observatory on the island. Planning to buy Fair Isle and do some real scientific work up there to unravel the mysteries of bird migration, was a way of escaping from the camp into the freedom of the future.

"Getting a chance to do so much birding in the camp whetted our appetites, for so relatively little was known about the detailed lives of individual species. Even in camp we made contact with German ornithologists. I had records of German bird notes sent to me by Professor Erwin Stresemann. I sent him my notes on the birds of Crete, and when he published them along with his own in the middle of the war in a German journal he acknowledged the help of a certain Lieutenant Waterston.

"Funny how things work out. When Crete was retaken by the Allies, Heinz Seilmann, the great German cameraman, was captured. But when he explained he was filming the life of Eleonara's falcon, he was allowed to go back and finish his work. And years later in America, Professor Stresemann, Seilmann and I faced an audience on the same platform at an International Ornithological Congress. When Stresemann stood up to give his address, he introduced us: 'On my left George Waterston and on my right Heinz Seilmann.' Then he told how our friendship through birds triumphed over the stupidity of war."

George's brown eyes fairly sparkled in his dark gipsy face as he spoke of how the *ups* of life so wonderfully make up for the *downs*. It was ill health which caused him to be sent back to Britain for hospital treatment in 1943. His homecoming was by way of Sweden and the coast of Norway, then across the North Sea.

206

"I think the most emotional moment of my life was when somebody shouted 'Land ahead,' and there, only two or three miles off, was the Sheep Rock of Fair Isle standing out in the sunshine. The tears ran down my cheeks – I knew it so well, and it had been so often in my thoughts."

George's interest in the three mile-long island lying midway between Orkney and Shetland had begun in the mid-thirties when it held 130 folk. "Oh, they were great fun, always good for a laugh, and really keen on birds, for it's such a marvel-lous place for migration."

But Fair Isle had to wait meantime, as the ship bore him home and he went into hospital for kidney treatment. He was expecting to be given a Home Guard command when he came out, but instead found himself being persuaded by the ornithologist James Fisher to undertake a study of rooks to assess their effect on agricultural output at a time when Britain was desperately short of food. (Evidence that has built up since George's confirms his finding that any harm the rook does to crops is counterbalanced by the pests it eats.)

The end of the year saw George back in the Edinburgh family business of stationery and printing, but his heart was not in sales management. The Fair Isle dream was as fresh as ever. Typically he had prepared a careful memo stating the ornithological objective and presenting it to friends and likely people to win their backing and some of their cash. The purchase price of £3500 was raised and George became the owner of Fair Isle.

There was a hutted camp on the island, built for the Navy, which was to become home to the noted ornithologist Kenneth Williamson. His work there soon proved that the island was even more remarkable for migration than anyone suspected. Visitors stayed at the observatory and stimulated the demand for knitted Fair Isle patterns. The 'laird', who has stayed in every croft, was simply George to all the islanders through his hundreds of visits. However he could not close his eyes to the fact that, even since the purchase of the island in 1948, it was running down; crofts were deteriorating as young folk left and the population eventually dropped to under fifty.

Money would have to be spent on it to prevent it from becoming another St Kilda. Houses needed modernisation, a better harbour was an urgent need. The island needed a new boat and better roads. The solution was to offer Fair Isle to the National Trust for Scotland since they were in a position to launch an appeal to charities and the public.

The Trust took it over in 1954, with George as their official adviser, and great work has been done since, an air strip has been built, renovated houses have electric light, and the new island boat can come into a deep-water pier for the first time in history. There has been a drift back to the island by the young, and the population has stabilised at around seventy.

And in the year the National Trust for Scotland took over responsibility for Fair Isle, George broke with the family business of George Waterston & Sons to become Secretary of the Scottish Ornithologists' Club and Scottish Representative of the Royal Society for the Protection of Birds. "Yes, there was some opposition, for I was the sixth generation in the oldest family firm in Edinburgh – it was established in 1752.

"Nobody could have foreseen then the rapid growth of bird interest or the urgent need for action to combat toxic insecticides which were poisoning our birds of prey. And the nesting of the ospreys on Speyside did a lot for us. Remember the original pair in 1959 when we could muster only six watchers? Last year we had over a dozen breeding pairs, and we have had over 70,000 visitors at the Loch Garten hide in one year."

I remember the young black-haired George of these early days on the occasions when meetings were held in a Glasgow hotel. A hearty laughter with the gift of putting everyone at ease, his drive and enthusiasm was persuasive. Even at school in Edinburgh Academy it was natural that the bird club should meet in his house, talk ornithology and plan week-end outings. The accent was on conviviality.

"After the stir of Edinburgh we really enjoy living full-time in the country. Irene and I are both fond of gardening. Planting things and watching them grow until you can eat them, satisfies something deep down."

I was impressed by the amount of work they had done between them as we looked at the orchard, the neat vegetable plot and the flower garden. "This place used to be a croft with a cow and hens on three acres. Part of the house was a wee shop. We bought it eighteen years ago for Irene's mother with a view to having it ourselves eventually. We moved in last year after she died at over ninety."

"I'd be nowhere without my wife Irene. We've worked together on everything, and we have had so many tricky problems and exciting times. Last year was terrific. We had the good fortune to be asked to go as guide-lecturers on the *Lindblad Explorer* for two months on a sail of 7000 miles in the Arctic. [*He showed Tom albums of this voyage and earlier Greenland and Ellesmere Island surveys.*]

There were photographs at the ospreys' eyrie in 1959 when there were only six people to do the round-the-clock-watch. A photo shows George with a string attached to his wrist as he takes a nap. The string was attached to me in the hide. At a tug from me he would raise the general alarm, since a tug meant an attempt was being made to rob the nest. Alas, that first nest was robbed despite our safeguard, and the raider got away after substituting hens' eggs in the nest.

It was after that robbery the hide was thrown open to the public. "Colleagues thought it was a rash decision when I said we should invite visitors to come and see the ospreys. Response was fantastic. It did more good for conservation than anything else we could have thought up." Irene is a keen ornithologist, but has been taking more and more interest in Arctic botany, perhaps as a relief since her job was secretary of the Scottish Ornithologists' Club when George took over full-time directorship of the R.S.P.B. in Scotland.

I remember her with a big book on alpine plants at the hide

in Fetlar when the first pair of snowy owls nested, making it a first for Britain. Protection was vital, so George was there mustering a guard of helpers, as he had done with the ospreys. Glad to say the Arctic owls are still nesting after eight years, and the Fetlar hill has reserve status. [*The owls are no longer present.*]

"Right now [*1979*] the Society are trying to raise £290,000 to buy the whole 1500 acres of Loch Garten to protect the whole forest environment of that wonderful bird country." And with a swift motion he passed me an appeal form – the old fund raiser was still in action! [*The reserve was bought and today is a major attraction in the Highlands.*]

It was for outstanding services to ornithology and conservation that George Waterston was awarded the O.B.E. in 1964 and last year this modest man was capped LL.D. by Dundee University for his outstanding work. Then around last Christmas he had a return of the old kidney complaint, suffering pneumonia and pleurisy as well. For two months he lay in Edinburgh Royal Infirmary, weak and depressed, seriously ill; but he didn't want anyone to hear about it. He is now tied to a kidney machine which he has to visit three nights every week for five hour stints. "A tedious bore and very time-consuming," was all he would say about it.

He looks upon the restrictions imposed upon him as an exercise in adaptation. "I have a lovely place to live, plenty to do and I can lead a pretty normal life. I'm lucky." Lucky he is, certainly to have achieved so much in his most active years against the background of the kidney trouble which has plagued him since boyhood. Lucky to have retained his youthful enthusiasm for all the things he holds dear.

His beloved Fair Isle has been foremost in his mind recently. George explained why the present air service is so vital. "The economy of the island depends on the visitors who fill the 24-bed hostel, which is part of the observatory we built in 1969. [*And was rebuilt two years ago.*] To keep the hostel filed we need the Loganair service, since the boat could never carry enough passengers to make the observatory pay its way. Because of the observatory the islanders have a good market for their produce. It is also their community centre. It cost £50,000 to build."

Speaking about the future for himself. "My hope lies in a kidney transplant, and I am pressing hard for it."

George was given a transplant operation but it did not 'take'. He died on 20 September 1980 but not before he had some brave days in the Highlands and on Fair Isle, thanks to a mobile kidney machine and the support of his wife Irene who shared his great days.

WEIR'S WAY

TRAMP-ROYAL

Some Stravaigings was the title of Matt's diary which I have just been reading. Actually it is more than that, for it contains quotations, poems and photographs from various sources, including some of his own. The book has all the ardour and idealism of youth, and its pages shine with love of the Highlands and everything about them – especially the wildlife and the mountain tops. The experiences were snatched from a life in Glasgow which gave the writer only Saturday night and Sundays for week-ends, and a fortnight's holiday each year. I'd like to tell you something of this man, my closest friend, who knew how to use his time so well.

I was travelling half-fare on the train to Tyndrum when we met. Small for my seventeen years, I wore a schoolboy uniform to fool the ticket collectors. The big, ginger-haired lad in the corner with the outsize rucksack told me he was out for the May holiday week-end, and I was envious because I was out only for the day. It was a Sunday excursion, and I was going to snatch Ben Lui before the train went back.

At this time I had no regular climbing companions, though

211

I was on the hills every week-end. Here was another like myself – except he had been more places. Moreover, he was keen on the rocks. By the time we got to Tyndrum I was no longer out for the day but ready to accept his invitation to share his tent. "I've bags of grub and a couple of blankets, we could do the four peaks of Lui and have a day on Ben More and Stobinian tomorrow if you could get a message to your mother that you won't be home.

She got the message, and I took the blessing when I got back, but that sunny week-end, the glitter of blue skies and snow was unforgettable as we kicked steps up the Central Gully, traversed Oss and Dubhcraige, met an orphan lamb that ran up to adopt us as mother, saw ptarmigan and wheatears, identified summits for future exploration, and camped beside a burn where oyster catchers and sandpipers were nesting. In the morning we tramped to Crianlarich, did another three Munros, then I went home to the reckoning.

That was the beginning. Both of us worked Saturday afternoons, I in the Co-op as a grocery apprentice, Matt in a butcher's shop. So the earliest we could get away was 8.30 in the evening, which meant arriving in Aberfoyle or Callander or Balmaha or Blair Atholl very late after a tiring day in the shop. We pooled our money and bought an 80-foot Alpine Club rope to climb rocks wherever we found them.

Matt was the man with the imagination. I was the one with ambition. Given half a chance I would have spent all my time on hard climbs. Matt was more liberal-minded. He loved big journeys. "How about this?" he would say, producing a couple of maps. "We could get to Blair Atholl at Midnight, walk up the Tilt, doss out for a few hours, then cross all the tops from the Tarf to the mouth of the Feshie."

We did it, too – at an Easter Week-end – though a better variation was at the May holiday when we slept out on the top of Ben Bhrotain and traversed everything from Monadh Mor to Braeriach, drumming-up high on the Larig before dashing down to catch the train at Aviemore. On these big journeys we travelled light, no spare clothes except socks: no tent, no tins, only tea and sugar and lots of butcher meat, steak, chops and special beef sausages (prepared by the master!) Twice we crossed Sutherland into Ross by different routes, exploring Glen Golly and the Dionard to Cape Wrath, and from Ben More Assynt to Coigach.

Matt had began his outdoor life as a fisherman – a passion which evolved from catching 'baggies' in the Molendinar, which he used to follow down from Hoganfield Loch. And it was here, when this clear burn had sheep and horses grazing on its wooded banks that he learned his birds. We were poor in the thirties, but Glasgow was rich in green space, before it was swallowed up in housing schemes. In those days there was plenty to explore on our doorstep, and when motor cars were scarce, cycling was a pleasure.

The outdoor men of that time used to gravitate to the Craigallian fire, a 'howff' near Milngavie, in a hollow by the loch encircled by pinewoods and backed by the steep front of the Campsies. Here, only ten miles from Glasgow, was a crossroads of adventurers. Here is a fragment from Matt: 'Coming along a track of a winter's evening, the glow of light and the merry shouts of laughter brought joy to the heart. One could always be assured of company there, good company, and pleasant tales of the countryside'

Alas, the popularity of something which had became known as 'hiking' put an end to Craigallian. The fire was banned because of litter-louts and despoilers. Notice boards went up, and traditional routes to the Campsies were closed. But the true outdoor men knew the ways round these obstacles. They met in caves and 'dosses' – and this is where Matt learned much of his climbing lore. Yet he was pretty much a loner until we met. So was I.

We never had a relationship of absolute togetherness however, for Matt loved his company more than I did mine. He liked to spend some holidays by himself, so when he said, "I think I'll go to Glen Lyon at Easter," I knew he didn't want

me. And often enough we opted to spend our annual fortnight separately.

These breaks deepened our friendship, and when we met
again we would begin planning something exciting, such
as an ascent of Crowberry Ridge, which in these days had a
fabled reputation as one of the hardest climbs in Britain. Our
ascent was made possible by the inauguration of the first bus
service through Glen Coe on the newly-built road.

It was the September week-end, and the ridge seemed a
very serious undertaking as we drew close to the square-cut
crag rising massively to the narrow top of Buachaille Etive
Mor. It deflated some of my pent-up ambition, and I knew in
my heart that I was depending on Matt to see us up. And I can
still see him out on Abraham's Shelf, nailed boots scraping as
he worried over the hard move. I remember his "Pheeeee" as
he got round the holdless corner to better holds. He was not
a neat climber, but there were few things that he couldn't get
up, including the famous Jenny's Lum Arête on the Campsies,
which had only been done once until his ascent.

In 1939 Matt and I talked about being abstainers from the
folly of going to war, but in the end let ourselves be called
up, I to the Ayrshire Yeomanry, Matt to the Scots Guards. His
was a hard war, but he enjoyed the training in Moidart and
Galloway, practising cliff landings from the sea and night
marching over huge chunks of hill territory.

Then came North Africa and the battle for the desert. Letters he sent me at this time were full of bird migration notes
and interesting species seen, though he was in the thick of
battle, moving from foxhole to foxhole. He was wounded in
this campaign, but recovered in time to go in with his landing party to Anzio, where his battalion died almost to a man,
holding a forward position for the relief that never came. The
journey across the Brenner in overcrowded cattle trucks to
prison camp was so desperate that ever afterwards he suffered from cramp if his knees remained bent too long in one
position.

Demobbed, we continued our mountain trips, but the emphasis was now mainly on ornithology. We had a marvellous week in the Cairngorms in early June, sleeping out in a cave in Glen Slugain in the afternoons, and climbing at night to avoid the heat of the sun, which softened the considerable snow cover and made it heavy for walking.

The Cairngorms can be called an Arctic island in Britain, in vegetation, wildlife and scenery. Atlantic islands give us the same pleasure – and good climbing, too – as we explored the coast and hills of Eigg, Rum, Tiree, Canna, Iona, Harris, Gigha, Colonsay, Coll and many another. Islay was a special favourite with Matt, for its astonishing variety of birds, and his energy on it and other islands was a never-failing source of wonder to me. Leaving me asleep, he would have something of interest to recount as he made my breakfast, for he believed in early rising and late bedding when he was on holiday. It was due to him that I made a film of Hebridean birds in exactly one week. While I was in the hide filming a sequence of little tern, ring plover, or oyster catcher, he was finding twite, dunlin, or red-necked phalarope. His patience was endless, for the watching and tracking of birds was a joy to him. He got happier and happier every day he was out, singing Scots airs or Gaelic songs and he was always ready to recite a piece of poetry appropriate to the occasion.

It was Matt who started me off writing and printing my own photographs. He enthused me with his own passion for literature by showing me passages from his favourite books, for we used to meet every Friday night in Townhead Library to plan the week-end. It was only after a time he showed me some of the things he had written himself, some of it published work.

I had always been a diary-keeper. Matt encouraged me to join an Art of Writing class at Glasgow University, where I had many a red face as my poor efforts were analysed by Edward Scoular, the W.E.A. lecturer. Curiously enough, as I started to break into print myself, Matt stopped writing for

215

publication, though he never lost the scribbling habit.

In my first nineteen years as a professional writer Matt was a tower of strength as a sort of instant encyclopaedia, for dates, historical events, or bits of personal information gained from practical experience on the ground. Matt had a grasp of history which I lacked, and I profited much from his informed mind. By merely lifting the phone, I could get an opinion I valued. Nor did I fear anyone's censure more than his.

On our very last outing to Loch Tay we talked about the early days and compared them with what we get from our lives now. "No matter what erudition you bring, you can never recapture the thrill of these first days," said Matt. "It comes only once, and the mere act of repetition tarnishes it. I remember the first time I went to Mull. I thought it was a marvellous place, but when I went back there I couldn't find it. It's something in yourself, not just the countryside or the weather." I knew what he meant – the joy of being alive that makes a young colt gambol and fox cubs play – that, plus the thing of the mind that we call idealism.

Home by Glen Lyon in a snow flurry, I remember how relaxed Matt looked in the house that night. The next time I saw him was in hospital and a month later he was dead. Matt, the invincible enthusiast, wasted away in seven weeks of a tumour.

Matt was fifty-eight when he died. He was part owner of the butcher's shop in Lenzie where he had worked for over thirty years. He lived with his brother and sister in Glasgow, in a house which was my second home when his mother was alive. And I got the rough edge of her tongue too, at times, especially when we came in late on a Saturday night to eat dinner that had been kept hot for us long past our expected time.

The morning of the day he was cremated was so beautiful, sunny and warm after night frost, and I took my thoughts for a walk down by the lochside. I doubt if I have ever felt the songs of birds with such intensity, especially three tree creepers in different locations, singing their marvellously sweet four-second song – yet I had only heard it once or twice in my lifetime.

Above the torrent of skylark, blackbird and thrush song you could hear the marsh and water birds, the whistling of wigeon and teal, the quark of mallard, the whinnying of curlews and the melancholy wheezings of reed buntings. Wherever I walked there were birds: rooks, herons, grey lag geese, swans, long-tailed tits, a buzzard and thousands of shouting gulls.

TOM WEIR'S SCOTLAND

Matt Marshall wrote occasional pieces for publication and one book, The Travels of Tramp-Royal, *an idiosyncratic, Borrow-like account of Highland journeys. Tom's copy was heavily marked and was a treasured possession. Being a butcher, Matt always had the best of meat on their expeditions, and for the rest of his life Tom would be equally fussy; no mistakes, the best of steaks.*

SETON GORDON – MAN OF NATURE

I was driving north to spend the day with the doyen of naturalists, Seton Gordon, at his home in Upper Duntulm, close to the spot where Flora Macdonald lies buried. For me it was a voyage into another historical period with a tall kilted figure whose liveliness made it difficult to grasp that he had just celebrated his 90th birthday. As we sat down to talk, he said, "The last time we met was in Edinburgh. You gave a lecture, and I played *Farewell to St. Kilda* on the pipes. We were fundraising for the National Trust." At which I could only reply, "And twenty years later you are still hanging on to your own teeth and looking remarkably unchanged. Are you still playing the pipes?"

"I still have a blow," he chuckled. "They are in Portree getting a new bag put on. Angus MacPherson of Invershin, who died in April this year, would have been ninety-nine in July if he had lived. He played until he was ninety-seven, which is the record I have to beat. He was the last of the old type of pipers who put the soul of the tune above all. Fingerwork is not enough. To go by the book is to have technique without expression. Piping is in a state of flux. People are all fingers. You have to put away the book to realise the music and the beauty of the tune.

"Without the pleasure of piping and judging at the competitions my life would just not have been the same. I remember long ago when the Corrour Bothy had a lock and I had a key. It was December, and I went up with a companion to climb Cairn Toul. It was deep snow, and a severe blizzard turned us back. On the way down we found ptarmigan sheltering at the bottom of every footprint. They were more numerous then than they are now.

"Back in the bothy we drew lots to see who would go on to the springs for water, which was a fair distance. My companion had to face the blizzard. He didn't come back, and I could not see a thing from the door, so I played the pipes and the sound enable him to work his way back. In twenty yards he had lost sight of the bothy."

Brought up in Aboyne, and author of his first book, *Birds of the Loch and Mountain*, at the age of eighteen, there seems to have been no time when Seton Gordon was not interested in writing and nature. "I remember as a small boy, before the turn of the century, a pike used to live in a backwater near the bridge at Aboyne. I was determined to catch it, and with a small fish on a cast, hooked it. My governess held me round the middle and went backwards with me as I drew it in. Lord Huntly happened along just as I got it to shore, and couldn't believe such a small boy had caught a seven-pound fish."

I asked about his writing. The only thing his memory was weak on was the exact number of book he has written.

"Almost thirty, I think. For me, writing has always been 99 per cent pleasure, I think I got it from my mother, who was sometimes called 'the Queen's poetess.' As an author and nature photographer I was able to support myself, helped out by lecturing."

Luck played it part, too. "I remember coming from Oxford to Aviemore, hiring transport to Loch Einich and walking to Corrour carrying kit, and listening to the snow bunting singing. My memory of collecting bog fir for the Corrour fire, and exploring the corries collecting alpine plants to help in a forthcoming examination.

Back at Oxford the luck came when the question on his examination paper read, 'Write all you know about alpine botany.' His detailed answer gave him the distinction of being the first student at Oxford to get an honours degree in botany through writing of the alpine flora of the Cairngorms. "My idea was to get a job with the Board of Agriculture. I took a diploma in forestry, and an honours degree in natural science, but didn't get the job. I went to Russia in 1912 with Prince Felix Youssoupoff. He was with me at Oxford; he owned thirty-two properties and wanted me to be one of his foresters. He was the Prince who killed Rasputin and married the Czar's niece, and if I had taken the job I might have died in the Revolution."

Instead, the outbreak of war in 1914 found him planning to join in the action by driving an ambulance. Then out of the blue came the offer of a job organising a secret coastguard service under the guise of being a travelling bird watcher. Based on Mull, and with his own fishing boat, *Lustre Gem*, a whole new world opened up as he got to know the Inner Hebrides while watching out for enemy submarines. "It seems all wrong that I had this marvellous chance to go where I pleased, landing on uninhabited islands and enjoying wild life, while friends were being killed in France."

Married in 1915 to Audrey, who was to be a tower of strength to him for forty-four years, he had no doubt that

219

his two years at Ardura from 1914 to 1916 were the happiest of his life. "I don't think anybody got to know Mull so well. And even although I am a bad sailor, I enjoyed the freedom of that boat to go anywhere." Then came a move to Aultbea as Naval Centre Officer, and here he met 80-year old Osgood Mackenzie and helped him write one of the classic books of this century, *A Hundred Years in the Highlands*. "Osgood was so thrilled, like a boy, with the book, that he began writing another. He died as he was writing. I can't really say I got to know him for the gap in our ages was too great. He had no use for English, and his wife left him because he spoke nothing but Gaelic."

At this point Mrs Gordon [*Seton remarried*] came in to ask us through to lunch, and now I had a real chance to speak to her, for she had tactfully stayed out of the way to let us get on with our talk. "Betty was a great friend of ours before my wife died in 1959," Seton Gordon had confided. It was a happy meal, with whisky to go with our soup and chicken, and I heard about a walk they had done in 1960, lasting from 7 a.m. until 4 a.m., twenty-one hours, and causing a police search-party to be raised.

Mrs Gordon took up the tale. "We set off from Luibeg. I am used to the Kintail hills, and have been deer-stalking on them for twenty-two years, but it was my first time in the absolutely vast country of Braeriach, so rough with stones. The real surprise to me was to find the whole summit pink with flowers of *Silene acaulis*, growing from gravel. We saw ptarmigan with young, and a red deer hind with a spotted calf . . ."

Recollection stirred Seton Gordon, "I'll never forget the richness of colouring as the sun went down, intensifying the blaze of red from the flowers, I've never seen anything like it. Ben Nevis was clear. So were Cruachan and the Glencoe peaks."

As he talked I made a small calculation in my mind, that he would be seventy-four when he saw that sight in the remotest top of the Cairngorms. Also, that fifty years earlier he had written the *Cairngorm Hills of Scotland*, which was one of the finest mountain books I had read as a teenager, gripped by climbing and wildlife. It profoundly influenced my own desire to see those things and write about them when I grew up.

The memory of that visit to Braeriach sparked off another. "I remember going every day to the Wells of Dee to get the incubation period of the dotterel at 4,000 feet. In twenty- six days the dotterel got to know me, and as I watched on one occasion a daddy-long-legs landed on my arm. The dotterel ran on to my sleeve, swallowed it, and instead of flying away, gazed into my face steadily, then went back to the eggs. I felt I had been recognised as a friend.

"But if my collie got up from where it was lying the dotterel would do the broken-wing trick. I recall one day of showers when the eggs were chipping and a storm of hail was batter-ing the hill, when the bird came running to the nest at top speed and looked up as it covered the eggs as if to say, 'Just got back in time.' It hatched them all safely."

With such a love of the high Cairngorms and the ancient Caledonian pines of its glens, I asked him how he came to choose a headland as bare as Upper Duntulm in Skye as a permanent home. "We came here in 1931. The house had originally been a manse and has seventy acres of croftland. We liked the place. I could write, and my wife worked the land. We had eight or nine cows, some sheep. We grew oats and potatoes. There were men in those days to cut peats. We planted the shelter belt around the house."

I asked about his working discipline. "Six hours writing a day was my usual, three in the morning, off in the afternoon, then another three hours after tea. The roads were quieter and travelling was easier. A car was essential. I used to go lectur-ing during February and March, travelling all over Scotland, Ireland and England. At the Royal Institution I was the only nature man to be honoured.

"I always showed my own slides taken with a half-plate camera. You had to be strong to be a nature photographer in the old days, everything was so big and heavy for the distance you had to carry it. I always finished my lectures so as to be back at Duntulm for the nesting of the golden eagle. It is four miles to the eyrie from here. I used to leave in the morning for the walk, sit for five or six hours, then home. The eagle didn't mind. I saw the mating of the pair once. There was twenty inches of snow on the ground at the time – soft snow. The bird came straight down on the hen, pushing her out of sight as he mated her. Come through to my untidy study and I'll show you some of the things I've collected over the years."

It is not very often that I meet my match for untidiness, but this was getting close to it – desk and tables covered in letters and papers, books everywhere, lively bird paintings on the walls and photographs jostling each other for room to show themselves on the ledges. "My typewriter," he smiled. "It's a genuine antique, but still in use. I don't do much real writing now, but I get a lot of correspondence from readers, and I always answer it."

Anecdotes flowed from him as we went around the walls, and here is a point I must make about Seton Gordon. He is a much more humorous man than is apparent in his writings. He is also a very good mimic, and I only wish I could tell some of the stories he asked me to keep secret in case of giving offence. Tact and kindliness are built-in responses. Lairds in the old days, it would seem, were not only jealous of stray tourists, but of other lairds who might dare to walk over their property. On Deeside the situation was particularly critical. At the beginning of the century, when Mar Lodge was really private, you could not cross Victoria Bridge to the Lodge without special permission. Now it is a hotel, and a jeep road goes almost to the top of Beinn a' Bhuird. [*No longer.*]

"I've taken advantage of that road, too. I'll tell you what we did when we were staying with Farquharson of Invercauld. We went to church in the morning at Crathie. Went home for lunch. Then drove to Mar Lodge, got the key of the lock on the gate, and drove off for the top of Beinn a' Bhuird at 2.30 p.m. It's a terrible drive, as I'm sure you know, but it got us up there so quickly there was time to walk over the tops and look at the snowfields. The sun was low, lighting the zig-zag shore of Loch Etchachan when we got back to the Land-rover."

We talked about Aviemore, where Seton Gordon and his wife Audrey had lived for sixteen years, doing some of their best golden eagle work, spending no less than 167 hours in one season at a Speyside eyrie. "Our old home is now the Nature Conservancy Office, which shows how things have become organised in the interval of time since we lived there.

"I think seventy-five per cent of my enjoyment of the Highlands now is made up of memories, of times when you knew everyone, landowners, keepers, countryfolk. Wherever you went you stayed the night with friends – they would have been offended if you had done anything else.

"There is less to do here at Duntulm when you lose the strength to go long cross-country walks. You realise how terribly exposed to weather the headland is. My wife's home is Biddlesdon, in Northamptonshire, and we winter there. She [*Betty*] has a little house in Kintail where we stay, but I like to spend the summer here and take a walk every day. It is a wonderful place for sunsets."

Seton Gordon would agree that life has been good to him, blessing him with exceptional health, a good brain and a creative imagination to use it. In terms of stickability and sheer stamina in the field of natural history he has set an Olympic standard. One of the great strengths of his writing is the strong personal thread that runs through all of it. Few reference books are more valuable to a writer than his *Highways and Byways in the Western Highlands* and *Highways and Byways in the Central Highlands*.

My problem in talking to Seton Gordon that long day as wind and rain beat upon the windows of his home was to keep the conversation oriented towards him and not on me.

Then as I got up to go, I told him that I was heading up to Uig to meet up with sailing friends who should now have pushed their way up from Ardnamurchan.

He was intensely interested in our plans, and I could see the old coastguard officer was envying us the option of the wide seas and the kind of landing on remote skerries he had made himself. But, being a bad sailor like me, he was apprehensive about the weather. We shook hands. It had been a grand day, but it was not quite goodbye. At the end of my sailing trip who should be waiting on the Uig quay but the old kiltie himself, balmoral bonnet at a jaunty angle. "You came past Duntulm in the white boat. I was watching you through the long glass. Where have you been and how did you get on?"

His face wore a happy smile as he cupped is ear and listened to me telling him of threading a way through the Cathedral Cave on the Shiants and clambering over the boulderfields under the great organ-pipe formations of columnar basalt. I talked of the brilliant orange colour of the lichens and the clouds of puffins hurrying back and fore between the sea and the hanging ribbons of greensward. Then up to the top of Garbh Eilean, through housing schemes of guillemots and razorbills, with the reptilian heads of shags poking up from dunneys in the boulders, mouthing threats and guarding eggs or young. Up top we were amongst singing skylarks and looking across the North Minch to the strange monoliths of Sutherland. In North Uist we had climbed Eaval, only 1,138 ft, but one of the most awkward hills in Scotland to reach because it is almost surrounded by fresh and salt water. To reach it had been a wild sail from Harris, twelve hours in a Force six wind, with no snug anchorage at the end of it in a bay called Bagh a' Bhioran in Loch Eport.

The light of memory was in his face as I spoke. It was my last conversation with him. The grand old man of Scottish Natural History died just short of his ninety-first birthday. But in his very last summer of life he had been up on the Cairngorm plateau with my friend Adam Watson. These two had become aquainted in 1944 when Adam was thirteen and Seton Gordon had showed him his first golden eagle eyries. Until then they had only known each other through correspondence. Adam still has an early letter which says "It is a fine thing for you to have a love of the hills, because on the hills you will find yourself near grand, beautiful things, and as you grow older you will love them more and more." The truth of experience from a great man who had discovered it for himself.

Tom Weir's Scotland

Seton Gordon's books were often reprinted, some quite recently and, particularly recommended are his Highways and Byways pair mentioned above. The anthologies, Seton Gordon's Scotland *and* Seton Gordon's Cairngorms *are still available and both have a full bibliography.*

SAILING WITH THE *CAPTAIN SCOTT*

It was the chance to board the *Captain Scott* and talk to her master, Commander Victor Clark, D.S.C., R.N., which brought me to Plockton. As I swung under Duncraig Castle crags, suddenly she was there – Britain's largest sailing schooner – slim masts shining above the white houses of the former fishing village. She was even taller and more elegant than I had expected. The problem of getting aboard was solved when I heard that some gear was to be lifted from the jetty at 5 p.m. A message from the master gave the assurance that I would be welcome.

I had heard a little about the *Captain Scott* from her builders, Herd & MacKenzie, of Buckie. She was launched in 1971. I know that she looked like a traditional t'gallant trading schooner above water, below she had more the design of a yacht. Today I was seeing her as a black and white skeleton, bare of canvas, rocking gently at anchor as I climbed from the rubber dingy up the ladder and over the side. Immediately I was ushered below decks to the master's cabin.

He apologised for its untidiness. "I'm just off leave and trying to catch up with paperwork." He had been on a Dormobile trip, visiting friends and exploring old haunts in the South of England. His easy manner, friendly grin and twinkling eyes were not quite what I expected. I had been prepared for austerity because of his high ideals of living and a background commanding destroyers and frigates.

I knew something of his record. He had been at Narvik in the big raid of 1940, when *H.M.S. Warspite* blasted several enemy destroyers and chased another three up a side fjord until they ran aground.

Commander Clark's own turn of ill-fortune came in the *Repulse* when Japanese planes sunk the ship off Singapore. Then after commanding the west coast raiders in Malaya, he was sunk again off Sumatra. This time he was one and a half days in the water with a broken arm, but this did not prevent him from paddling a canoe for four days up a river. The Japs got him after six weeks, and for the next three and a half years he was held prisoner and so starved that his weight dropped over three stones.

Retiring from the navy in 1953, he now became a single-handed sailor, buying a 9-ton ketch and sailing it 48,000 miles round the world. His book, *On the Wind of a Dream*, describes his six years in the ketch *Solace*. Knowing that his motto is *Auxilio divino sic parvis magnum* – With God's help, little people can do great things – I listened with interest as he told me how the *Captain Scott* came to be lying at Plockton.

The dream of such a vessel originated when Commander Clark was master of the *Prince Louis*, the Outward Bound sea-going schooner used by the Moray Sea School. Appointed to this ship in 1962, he found it a "terrible decision" when, in 1966, the ship had to be relinquished on the grounds of expense. "So I asked if I could borrow the ship for six months and run it as an independent unit. Thanks to financial backing and the help of Kurt Hahn, the try-out was a great success. The money ran out, but I had proved the value of a combined sea and mountain course. Now we needed a ship to carry on, so I spent the next two and a half years searching for one.

"Then Lord Dulverton, hearing the tale said, 'I'll build you one.' I was given carte blanche in the planning. The ship was laid down in the Buckie yard in 1970, and I chose Plockton as the base, though we shall be moving shortly to Loch Eil. We run our courses on Outward Bound lines. We have definite training aims. We present various challenges which have to be faced. In the 26 days of a course among the hills and on the sea, no one is allowed to evade any single challenge.

"There are two ways of meeting challenge, the positive and the negative. The positive is to accept and go for it, as in taking on a mountain, be it Ben Nevis or Mount Everest. The negative is to shrink away from it and avoid the challenge. In 26 days, we aim to show that there is no such thing as 'I can't,' and we do it by making a man prove himself to himself the whole time.

"Out of thousands of young men, I have met only one since 1962 who was not prepared to try to overcome his fear of going up the rigging, He was an army N.C.O. I gave him an order and he refused to obey it, so there was only one course of action left – to send him off the ship. We weren't asking him to take any risks. We offered every help, as we do to everybody. [*Clark, 65, would climb to the yards to show it could be done.*]

"Discipline is no problem aboard a ship like this. The new crew will see the need for it immediately they come aboard on Monday, for the deck will be a mighty mess of ropes and halliards. To master it needs teamwork, and they see the commonsense of discipline. They like it once they see the reason for it.

"I believe in full employment. It is better to be hard worked and fully extended, even to the point of not getting enough sleep, than to have an easier time and get bored. We work them from 6.30 in the morning until 8.30 in the evening, and the secret of keeping the boys fully extended is variety. We have three watches in competition with each other for speed and efficiency in handling the sails. We have lectures, debates and discussions. Each boy has to give a five minute lecturette.

"And every course includes three mountain expeditions into the hills with camping equipment, each one harder than the one before, as experience is built up. It is a unique combination of sea and mountain experience. There is no other training scheme like it. For most people it is more than just 26 days away from industrial backgrounds.

"For the permanent staff it is a gruelling life, 'Quite mad by naval standards,' to quote someone we had here. For the instructors each course is 28 days of unremitting work, so it is only to be expected that the average member sticks it for about 18 months to two years. It is not easy to find the right men."

Well, I knew they had found the right man in Commander Clark, whose home is the ship, whose love is the sea, and whose work is also his hobby. I could see his eyes light up as he talked about rounding Barra Head for St Kilda and heading north for Orkney and Shetland, or turning southward for Arran and Mull in a ship driven by wind on sails stretched from 98-ft. masts. There are, however, two sides to every story. Before leaving the ship I went up the rigging to see what it was like on the cross-trees above a heaving sea. And before I left Plockton I sought out Calum Finlayson MacKenzie, who had been on one of the first courses organised by Commander Clark on the *Captain Scott*.

Calum happens to be a relative of a climbing friend of mine. At nineteen he has sponsored himself when he got the chance to go at a bargain price when the normal fee in winter for his age group was about £70. Most who go on these courses are sponsored by their firms. When I asked him if he thought it had been worth it, his reply was that he intends to go back this winter by taking a week of his annual leave to be the bosun's mate.

He explained why he wanted it to be winter. "I don't get the same thrill out of calm water. You have a better chance of getting it rough in February or March. I like to feel the ship listing along. In a Force Nine you can be doing ten or eleven knots, really moving with all sails set."

"What about working up there in that weather, reefing the sails when the ship is lying away over at an angle and swaying?" I asked.

"I liked it. It gives you a great feeling working high above the waves. When you are listing along the wind in the sails holds the ship steady. I didn't feel frightened. You have a safety cord so you can't fall off. I got to like the sea more and more. So did the other boys.

"The first day up the rigging two or three boys weren't sure and came back down. But the instructors were very good. The boys were encouraged, and they were soon swarming up and down like the rest of us. They had to for at 'Divisions' every morning, everybody has to go over the rigging, and you try to see who can do it the fastest. You can do it in two minutes once you get the hang of it. You think nothing of the height."

With pride he showed me his certificate of a trip that had embraced sailing to St Kilda and back by Lewis and Skye to land on Rum for a mountain expedition. He showed me his report on his character and conduct, which was a candid statement, with failings as well as good points detailed. Each sponsor gets one on his candidates.

I asked him what he thought he had learned from his trip. He had obviously given this some thought. "I have learned to have more respect for other people. You can't do everything on your own. You have to work together. I didn't think I would get on so well with strangers from England. But they were a terrific bunch.

"You see each watch works as a group on one sail, so you all get to know you're particular job, and get better and faster at it. The talks and discussions were good, too. I gave my five minute lecturette on Plockton, what it's like living here. But I wasn't so keen on the mountain expeditions, I prefer the sea to slogging over hills with a heavy pack. We got wonderful meals on the ship."

David Osselton, Expedition Officer, talked to me about his own view of the hill-walking aspect. He was not out to make the boys suffer, but the three mountain trips bring home to them the satisfaction of undertaking hard journeys through difficult and uninhabited country in places such as Knoydart and Kintail. No risks are taken that cannot be met with knowledge and technique, which it is his job to impart before they go off on their own in small groups. Osselton himself is a man with Alpine and Himalayan experience, with a comforting warmth of personality.

He was followed as Chief Instructor by John Hinde, with whom I was able to instruct on three very wild successive Novembers, courses which were marvellously effective. Alas, sponsorship dried up and nobody would pay the price, then, of a thirty sixth part of a jet fighter to keep the Scott *in Scottish waters. She now sails the Gulf, renamed* Youth of Oman.

SCOTS MAGAZINE 1977

RETURN TO 1912

"Have you ever heard of the Glesca Buchts?"

I had not, until Bob Mackay told me it was the principal feeing fair for the West of Scotland, held near Queen Street Station.

Bob had run away from home in 1912 and at May term was feed, contracted to a Gartocharn farmer for the lad's wage of the time, £6 the half year. On holiday from England with his wife, he'd come to see me and show her East Cambusmoon Farm where he had unloaded his kist all those years ago.

His chief memory was of the gaffer who showed him a cubby-hole at ground level with a window looking out on the clairty yard. "A grand view disnae pay the rent," said the gaffer by way of explanation. Things looked better in the kitchen where the farmer was tucking into a tasty looking meal, but all Bob got was a bowl of brose and a girdle scone.

Bob certainly had a fine welcome from the present farmer and smiled his surprise when she led him into the cubby-hole, now a nice wee bathroom in the modernised old house. Mrs Wilson was as delighted as I was to hear the old man's memories.

"Up at five in the morning, it was into the byre to milk the kye, and without a bite to eat yoke the horse and cart and take the milk to Balloch where I bought half a dozen rolls and ate the lot. The breakfast when I got back was a bowl of porridge and a herring with a slice of bread. Then out to sow the turnips. At lowsing time there was more brose, but before bed I went for a walk to find the railway line and the nearest place where I could get a train.

"I never took off my clothes, I just dozed, waiting for the grey of the morning, eased the window, and in stocking soles crossed the yard and got the dung barrow. The yard was cobbled then, so I tied wisps of straw round the wheel and tried to slide my kist from the window on to the barrow, but bang went barrow and kist on the cobbles. I held my breath but nobody wakened. With tackety boots round my neck I warsled the kist and barrow bumpety bump over the cobbles, often keeking over my shoulder. On the loan, puffing and blowing, I came to the level crossing I had seen the night before and I knew I would come to Croftamie Station if I kept along the line. Pushing the barrow on to the platform I found some old newspapers and was cleaning my kist when out came the station master.

"Where do you hail frae?" says he. I named the farm.

"Cambusmoon; I thought you might be frae the Moon. But what about the filthy barrow on my platform?"

231

" 'Right,' says I. So I took the barrow outside and shoved it through the hedge. 'Are you hungry laddie?' says he. 'I could eat you,' says I.

"The workman's train came a half hour later and soon I was in Stirling. That day was Stirling Fair, and between penny reels at the Corn Exchange I was feed to Rab Armstrong at Cambus near Alloa."

Fascinated by his total recall I asked what happened next.

"The war. I joined up in the Argylls and went to France with them in1914, got seriously wounded in 1917, and in and out of hospitals until 1921. Then four years later I married one of the fine girls who had nursed me in Chichester, and there she is. I retired after twenty years with the Duke of Richmond and Gordon at Goodwood, in charge of the forest, racecourse and motor circuit.

"We have a house on the Duke's estate and I have a good pension, so in our old age we are quite comfortable. My mind has often wandered back to Gartocharn, wondering if the farmer got back his barra, and what did he think when he saw the bed empty and the laddie ower the hill."

At Cambusmoon you don't need a barrow now. The byre has press-button automatic cleaning, and the milk from the cows extracted from them by machine is piped direct into a bulk tank for collection. And with extra grazing on another farm the stock of cows is 180, 62 of them milkers.

WEIR'S WORLD

IX

ALWAYS A NATURALIST

The first item, written during the war, shows that Tom was already a keen bird watcher, an enthusiasm that made him an expert all his days. On one occasion he was caught sneaking into camp at dawn and hauled before his C.O. He escaped with a mild telling off; his excuse he'd wanted to hear nightingales singing was so improbable it had to be true.

NE'ERDAY

Ne'erday (New Year's Day), the Scotsman's big day and I was in the English town of Folkestone with the day to myself. It was a concession I did not expect an English Regiment to grant me. What to do with it? The mists of morning were being broken by a yellow sun and patches of blue overhead indicated a perfect day to follow. Too good to spend in a town.

I took my binoculars and wandered along to the bus station. The luck was in. A little bow-legged man dressed in decrepit shooting clothes and carrying a gun was standing there. We were soon in conversation. If it was birds I wanted to see, he knew the very place. "Get to Fordwich and follow down the River Stour to the marsh. Best place in the district."

And what a day it turned out! The old church was no sooner at my back when things began to happen. Across my path flew that villain of the Scottish Highlands, a hooded crow. His grey tunic was unmistakable and to convince me, he gave his harsh rattling call. Then a redshank flew up, its jerky wing-beat a delight to my eye. On the river a little grebe plunged to safety, gaining sufficient confidence when it reappeared to let me inspect its light winter colours. From the ditches jacksnipe sped to safety in silent zig-zags. Ahead of me now stretched the marsh proper, a brilliance of golden reedbeds, frozen water, and under the hulk of a colliery several sheets of open water. Reed buntings drooped their tails at my side, and stonechats, goldfinches and linnets were unexpected touches of charm.

I was examining a ditch for a way across when the find of the day came. Straight towards me it flew, a great grey shape with effortless buoyant flight. I fastened my glass on it and caught the wonder. After every few wing beats it soared and swayed and planed in glorious manner, wings uptilted. I could not but whoop for delight. It was a hen harrier, the finest bird I have ever seen. Not even my first golden eagle impressed me as did this bird.

On the flood waters there were thousands of duck: mallard, pochard, teal, tufted, wigeon, and once with the sunlight full on its snowy neck and breast, a pintail passed over, surely the last word in streamlining from long slender neck to pinpoint of tail. Cormorants too were fishing and perching on convenient posts.

It was just as the light was beginning to fade I caught sight of my harrier again. He was distant and as shadowy as the encroaching mist; a grey shape skimming over the reeds. Back and forth he flickered, cutting in to the reeds with a swishing V movement, down and up again.

I saw over forty different species on that marsh and I voted it my most exciting bird watching day – with the gift of a hen harrier for my Ne'erday.

Typescript in National Library of Scotland Collections

THE GANNET CITY OF THE FORTH

The Bass Rock whose great buttresses rise from the Forth at North Berwick is one of the most crowded gannet tenements in the world. It was to look more closely at these crash divers of the ocean I landed in July, leaping out of a heaving boat on to the jetty which is the first step on a staircase winding through the ruins of a fortress.

This is the only breach in the great precipices of the Bass and the fortress wall effectually closed it to invaders. You zig-zag through the fortress, gaining height at every step and suddenly you are amongst a dazzling housing scheme of birds, row upon row, birds crashing down or taking off amidst a torrent of growls which drown the noise of the sea.

The poet Dunbar [CI5] expressed the scene in these lines:

> The air was dirkit with fowlis
> That cam with yammeris and with youlis,
> With shrykking, skrieking, skrymming scowlis.
> And meikle noyis and showtes.

The gannet is the most spectacular bird of the British coast, and anyone who has sailed the Clyde or the Forth knows its wonderful flight as it glides over the water, spear-bill down-pointed, the black tips of its white wings horizontal till it sights a shoal of fish when suddenly it seems to commit suicide by hurling itself into the water from heights of 100 to 150 feet, reappearing in about ten seconds to show that this is all part of the day's work.

Normally you only see gannets from a distance as they swing over the ocean. Here on the Bass you can walk among them — apprehensively at first as the gannets menace you with their huge bills and growl like angry dogs. But mostly this is display, more intended for the gannet next door for no gannet trusts any other gannet. That is why they are so reluctant to fly. The job of the sitting bird is to guard the nest against thieves for the moment a back is turned one will snatch up a beakful of the other's nesting material.

At close range the gannet is a superb bird, so well feathered that you see why it does not feel the shock of its dives. The thick neck is itself a shock absorber of cellular tissue extending to the breast. Moreover it is air-filled mechanically at the moment of diving and it is a safe bet that the higher the gannet is flying the deeper the fish are swimming. So safe is this rule that some fishermen set their nets for depth by gannets. The fish are caught but not swallowed during the dive, but as the gannet swims with its wings to the surface.

In July it is astonishing to find such a diversity in nesting progress. Some nests were still at the egg stage and contained the usual single brown-stained egg which takes 42 – 45 days to hatch. Others had a repulsive looking chick, quite black and naked, yet even at this feeble stage it would retch up its food at our approach. Most nests however had chicks in the downy white stage when they are at their most beautiful and pleasantest to handle.

Quite a few were handled that day to put rings on their legs in an effort to discover something of their movements after they leave the Bass. It has been shown that recoveries of ringed birds that first year gannets are travelling beyond the Bay of Biscay to North Africa, West Africa, Norway, etc. Older birds do not feel the wanderlust so keenly, and few adults go beyond the bounds of Europe.

Indeed, one of the most interesting of recent observations is that the Bass Rock gannets are tending to become all the year round birds instead of summer migrants to the rock. This may be due to the warming up of the Northern Hemisphere. Whatever the cause, many birds now come back to the rock in December and do not leave again until November, thereby staking an early claim to the best nesting sites even if actual nesting does not begin until April or May when the three inch egg is normally laid.

No one knows much about the mating of gannets, but the probability is that they mate for life and come back again and again to the same rock, to lay the egg and to keep it warm by placing webbed feet over it, for the gannet has no brood spot like most birds. The naked and blind bundle of black skin which is a newly hatched gannet is unattractive at first, but soon the white down covers it, and in six weeks it will be fully fledged.

The gulls darting in and out amongst the gannets were one reason for the vigilance of the parents in keeping constant attendance on the young. These pirates will force a young gannet to disgorge its food, or at worst swallow the youngster if it is small enough. So the adult gannet sits with the young and is very tender to it, feeding it on regurgitated herring or mackerel, haddock or whiting or other surface-feeding fish until the youngster's bill is so large that it can no longer thrust it down its parent's throat. This is the stage when at three months old it suddenly finds itself deserted and it is time when gannets are best to eat, just before they take to the sea for the first time in their lives, at the fat stage when they are known as *gugas*.

No gannets are harvested on the Bass Rock now, but until late in the 18th century over 1,300 were slaughtered yearly, being advertised in the Edinburgh Press under the heading:

Solan Goose

There is to be sold, by John Watson Jun. at his stand at the Poultry, Edinburgh, all lawful days of the week, wind and weather serving, good and fresh Solan Geese.

Any who have occasion for the same may have them at reasonable rates.

The reasonable rate was about 'twenty pence apiece'. That advertisement was August 5th, 1768, just 321 years since the first record of gannets nesting on the Bass. Wandering over the seven acres of the cliff top you walk historic ground, for this rock was once hermitage for a Saint and later a prison where Covenanters were imprisoned for their beliefs, but the most outstanding thing is that here was the last bit of Scotland to surrender to the Union of the Crowns.

The story is a good one. The impregnable fortifications had been used as a State prison since 1671, most of the prisoners being ministers of the Church whose love of liberty and truth prevented them from accepting the Act of Supremacy, entitling the King to act as supreme judge in civil and ecclesiastical cases. The fact is that Charles II really hated the Presbytery and perjured himself to the Covenanters to gain support since he had no intention of maintaining the Church of Scotland. Many of these fine men suffered privations that enfeebled them for life. But on June 15th, 1691 four young Jacobites were to get something of their own back, for while garrison troops were unloading coal at the jetty, the prisoners saw the chance to shut the gate of the fort and lock the troops out. It was a bold stroke which paid off, for not only did they hold out, but their numbers were reinforced to sixteen with the help of two French Government boats which kept them victualled, and for three years they held the Bass in defiance of King William III and all his forces. Such was their secure position that when they did capitulate they did so on highly honourable terms.

So it meant something to wander through the old prison and see little puffins and bronze-winged shags staring out from narrow window ledges where martyrs had stared out on a hopeless future. The birds have taken over the prison and by a strange chance it is these fortress walls which have saved from extermination a rare plant which is peculiar to the Bass, the Tree Mallow or Bass Mallow whose pink clusters of flowers on tall stems make such a fine show of colour round the old prison. But for the wall excluding grazing sheep, the animals would have exterminated the mallow as they have done on other Forth islands. [*Currently a problem again.*]

The only link with the saint, St. Balthere or Baldred is the ruin of a tiny chapel erected in the 16th century on the site of the Hermitage where the saint lived and died on the rock in 756. Near it too is the garden and a poisonous looking well with water so bad that the prisoners had to sprinkle it with oatmeal before they could drink it. There is no real spring on the island.

It was a strange chance that nature created a rock that could be made impregnable by the building of a single wall to bridge the only link in the cliff face. Stranger still that a band of devoted Scotsmen should be able to snatch it from their captors and live as outlaws for three years. It is appropriate therefore that the Latin name of the Gannet should be taken from the Bass Rock, because there are more gannets in Scotland* than anywhere else in the world. *Sula bassana* is thriving, and so for that matter is Scotland.

* *Of the world population of 167,000 breeding birds, 109,000 are estimated to breed in Britain; St. Kilda with 18,000 pairs being the greatest breeding station in the world.*

Howden Quarterly

ENCOUNTERS

As Ward Clarke in *Scotland's Magazine*

DAWN DANCERS

Let me tell you of a night-out I spent in the Loch Ard region after following a track into the hills at 10 p.m., to stretch my sleeping bag in a concealment of ruins overlooking an acre of grassy clearing in young forest.

That green is a blackcock *lec* – a jousting place where these fat birds of the grouse family meet at dawn and tournament with each other before the eyes of the ladies who may reward their performance by allowing them to mate.

I hoped the birds would be my alarm clock, and so they were at 4 a.m., though it was too dark as yet to read the time – only light enough in fact to see white saucer discs whisking about the grass like will o' the wisps. Cat-like whimperings and sharp hissing sounds added to the supernatural effect, then a vibrating bubbling like stewpots on the boil began, and dimly I began to make out the birds, their necks blown out, wings projecting stiffly like little arms, the tails as neatly spread as a fan of white feathers.

Peering cautiously between the stones, I was spectator of a preposterous puppet show in which every action was stiff and exaggerated. Even gliding along the ground was like the action of an automaton. Hopping as if on hot bricks, they would jump in the air, hiss and bubble as if about to explode. Then two would face up to each other, thrust and parry like fencers, then separate without as much as a mock fight. At other times the feathers would fly. Breaking off the engagement was usually accompanied by a sharp jump in the air and a loud sneeze and a fit of bubbling.

The tension became tremendous as daylight broke and the orange of sunrise struck the mountaintops. Now the birds had a sheen on their blue-black bodies, the red wattles over the eyes and white scuts edged with black making vivid contrast. I realised it was more than the morning light which was causing it when I glimpsed three grey hens on the perimeter of the *lec*, slender necks and slim heads held high as they daintly stepped round the 'bubbling' cocks, hardly stopping to watch any particular joust.

I kept my eye on one particular hen and noticed that she kept coming back to a certain strutting cock. Time and again she crouched close to him, but always she retreated when he came close. Then came a time when she did not run away, at which the cock did an about turn, raced madly for about 20 feet to wheel about and come back, this time to mount and tread the willing hen.

The birds were still displaying at 7.30 a.m. when, with a whirr of wings, the whole lot went over my head, perhaps a dozen or so, and I saw the reason was a slow flying hawk, pale as a sea-gull with long narrow wings edged with black. Head down and searching only six feet above the ground, it seemed to stall from time to time as its wings went back in an elegant V and down came yellow legs. It was a cock hen harrier out vole hunting and a sight to make anybody's day.

ANIMALS AT HOME

The keeper who told me this story found a young otter curled up in a barrel in a sheltered spot at the back of the house. There was not much life in it, until he put down a bowl of milk and bread, when it accepted him as a friend and to his surprise decided that the barrel was its home.

In no time it was nosing into the house, playing with the children, rolling about on the carpet, and snatching at anything liftable within reach. But the keeper knew that otters have a bad reputation of getting jealous and turning savage so he decided to lose his new pet by taking it ten miles down a loch and slipping it over the side of a boat. Returning home a few hours later he found the otter had beaten him to it and was at the fireside, to the annoyance of his wife.

He tried giving the otter away, but knew nobody who wanted it, so he decided to try to lose it, using the car to try to bamboozle it; hoping that the otter would be completely disoriented by all the twists and turns between the house and where he set it down fifteen miles away. But again the otter beat him home . . .

Then there was the story told to me by Dick Balharry, of being given a blind bedraggled little animal about the size of a mouse, which never stopped squeaking. Dick knew what it was, a baby pine-marten, but the extraordinary thing was that it had been found in an empty golden eagle's eyrie which the marten must have been using as a den. Dick thinks the infant had probably been left behind when the marten shifted its kits as a frightened parent sometimes does.

Now followed sleepless weeks for Dick, his wife and two children, taking turns to feed the squeaker every four hours. Despite such frequent applications of milk from a tiny filler the fractious infant hardly seemed to grow, and was refusing to open its eyes it seemed. They were getting tired of it; boring.

Then magic; the eyes opened, it changed into a sharp-eared,

yellowish bibbed, bushy-tailed brown acrobat, lightning quick, and with a sense of humour. Nocturnal by instinct it became most active as daylight ebbed, and it was great fun when it would leap from Dick's shoulder to mine, wriggle into my pullover and come down my sleeve, then back on to my shoulder and leap ten feet onto Dick.

Offered its freedom, it refused, and now, it is too confiding to be released, or it would be shot for certain. It is time we revised our laws to give these rare and marvellous animals protection.

[*Which they now enjoy.*]

A GLEN LYON CAPER

The *capull-choille*, the horse of the woods, is the greatest grouse in the world, turkey-sized and notably aggressive in the breeding season. The cock bird who was the villain of my story had taken to attacking humans rather than rival cocks, Alas, he died when he attacked a Landrover, but before that time he had drawn blood from ornithologists who had come to see him. He was very much alive on the day when I visited the keeper to find out where the crusty character lived.

"I'll take you, but you'll be on your own for the last bit, for I'm not going near," laughed the keeper as he pointed to a distinctive knoll. "Go up there and he'll come to you." Armed with cine-camera to capture the action, up I went. In a trice I was watching through the viewfinder a great bird climbing fast up the knoll, legs moving in a mechanical glide over the ground like a life-sized clockwork toy.

It stopped just as its great hooked beak and hanging ruff of feathers filled the frame, and I had just time to put up my boot as it leapt, colliding against it, and began biting at the rubber sole. Then, as if dignity had asserted itself, threw itself back, stood tall, and virtually blew itself up as I watched. The neck swelled, the tail became a huge fan, the red wattle round the eye enlarged, the feathers of the neck projected. Head up and wicked beak open, its display was an unmistakable display to all-comers.

This was too good to miss. I resumed shooting (the film has been shown on BBC Television) when it leapt again, colliding with my heavy boot once more. Involuntarily I stepped back a yard and, as if taking a cue, he did the same. So I played a game of advance and retire with him; great fun.

What a colourful sight he made, a grotesque greenish-blue bird with brown wings ornamented with a white spot, puffed up with anger. I did the decent thing, I began a decisive retreat, at which he bounced off the ground to land on top of a fallen pine trunk, pirouetted like a ballet dancer, then from his wide open beak delivered a tiny rattle of sound, laughable to hear, coming from one so huge and noble.

The capercaillie has been increasing steadily in my life time, and we are lucky to have them, for they became extinct in Scotland in 1785, and the population we have today is descended from birds brought over from Europe in the nineteenth century. We are fortunate, because the capercaillie is in serious decline on the Continent, while in Scotland there is still enough natural forest to support it. Native pine-woods with old trees are its stronghold. Europeans will now pay £1,000 for ten guns to shoot capercaillie for one day in Scotland. In economic terms this is good, but no wood should be driven more than once in a season or Scotland too will lose its capercaillie.

They are now protected but in decline once more. On regular visits in the Sixties I encountered a similar attacking caper in the Black Wood of Rannoch.

SNOW BUNTINGS

It's an ill wind that blows snow buntings to a farmstead in Gartocharn, and there they were, feeding on seeds dropped from hay bales put out for the cattle, brownish and undistinguished as sparrows until they fluttered over the snow on white wings, living up to their old country name of 'snowflakes.'

It was the call note, a sharp drawn-out "Pseet" which drew my attention to them on a dour morning dark with the threat of more snow. I love Saxby's writing about the snowflake in Shetland. "I am acquainted with no more pleasing combination of sight and sound than that afforded when a cloud of these birds, backed by a dark grey sky, descended as it were in a shower to the ground, to the music of their own tinkling notes." My little party were hardly a shower, but they gave out the authentic tinkling notes as they darted about before settling.

The snow bunting flock he was referring to would be immigrants, from Iceland, Greenland or Scandinavia, Arctic nesters wintering on sea-shores and high hills, forever on the hunt for grass seeds. Here in Gartocharn we get them only in the hardest weather, and normally I have to go to the Campsies or the Luss hills to find them.

But last year produced an exceptional number of breeding records from the high Grampians, together with unique records of Lapland buntings. Why should this be? I think it was because of a similarity between Scottish hills last Spring, and the conditions which normally prevail in the Arctic in June and July.

The biggest flock of snow buntings I have seen was on Culloden Moor in April on a day when snow showers were sweeping the battlefield, and the flock of hundreds flying and settling truly fitted the Saxby description. And once when I was walking up a path in Torridon I had a merlin go over my head and take a snow bunting at ground level in front of me.

But that first morning of the snow brought in a few other immigrants to us, flocks of skylarks and meadow pipits, hosts of Scandinavian thrushes, and the fine sight of seventeen partridges rising from a little oasis of green with querulous calls, showing me their lovely soft chestnut and lavender colours as they whirred away on brown wings, rufus tails conspicuous.

Snow buntings are now as active as sparrows round the carparks and buildings of our ski centres. Plenty crumbs available.

A BIBLIOGRAPHY OF SORTS

Highland Days Cassel 1948, reprinted Gordon Wright 1984, Steve Savage 2010 *

The Ultimate Mountains Cassel 1953 (The first post-war Himalayan expedition)

Camps and Climbs in Arctic Norway Cassel 1953 (Lofoten and Lyngen)

East of Katmandu Oliver and Boyd 1955, Travel Book Club [1955], reprinted Steve Savage 1981

Focus on Mountains 1965 (small children's hardback; practical and stories, forward by John Hunt)

The Scottish Lochs Vol 1 Constable 1970, Rept. 1973, Vol 2 Constable 1972 then a one-volume edition, Constable, 1980. (Packed with information)

The Kyle Line Famedram 1971

The Mallaig Line Famedram 1971 (Informative booklets on the various railways in the Highlands)

The Oban Line Famedram 1971

The Highland Line Famedram 1974 (An illustrated, data-packed centenary booklet)

Scotland's Threatened Lines Famedram n.d. [1974] (Reprints of the Kyle, Mallaig, and Oban Lines, a different layout of the originals. Illustrated)

The Western Highlands Batsford 1973 (a 184 pp description)

Batsford Colour Book of the Highlands Batsford 1975 (one of series: 24 full page pics)

Scottish Islands David and Charles 1976 (A 125 pp. description)

Tom Weir's Scotland Gordon Wright 1980 (collected essays and articles)

Weir's Way Gordon Wright 1981, reprinted Steve Savage 2007 * (more collected works)

Exploring Scotland with Tom Weir Pelham Books 1991 (a more lavish collection, well-illustrated)

Weir's World, An Autobiography of Sorts Canongate 1994, reprinted Steve Savage 2006 * (a tour de force written in his eighties)

* these may still be in print and could be ordered in bookshops

'My Month', a monthly feature in the *Scots Magazine*, 1956 – 1999 was enormously popular. A series commissioned by *Scotland's Magazine* was published under the name Ward Clarke. Many magazine articles were later recycled into books (all with his own photographs) or became part of his TV presentations. *Weir's Way* TV series was made available in 4 DVDs.

Articles in the *Scottish Mountaineering Club Journal* featured: A Camp in Rum, 1948: Sutherland Crossing, 1949; Snow on the Cuillin, 1950; Lofoten, 1952; Nepal Himalaya, 1954; Spring in the High Atlas, 1957; The First Ascent of Dalness Chasm, Central Prong, 1958; Peaks and Passes in Kurdistan, 1958; Lochnagar, 1960.

W.H. Murray: *The Scottish Himalayan Expedition* Dent 1951 covers the same expedition as Tom's *The Ultimate Mountains* and Douglas Scott also wrote an unpublished account. Tom Weir's archive of photographs, slides, articles, diaries, scripts etc in the National Library of Scotland (Acc 13059)

Tom Weir was also a contributor to, or wrote Introductions to other works:

George Scott Moncrieffe: Kintail, Balmacara and the Falls of Glomach NTS 1965, *Wildlife in Britain* AA 1976, *In Search of Country Holidays in Scotland* 1978, *Wildlife Scotland* MacMillan 1979, *In the Country* MacMillan 1980 and an *AA guide to Scotland*. He contributed, at times, to *World Wide Magazine*, *Howden Quarterly*, *Motor World*, *Country Life* and the *Glasgow Herald* and many other publications.

Titles of related interest:
Matt Marshall: *The Travels of Tramp Royal* 1932
Molly Weir: *Shoes Were for Sundays* 1970
W H Murray: *Evidence of Things not seen* (autobiography) 2003